Childhood Under Siege

Also by Joel Bakan

The Corporation: The Pathological Pursuit of Profit and Power

Just Words: Constitutional Rights and Social Wrongs

Childhood Under Siege

How Big Business Ruthlessly Targets Children

Joel Bakan

THE BODLEY HEAD
LONDON

Published by The Bodley Head 2011

2 4 6 8 10 9 7 5 3 1

First published in Great Britain in 2011 by
The Bodley Head
Random House, 20 Vauxhall Bridge Road,
London SW1V 2SA

www.bodleyhead.co.uk
www.vintage-books.co.uk

Addresses for companies within The Random House Group Limited can be found at:
www.randomhouse.co.uk/offices.htm

The Random House Group Limited Reg. No. 954009

A CIP catalogue record for this book
is available from the British Library

ISBN 9781847920577

The Random House Group Limited supports the Forest Stewardship Council® (FSC®),
the leading international forest certification organisation. All our titles that are printed on
Greenpeace approved FSC® certified paper carry the FSC® logo. Our paper procurement
policy can be found at www.randomhouse.co.uk/environment

MIX
Paper from
responsible sources
FSC® C016897

Printed and bound in Great Britain by
Clays Ltd, St Ives PLC

For Rebecca
Myim and Sadie
Rita (in loving memory) and Paul
with all my love

Contents

Acknowledgments

Rebecca Jenkins, my wife, love, muse, best friend, and trusted editor, inspired, encouraged, and believed in me. She improved the prose and ideas of this book, draft after draft, with her deep intelligence, certain intuition, and remarkable ear for good writing, while also keeping me focused, confident, and connected to the joy and beauty of life. My kids, Myim and Sadie, inspired me and gave me hope, their lives and love, and my love for them, the surest answers to the sometimes nagging question "Why am I doing this?" I thank Myim for his intelligent and probing insights about, and help with, earlier drafts, as well as his unrelenting optimism and curiosity about the world. I thank Sadie for her teachings about the worlds of youth, and the deep emotional intelligence she brings to everything she does. Paul Bakan, my father and lifelong intellectual mentor, helped me with the research, provided sage advice and ideas in relation to drafts, and instilled confidence with his love and faith in me. Two other wise and brilliant souls, no less important in my life and work for the fact they no longer walk the earth, are Marlee Kline and Rita Bakan. I owe so much to both of them.

My editor at the Free Press, Emily Loose, has been an enthusiastic and unflagging supporter. She improved the book with her always insightful editing and her sure and impeccable sense of what needs to be said, and when it is best to say nothing. My agent Tina Bennett had faith in the project from the very start and made the book better with her original and intelligent ideas. Diane Turbide at Penguin Canada and Will Sulkin at The Bodley Head provided helpful insights and encouragement, as did Cecile Barendsma and Dan Hind. Ken Davidson helped with thoughtful comments on earlier drafts and also, along with his wife Reva and their family, with friendship and support. Dawn Brett did much of the research for and contributed thoughts and insights to chapters 2 through 5. Lisa Nevens and Claire Immega also did research for the book. Gary Burns, Bruce Lanphear, and Larry Raskin commented helpfully on earlier drafts, and discussions with Eleanor Feirestein, Mark Achbar, Danny Bakan, Andrew Petter, and Derryk Smith provided helpful ideas at various stages of the research and writing. I am grateful as well to the individuals who agreed to be interviewed for the project and thus took the time to provide me with their stories and insights.

I thank members of my family, in addition to those who I have already mentioned, for their love, support, and encouragement: Laura Bakan, Michael and Megan Bakan; Marilyn Jenkins, Carol and Terry Kline, Pauline Westhead; John and Glenna Jenkins, Ellen and Peter Colley, Carol Jenkins and Philip Tietze, Lucia Jenkins and Bob Cox, and Ruth Jenkins; Ronnie Kline and Ruth Buckwold, and Sandy Kline; and all of my nieces and nephews—Isaac and Leah, Adina and Zevy, Adam, Jackie, Sandy, Morgan, and Martha.

I could not have completed this work without the support of the University of British Columbia's Faculty of Law, and I thank its members, and particularly Dean Mary Anne Bobinski, for their patience and constant encouragement.

Introduction

I remember vividly one hot summer night in the early 1970s. I had escaped the cramped and humid hell of a Catskills bungalow (my extended family had met there for a "vacation"), and made my way to the Teen Glow Ball Disco at the big hotel down the road. Girls, a mystery to me (I was thirteen at the time), had become intriguing over the previous year, and one of them on the dance floor caught my eye. After mustering the courage to ask her to dance—she said, "Yes"—I knew my luck was doubly blessed when a slow number came on. We embraced, awkwardly, and began to move together to the music. I thought I was in heaven.

But suddenly the lights came on, the music stopped, and the glow ball ceased to glow. Two men, their necks craned and eyes squinting, made their way slowly to the middle of the dance floor. One of them, my father, had a flashlight tied to his head with a bungie cord; the other, short with bandy legs, knee-high white socks, and Bermuda shorts, was my uncle Ben. Later that night I would learn the two men had been dispatched by my panic-stricken family to track me down and bring me home when they realized I had gone missing. But at that moment, standing there stunned on the dance floor, my dark-adapted eyes stinging in the harsh, unwanted light, I knew I had to do something, and fast.

I pulled my princess close, kissed her hard on the lips (a first for me), bolted the dance floor and fled the hotel. When I hit the unlit road, I took a last look behind me. There I saw the strangest sight—a disembodied light bobbing eerily up and down, about six feet off the ground. It was, I realized, the flashlight attached to my father's head.

"It's me, I'm over here, I'm okay," I shouted.

Now, for most kids, certainly for me that night in the Catskills, parents can be a real drag—clueless, embarrassing, sometimes humiliating, overprotective, and always uncool. They make rules, curtail freedoms, spy and monitor, assign chores, require homework be done, limit computer use and TV watching, curb candy and soda consumption, forbid sex, alcohol and drugs, impose curfews, and vet friends. Even young children, and certainly tweens and teens, understand that parents get in the way of fun.

But—and this is the tricky part of it all—kids still want their parents to parent. Despite all the eye rolling and door slamming, they want parents to care about where they are and what they are doing, to care about them.[1] My father had ruined my night and humiliated me, but even my snarky teenage self knew that as a parent, he was just doing his job. I hated what he did, but at some level I felt cared for, even loved, by the fact he had done something, however awful (did he really have to wear that flashlight on his head?), to keep me safe.

Parents, like my father that night, know their job is to keep kids safe, and to make sure they feel and are loved and cared for, protected. It is the most difficult job in the world.

I should confess: I was not a model child. There was nothing innocent, idyllic, or calm about my childhood. I shot squirrels with BB guns, pelted cars with rocks, taunted trains for the sake of a thrill and a flattened penny—even blew up a small tree with a bundle of fireworks. I hung around the local drugstore plugging quarters into pinball machines and sneaking peeks at *Playboys* on the magazine rack. Later, as a teenager, I experimented with sex, drugs, and alcohol, played rock and roll, smoked cigarettes, drove cars before I got my driver's license (my friends and I would "steal" our parents' cars and drive them around town in the middle of the night), and attracted the ire of teachers, principals, and the police. I dismissed my parents' warnings and rules (they were so uncool), felt invincible, fashioned myself a rebel, and railed against anything that smacked of adult authority or sensibility.

I made my parents' lives difficult with worry. "May your own children cause you as much grief as you have caused me," my mother frequently cursed. But I was just a normal kid doing the things kids (or at least some of them) normally do.

Now, watching my own teenage kids grow up, a boy and a girl—each making good on my mother's curse in different ways—I remind myself, constantly, that this is how it goes. Childhood, the period between infancy and the end of adolescence, is not, and nor should it be, all purity and innocence. Danger, sexual curiosity, fascination with violence and horror, and intrigue with adult vices are all normal parts of growing up, as are rebelliousness, moodiness, acting out, and the belief that parents, teachers, and other adults are clued out and unfair most of the time.

So you will not find here a lament for youth's wayward ways, nor an ode to the lost innocence of childhood. Children, I believe, have stayed much the same over the generations, at least in terms of their essential needs and natures. They go through the same developmental stages, each with its own difficulties, confusions, dependencies, abilities, and vulnerabilities, and they require the same things from adults—love, protection, guidance, freedom, and respect.

Parents, for their part, have also stayed much the same—profoundly, instinctively, and universally loving their children; cherishing, nurturing, caring, and hoping for them. And because childhood is a dangerous time, with children small, inexperienced, still forming and vulnerable, parenting can be as much about fear as it is about love. Indeed, the two are inextricably tied. Out of love we cherish our children, wanting them to be safe, healthy, and happy, and to grow up into well-adjusted, productive, and life-loving adults. Out of fear we worry about anything that might deny them these things.

Knowing what to fear, and what not to—the "capacity to fear accurately," as psychoanalyst Erik Erikson described it in his landmark work *Childhood and Society*—is key to good parenting (and also to staying sane as a parent).[2] But it is not always easy to do, especially when, as in today's media-saturated culture, new dangers to children, or avowed denials of such, are headline-grabbing news every day.

Fearing accurately is made all the more difficult—and this is one of my central arguments—by the tendency of corporations and industries to incite and diminish fears in ways that serve their own purposes. Big business not only produces an inordinate amount of harm and danger to children, but also dictates the ways we fear (or do not fear) harm and danger. Whatever the issue—sex and violence in children's media, mental disorders among children, the ill effects of industrial chemicals on children's health, or failing schools—business interests, with the help of marketers, media, and public relations firms, craft "information" that creates and downplays fears in order to help sell products and justify harmful practices. The problem is further compounded by the fact the very institutions responsible for providing good and impartial information—government, science, medicine, and education—have, over the last few decades, come under industry's influence.

As a result of all of this, I argue below, we, as parents, are systematically misinformed, and our fears channeled to serve the interests of industry and corporations rather than those of our children. My hope for this book is that it will provide a corrective to this tendency; that it will help us fear accurately for the fates of children, and thus enable us, both as parents and citizens, to better protect them from harm.

I do not address every childhood issue, only those where for-profit corporations are centrally and directly involved in putting children at risk of harm. That is, however, a significant subset of issues, and one with profound and wide-ranging effects on children's lives. Needless to say, corporations are not the only culprits. Poverty, racism, sexism, neglect, violence, drug and alcohol abuse, exploitation, illness, and family dysfunction also undermine children's health and well-being.[3] These factors are, in their broader dimensions, beyond the scope of this book, but I do examine their intersections with the book's core issues throughout.

By way of a brief overview, then, subsequent chapters investigate the facts that:

- A massive and growing kid marketing industry is targeting children with increasingly callous and devious methods to manipulate their forming and vulnerable emotions, cultivate compulsive behavior, and addle their psyches with violence, sex, and obsessive consumerism.
- More and more children are taking dangerous psychotropic drugs—the numbers have increased severalfold since 1980—as pharmaceutical companies commandeer medical science and deploy dubious and often illegal marketing tactics to boost sales.
- Children's chronic health problems, including asthma, cancer, autism and birth defects, are on the rise as corporations dump thousands of new chemicals, in increasing amounts, into the environment, usually with the license of governments.
- Children as young as five years old are working illegally on farms in the United States, getting injured, becoming ill, and dying on the job, while the *legal* age for farm work remains a shockingly low twelve years old.
- America's public schools are becoming lucrative private-sector markets as education is harnessed to the immediate and self-interested needs of industry and learning is increasingly regimented and standardized.

What unites all of these scenarios is that, in each, for-profit corporations are either exploiting or neglecting (sometimes both at once) children's unique vulnerabilities and needs. There are other areas where this happens, no doubt, and within each area investigated there are legions more issues, stories, and examples than I can possibly explore. Hence, my aim is not to be encyclopedic, but rather to make and illustrate a larger point about childhood and society today—namely, that as governments retreat from their previous roles of protecting children from harm at the hands of corporations, we, as a society, expose them to exploitation, neglect their needs and interests, and thus betray what we, as individuals, cherish most in our lives.

I focus on wealthy countries, particularly the United States. While children undoubtedly suffer worse fates in poor and developing countries, where violence, dislocation, and hunger are pervasive and acute, it is my belief—and an animating belief of this work—that the practices of wealthy countries must also be scrutinized. Not only do children in these countries suffer too, and disproportionately so if they are poor, but the countries wield tremendous power and influence in the world, shaping, directly and indirectly, the policies and practices of poor and less developed countries. These are good reasons to hold wealthy countries accountable for how they treat children.

Another good reason to hold them accountable is that in wealthy countries we *can* protect children; we have the necessary means and resources to do so. The fact that we often choose not to, and instead allow children's interests to be sacrificed to corporations' self-interested pursuit of profit, is particularly objectionable. A society that refuses to protect its most vulnerable members from harm and exploitation *even when it can*, after all—even where the fewest barriers exist to doing so—has truly lost its way. As Nelson Mandela once stated, "There can be no keener revelation of a society's soul than the way it treats its children." Following that logic, and on the basis of what follows, we should be gravely concerned about our own society's soul.

Chapter One

The Century of the Child

Over the course of history, societies have struggled with the question of how to deal with children and childhood. During medieval times, for example, there was little sense of childhood as a unique and vulnerable time of life. Children enjoyed few special protections or benefits and inhabited alongside adults the worlds of work, social life, and even sex ("the practice of playing with children's privy parts formed part of a widespread tradition," states historian Philippe Aries).[1] "There was no place for childhood in the medieval world," according to Aries.[2]

Things did not improve with industrialization. Beginning in the late eighteenth century, children were scooped from orphanages and workhouses to toil in the "dark satanic mills,"[3] as William Blake described them, of Britain's early textile industry, places of "sexual license, foul language, cruelty, violent accidents, and alien manners," according to the historian E. P. Thompson.[4]

In the United States too, child labor was common in textile mills, especially in the post–Civil War South, where children as young as five years old worked long shifts in horrible conditions. "It's over eight o'clock when these children reach their homes—later if the millwork is behind-hand and they are kept over hours," according to one woman after she visited a South Carolina mill. "They are usually beyond speech," she continued.

7

> They fall asleep at the table, on the stairs; they are carried to bed and there laid down as they are, unwashed, undressed and the inanimate bundles of rags so lie until the mill summons them with its imperious cry before sunrise, while they are still in stupid sleep.[5]

As industrialization progressed, children were moved from mills to factories and mines, where conditions were often even worse.

A broad-based child-saving movement began to emerge during the nineteenth century.[6] By the twentieth century—the "century of the child," as one book published in 1900 prophesized in its title[7]—most modern nations had committed to the notion, historically rooted in the common law principle of *parens patriae* (a sovereign's duty toward children and other vulnerable groups), that societies, through their governments, are obliged to protect children and promote their interests. Legal systems were remade on a global scale to reflect that idea, and children came to be recognized by the law as uniquely vulnerable persons with special rights and needs.

Child labor was outlawed, as was the sale and marketing to children of adult vices such as tobacco, alcohol, and pornography, and consumer protection laws were designed to pay special attention to product safety and to advertising aimed at children. Governments undertook (to different degrees in different places) to provide children with education and health care, and to ensure their general welfare. Parents along with other adults were made criminally liable for neglecting and exploiting children, and juveniles who broke the law were spared the harsh treatment of criminal justice systems. Most modern nations embraced these kinds of reforms, which were also entrenched in international law when the United Nations proclaimed its *Declaration of the Rights of the Child* in 1959.

Despite flaws and limitations, the reforms of the century of the child were remarkable for their scope and impact. By the middle of the century it could no longer be doubted that society was duty-bound to protect children and invest in their futures; to help them survive, be healthy, and flourish as human beings.

The century's progressive momentum came to a sudden halt, however, near its end—in 1980 to be exact. That year, according to political historian David Harvey, marked "a revolutionary turning point in the world's social and economic history . . . [a remaking of] the world around us in a totally different image." Ronald Reagan and Margaret Thatcher swept into power in the United States and Great Britain, and a new economic ideology, usually described as "neoliberalism," was catapulted from the halls of academe into the driver's seat of public policy.[8]

The new ideology's core idea—that free markets are the surest way to achieve the greatest good for individuals and society—flatly contradicted century-of-the-child reforms. Society should have little authority to interfere with individuals and few responsibilities to help them, it held. Not even children should be coddled by an overbearing "nanny state," as Margaret Thatcher described it. Families along with other private actors, including corporations, should be left free to make their own choices and decisions. "There is no such thing as society," Thatcher famously pronounced, capturing the new ideology's essence. "There are individual men and women, and there are families."[9]

Individual freedom is essential and desirable, no doubt. But the freedom delivered by neoliberalism was, and remains, partial and problematic. In the name of that freedom, corporations were emancipated from regulatory constraints and enabled to ride roughshod over others' interests. Neoliberalism's freedom thus became a "freedom to exploit one's fellows [and] to make inordinate gains without commensurable service to the community," as political philosopher Karl Polanyi has described it, and, as such, a threat to a range of social interests, including the well-being of children.[10]

Children's well-being was, of course, precisely the purpose of century-of-the-child reforms. Those reforms extended protective rights and benefits to children, and entrenched the "best interests of the child" principle in law. Children were thus legally recognized as *persons* in need of special protection. Over the same period, however, corporations were also legally recognized as *persons*, and the "best interests of the corporation" principle was entrenched in law to protect *their* interests.[11] It was inevitable that the two new legal persons, and the principles protecting them, would clash. Century-of-the-child reformers sought to resolve the ensuing conflict in favor of children. The last thirty years of neoliberal reforms have reversed that priority.

In 2008 the economy nearly collapsed after years of reckless Wall Street adventurism. In 2010 the Gulf of Mexico was nearly destroyed as a result of an explosion on a British Petroleum oil rig. Both crises were devastating, acute, and highly visible, wreaking havoc and destruction on massive scales. During the years preceeding each, however, the recklessly self-interested behavior of the companies involved was openly tolerated by governments. Under the banner of neoliberal-inspired deregulation those governments had removed, refused to create, or inadequately enforced protective measures that might have avoided the disasters. In hindsight, it was no surprise that financial institutions, driven by promises of huge profits and with no regulatory constraints in place to stop them, would carelessly grant risky loans, repackage the resulting debt as securities, and build exotic derivative schemes.[12] Nor was it a surprise that BP, a company with a string of serious environmental and safety infractions dating back at least to the 1990s (though strategically hidden by its carefully cultivated green image), would, if it could, cut corners to save money when constructing and operating its deep sea wells.[13]

The crisis addressed in this book, however—the erosion and sometimes outright destruction of our capacity to protect children from economic activities that might cause them harm—is arguably the most chilling effect of the turn to neoliberalism. And though it may, unlike its more obvious and acute counterparts, unfold slowly rather than suddenly, take chronic as opposed to catastrophic forms, and engulf us so fully it sometimes disappears from view, it is driven by the same dynamics.

In my earlier book and film, *The Corporation*, I argued that for-profit corporations are legally compelled always and only to act in ways that serve their own interests. They are programmed to put their missions of creating wealth for their owners above everything else, and to view anything and everything—nature, human beings, children, the planet—as opportunities to exploit for profit.[14] Unable to feel genuine concern for others, to experience guilt or remorse when they act badly, or to feel any sense of moral obligation to obey laws and social conventions, corporations resemble human psychopaths in their essential natures, I argued. Free of regulatory constraints, they cannot help but act in dangerous and destructive ways—including toward children.

I was at pains to explain in *The Corporation*, however, that my critique was not aimed at the individuals who run and work for corporations, but rather at the institution itself. This is important to emphasize again here. As human beings, corporate executives, managers, and employees are no different from anyone else. They too are parents (and aunts, uncles, and grandparents), caring for children, loving, nurturing, and protecting them. They too are concerned about the issues raised in this book, likely even reading the book. My argument is not with them (or you).

Rather, the problem—and I believe the frustration for many who work in corporations—is that whatever may be our human inclinations, motivations, feelings, and beliefs, when we enter the corporation's world we become operatives for *its* imperatives, subsuming our own personal values to its institutional demands.

It is kind of like playing ice hockey. When you play hockey, you are in a different moral and legal world, a more brutish and nasty one than the one you inhabit off the ice. You do things—run people into the boards, trip them, punch them—that maybe get you two minutes in the penalty box. The same behaviors off the ice (at the grocery store, or at work, for example) would likely get you two years in prison.

Going to work in a corporation is like stepping onto the ice. The game is now defined by the rules of the corporation, by its institutional imperatives. The decisions made and actions taken follow from that. So now it becomes morally possible for individuals to do things that *as* individuals (off the ice) they would not do, might even abhor—such as developing and marketing products that are harmful to children, or unduly suppressing or discrediting information that raises concerns about such harms.

Traditionally governments restrained corporations, understanding that their purely self-interested institutional characters denied them the ability to restrain themselves. Legal limits were imposed in the form of regulations, and agencies were created to enforce those regulations. Such measures were believed necessary to protect children's health and well-being, among other important public interests. That was a key belief behind century-of-the-child reforms. Over the last thirty years, however, governments, under the spell of neoliberalism, steadily retreated from that belief and from the regulatory practices it inspired. Children were left unprotected as a result and are now openly exposed to corporate predation and harm.

Parents, by corollary, have become less able to protect children, their parenting choices limited and frustrated by corporations' profit-seeking maneuvers. Parents may choose, for example, to feed their children healthy food, but they have no choice about the powerful and pervasive marketing that fuels children's desires for and consumption of unhealthy food; they may choose to buy nontoxic products for their children, but they have no choice about the many other sources through which children are exposed to industrial chemicals; they may choose to limit their children's viewing of media violence, but they have no choice about the increasing ubiquity and brutality of such violence in children's lives.

We make choices today as parents, in other words, but not in conditions of our own choosing. And more and more the conditions in which we choose, and hence the choices we make and the effects they have, are determined, or at least heavily influenced, by the decisions and actions of corporations—by the choices *they* make.

In 1859, John Stuart Mill in his classic work *On Liberty* wrote that human nature

> is not a machine to be built after a model, and set to do exactly the work prescribed for it, but a tree, which requires to grow and develop itself on all sides, according to the inward forces which make it a living thing. . . . A person whose desires and impulses are his own—are the expression of his own nature . . . is said to have a character. . . . It is not by wearing down into uniformity all that is individual in themselves, but by cultivating it, and calling it forth, within the limits imposed by the rights and interests of others, that human beings become a noble and beautiful object of contemplation.[15]

Children should be enabled by society to develop unique characters, flourish as individuals, and become the "noble and beautiful object[s] of contemplation" of which Mill spoke. That is what childhood should be about. It is what it was thought to be about during the century of the child. But childhood, thus understood, is now under attack as industry and corporations freely exploit children's vulnerabilities and neglect their interests. This must, and can, be stopped. But first, it must be understood.

Chapter Two

Whack Your Soul Mate and Boneless Girl

W*hack Your Soul Mate*, a popular "casual game" (as simple, animated online games are described), available at numerous child-oriented sites on the web, allows players to determine "how . . . your soul mate meet[s] his or her untimely end." The game is easy to play. With a click of the mouse, a player chooses from among a variety of brutal murder scenarios between two animated "soul mates." In one scenario, the woman punches the man in the face, elbows the back of his head, and then defecates on him after he crumples to the floor dead and bloodied; in another, the man hands the woman a heart-shaped box of chocolates and watches as she opens the box and a spring-loaded cleaver pops out and cuts her head off, blood gushing everywhere; in yet another, the woman stands over the man, who lies prone on the ground, defecating on him as she beats him to death with her fists.[1]

Boneless Girl, another popular game widely available to children on the web, encourages players to smash an apparently unconscious woman wearing black thong underwear and a bra against various-sized spherical objects, and to squeeze her through impossibly narrow gaps, causing her limp body to be crushed and contorted. "Poke and pull this scantily clad babe all over bubble-land," the site exclaims. "You'll be amazed by the small spaces she can fit through, and throwing her across the screen never gets old."[2]

Brutality, violence, cruelty and murder, and finding humor and fun in it all, are common in casual games. *Stair Fall* is another example ("Pushing someone down the stairs has never been so awesome. The more damage they take, the more points you get. How bloody can you make this paper creation?"). Other ones are *Bloody Day* ("Back alley butchering has never been so much fun. It's like having your own barrel with moderately slow-moving fish. How many kills can you rack up?"); *Kitty Cannon* ("Make Fluffy bloody! The best thing you can hope for with these kitties is that they hit a pile of explosives. And even if they hit the spikes, it's still good"); and *Kill a Kitty 2* ("This kitty needs to die. All it takes is one click of your choice, and then watch as hilarity ensues. Will it be the killer bee or the killer heel?").[3]

Addictinggames.com is one of the web's premier casual games site. With 10 million players each month, the majority of whom are children and teenagers, the site hosts all the games described above (except for *Whack Your Soul Mate*, which it recently pulled in response to complaints). Kids love the site, and many agree with one ten-year-old's assessment that it is the "Best f_ing site ever!!!"[4] The fact kids flock to Addictinggames.com (and similar sites) is not surprising. For tweens and teens especially, the edgy and offensive content is a tantalizing lure. With their developing psyches "invaded by a newly mobilized and vastly augmented id as though from a hostile innerworld," as psychoanalyst Erik Erikson has described adolescence, they are fascinated by violence, horror, cruelty, and sex, especially when parents disapprove.[5] "I love this website but my mom thinks it's inappropriate (true, it is)," reports one twelve-year-old about Addictinggames.com.[6]

That most parents abhor games like *Whack Your Soul Mate* and *Boneless Girl* is equally unsurprising. Because "we try to instill in our children a sense of what's right and wrong; a sense of what's important, of what's worth striving for," as one father, President Obama, described it (while a senator), the nastiness and nihilism of these games is not something we want our kids to consider fun.[7] Despite that, Addictinggames.com has become a flagship site for its corporate op-

15

and both manifest in *Whack Your Soul Mate* and *Boneless Girl*. First, campaigns, products, and media content are aimed at the unique, forming, and tumultuous emotions of childhood and adolescence (the subject of this chapter); and, second, children are targeted separately from parents, with campaigns, products, and media content uniquely enticing to them, and often at odds with parents' values and concerns (the subject of the next chapter).

Growing up in Denmark in the 1980s, Martin Lindstrom, one of today's top kid marketers, was "slightly different," he says, than other boys his age. While they played with LEGO, he was obsessed with it. At the age of eight he began building a "Lego Mini Land" in his backyard. Three years later he opened it to the public, charging each visitor the Danish equivalent of a dollar for admission. Only two people showed up—his mother and father. Undaunted, he drafted an advertisement and ran it in the local newspaper. The next day, more than a hundred people showed up. "That's when," he says, "I realized that marketing and branding are magical." [10]

The next year Lindstrom, then twelve years old, started his own advertising firm. He sold the firm to a top international ad agency six years later, and after working at that agency (as an internet marketing specialist) and then at LEGO (as a brand developer and chief designer) he began his current career as a consultant. Advising the likes of Disney, Microsoft, Kellogg's, Pepsi, and Mars in that capacity, he has now become, in the words of the BBC, "the number-one brand builder" in the world. [11]

For Lindstrom, marketing to kids is all about discovering and then engaging the unique emotions of youth. Emotions drive everything for children, he says, and marketers, to be successful, must engage the most fundamental emotions at the deepest levels. *Love*, which connotes nurturing, affection, and romance, is one of these fundamental emotions, he says. *Fear*—as in violence, terror, horror, cruelty, and

17

war—is another. Then there is *mastery*, kids' aspiration to gain independence from adults, and also their desire to master new skills (in gaming, for example). Important as well are *fantasy* ("provide [tweens] the tools that will enable them to create the world of their escapist dreams," Lindstrom advises, "and voilà, you've got it made in the proverbial shade"); *humor* ("pushing the limits, making fun of adults and doing crazy things");[12] and *collection value* (the impulse to collect things such as cards, coins, stamps, and avatar accessories). Finally, there is the *mirror effect*, the desire of kids to imitate the grown-up world. "Products that allow tweens to act as players in an adult world are bound to succeed," says Lindstrom. "The younger you are, the older you want to be; nine-year-olds want to be fourteen so they can be categorized as *real* teenagers, but fourteen-year-olds think teenagers *suck*; they are waiting to become *real* adults." [13]

Successful marketing to children and teenagers requires more than just tapping these emotions, however. It is equally important, Lindstrom advises, to use the right kinds of media to do so. Today, he says, when "interactivity means everything," marketers must take full advantage of the deep and sustained engagement allowed by interactive media, such as games, virtual worlds, and social networks, if they want to reach children effectively.

Addictinggames.com is exemplary. Many of the site's games deliver emotional content interactively—players can act out and control virtual acts of brutality and murder rather than just passively watching actors or animated figures do so, as they would on TV. They can actually *feel* the emotions associated with these actions. That is what makes the games (and gaming more generally) appealing for kids, and hence profitable for Nickelodeon and Viacom.

The games illustrate another point as well, however, and the main point of this chapter. Having discovered that manipulating children's deep emotions is a formula for success, kid marketers push that formula as far as they can, doing whatever it takes, without apparent constraint or concern, to work the emotions of youth into profit. It is this dynamic, as I explain below, that drives them to ramp up media violence, cultivate addiction, cynically exploit social network friendships, sexualize girls, and promote hyperconsumerism.

In the spring of 2008 the video game *Grand Theft Auto IV* was released, selling in its first week six million units for a half billion dollars and thus smashing every entertainment industry record. It was now clear that brutal and sometimes sexual violence was a top entertainment choice for kids. Tween and teenage boys loved the video game (nearly half of all thirteen-year-old boys reported it as their favorite), which like many other popular video games allows players to choose among and create different, and usually violent, scenarios for a protagonist avatar.

In one possible *GTA IV* scenario, inspired by a promotional trailer for the game and posted on YouTube, protagonist Nick Bellic, a grizzled Balkan Wars vet, has sex with a female prostitute in his car and then murders her. The murder is brutal. Bellic beats her with a baseball bat and then as she runs away, he throws a bomb at her. The bomb explodes, she catches fire, and falls to the ground, engulfed in flames, her body quivering. Bellic then sprays her with bullets from a machine gun. Once she stops moving, Bellic reaches into her pants pocket to retrieve the money he paid her for sex. He then saunters back to his car.[14]

Despite its "mature" rating (the industry's designation that a game is inappropriate for kids under the age of eighteen), *GTA IV*, like other mature-rated games, is often sold to underage kids who happily buy and play it. Nearly one half of all twelve- to sixteen-year-olds and a quarter of eight- to eleven-year-olds own mature-rated games.[15] Much larger numbers of kids find ways to play the ever-growing repertoire of increasingly violent games even if they do not actually own them. When, for example, *Call of Duty: Modern Warfare 2*, a game both lauded and criticized for its cinematic experience of violence and

19

mayhem, was released in the fall of 2009, selling nearly 5 million units for $300 million, our then twelve-year-old son, who was not allowed to own the game, phoned around furiously to find a friend who had bought it and went over to his house to play it.

Then there is *Halo*, a space epic with immersive violence, poised to become the "No. 1 gaming title of all time," according to its maker, Microsoft, and recently released in its fourth edition (*Halo Reach*). Again, the game is hugely popular among tween and teen boys ("It's just fun blowing people up," explains one twelve-year-old) despite its "mature" rating. Even churches have begun offering *Halo* to recruit young members—that's how popular the game has become. "[It's] the most effective thing we've done," says David Drexler of the Country Bible Church in Ashby, Minnesota, who seems to have no problem turning his church into a den of virtual violence to lure youth. "We have to find something that these kids are interested in doing that doesn't involve drugs or alcohol or premarital sex." [16]

Numerous other popular video games are notable for their brutality and violence. Casual games too, such as the ones at Addictingames.com, are ramping up violence, and pairing it with sexual images and themes, in efforts to attract young players. The reason is simple: kids, especially tweens and teens, want to play games that engage emotions associated with *fear*, as Lindstrom observes. That is what draws them to violence, brutality, blood, and gore. [17]

But fear is not the only emotion game designers play upon.

At the opposite end of the emotional spectrum, in virtual worlds of pets and penguins, cuddly avatars frolic through landscapes of *love*. Yet the same formula responsible for video game violence—mining kids' deepest emotions with powerfully interactive media—is at work. "We thought virtual pets was a good idea because people would get attached [to their pets] and keep coming back," is how Adam Powell, creator of the world's first virtual pet website, Neopets, describes his achievement. The site, launched in 1999 and now boasting more than 40 million members worldwide, was bought by Nickelodeon for $160 million in 2005. "We couldn't help notice that there was this site that had an enormous number of kids," explained Jeff Dunn, Nickelodeon's president at the time. Dunn made the right decision, as Neopets quickly became a corporate goldmine.[18]

Numerous other virtual pet websites, Club Penguin and Webkinz notable among them, have also done extremely well using the two-step formula pioneered by Neopets—forge emotional bonds between kids and their virtual pets to create "stickiness" (a term used to describe the degree to which users keep playing at and coming back to a site); and then monetize that stickiness with sales of advertising, subscriptions, and virtual goods. Kids feel strong emotions for pets which, site operators have found, easily extend to those composed of pixels on a screen. Children name their virtual pets, feed and play with them, care for and build homes and habitats for them, and navigate with them through exciting virtual landscapes and adventures. They form deep attachments to their pets, and obsessively monitor the meters displayed at most sites indicating pets' emotional and physical states (with their own emotional states often determined by how their pets are doing and feeling.)[19]

Pet sites succeed by manipulating, using casino-style tactics, the intense feelings kids have for their virtual pets. Club Penguin, for example, initially allows kids to play for free in "basic mode," giving them time to bond to their penguin avatars, and then aggressively pitches more fun and excitement, and better and more things for their penguins if they buy costly subscriptions. The site, for example, will display in a "basic mode" pop-up box a special accessory for an avatar and then inform the player who clicks on it that he or she must subscribe in order to get it.[20]

Giving away "free" virtual things and cash is another tactic used by pet sites. At Neopets, for example, players are given 150 NC (short for Neocash, a virtual currency) when they register. With that, they can buy virtual goods for their pet avatars. But because premium goods cost a lot, as much as 800 NC for one item, the free Neocash (much like the rolls of quarters handed out on casino buses) quickly disappears. Players can win more by playing games, but the large amounts of Neocash needed to dress pets in the latest fashions, feed them good food, and buy them cool things, compel many to buy Neocash with real cash, at an exchange rate of $1 for 100 NC, either online or at retailers that sell Neocash cards.[21]

A final tactic used by pet sites, which would likely make even a casino owner blush, is to threaten children with ill fates for their beloved pets if they stop visiting the site or do not visit it enough. Webkinz, for example, takes away kids' pets and everything they have purchased for them if a subscription lapses, and threatens kids with sickness and unhappiness for their pets if they do not visit the site regularly to feed and play with them. "I am 6 1/2 years old and i am afraid that my webkinz will die; i feel like crying cuz i can't go on webkinz," complains one child at an online forum.[22]

These and similar tactics are craftily deployed by pet sites to draw kids in, entice them to stay, and keep them coming back (and thus to get them to engage with ads and hand over money for subscriptions and virtual goods). Virtual pet sites are "like gambling at the end of the day," says Martin Lindstrom. They are designed to make kids feel *compelled* to visit, play, and subscribe; to be, as *Wired* magazine once described Neopets, "so addictive that people would gladly suffer through ads to experience [them]."[23] It may seem diabolical—manipulating kids' emotions so as to "addict" and therefore monetize them—but that is accepted strategy at pet sites, and indeed throughout the gaming and virtual world industries.

There is, after all, nothing stickier than addiction. And that is why these industries have developed more and more addicting content over the years, from simple skill-based games in the 1980s, such as *Tetris* and *Pac Man*—"these games were designed so you would try fifty times, and when you finally got to the goal feel a great sense of achievement and joy," according to gaming titan Kristian Segerstrale—to the likes of *GTA* and *Halo*, Webkinz and Club Penguin, and scores of other video games and virtual worlds that, as Seger-strale describes it, "really grip you as a player, really take you on a journey." [24]

"Addiction" has indeed become the gold standard in gaming, the true mark of a game worth playing. "It's like injecting heroin," reports one online reviewer of *GTA IV*.[25] *BusinessWeek* describes new iPhone games *as* "immersive, addictive fun," [26] while a recent review of *Civilization V* says the game should have a warning label—"The contents of this package may be highly addictive and lead to lack of sleep, lost productivity and marital strife." [27] One game designer proudly proclaims that "parents have to drag their kids away crying" from a game he designed for preschool-aged kids;[28] another observes that "the perfect game is [one] that sucks you in and never lets go." [29] And then, of course, there is the aptly named Addictinggames.com where, in the words of corporate owner Viacom, "junkies gorge themselves" on "addictive . . . impulsive" games that "fuel their addiction." [30]

It is no secret, says gaming expert and psychologist Douglas Gentile, that designing games to be addictive is the main "indicator of success" in the industry. *World of WarCraft*, he notes, has 10 million members paying $15 a month. "Do you think they want it to be addictive?" he asks. "I don't know if they think in terms of addictive, but they certainly want repeat play, they want continued play, and they want you to like it so much that you get your friends to get on. That's much better for their bottom line." [31]

To achieve such repeat and continued play, successful game designers exploit not only deep human emotions, as Lindstrom and Seger-strale advise, but also the basic patterns and principles of human and animal behavior, as discovered by behavioral psychologists. A powerful way to "make players play forever," according to game design guru John Hopson, in his highly influential article *Behavioral Game Design*, is the "avoidance schedule." Put a rat in a cage with a small lever. Shock the rat at short intervals through the cage's metal floor. Hold off on the shock for thirty seconds if the rat presses the lever. And lo and behold, the rat quickly learns to press the lever at a rate that ensures the shocks stop. Human game players, Hopson says, will keep playing a game, just as the rat keeps pushing the lever, if emotionally painful consequences are inflicted upon them if they stop.[32] The "avoidance schedule" is the operative principle at children's sites such as Webkinz and Club Penguin, where bad things happen to kids' cherished pets if they stop playing, fail to play enough, or do not subscribe. It is a desirable strategy from the perspective of game designers, says Hopson, because it is "relatively cheap since they don't have to keep providing the player with toys or rewards."[33]

The "avoidance schedule," according to Hopson, is one of several "fundamental patterns that underlie how players respond to what we ask of them," all of which are "species-independent and can be found in anything from birds to fish to humans." The trick to successful game design, he says, is to manipulate these universal evolutionary tendencies in order to elicit compulsive and addictive player behavior.[34] So, the fact we know a chimpanzee will happily do some task in exchange for a piece of lettuce, but after having been fed a tastier item, such as a grape, will throw an offering of lettuce back at the experimenter, is a warning to game designers never to reduce levels of reinforcement. This "is a very punishing thing for your players and can act as an impetus for them to quit the game," says Hopson.[35] Instructive as well is an experiment in which a pigeon denied a food reward after receiving it every thirty seconds for an hour will beat up on another pigeon in the cage, despite the latter's innocence (it was tethered to the cage and thus unable to interfere with the first pigeon's food supply). The "frustration is irrational, but real nonetheless," a lesson to game designers, according to Hopson, that stopping rewards will generate anger toward the game and cause players to stop playing.[36]

In the end, says Hopson, the thousands of behavioral studies done over the years on rats, pigeons, chimps, and a Noah's Ark full of other animals, including humans, contain an important overall message for game designers. To make players play hard and keep playing they must reward them on a variable, though frequent, schedule (creating a "constant probability of reward, [so] the player always has a reason to do the next thing"), and/or punish them if they stop playing or stop playing hard (i.e., the avoidance schedule).[37]

For a game to be successful, then, it must, following Hopson, be structured to allocate rewards and punishments in accordance with our most fundamental behavioral tendencies, and, following Lindstrom and Segerstrale, deliver content that taps our deepest emotions. Understood in this way, it is hard to imagine a more cynical art than game design, especially when we consider that children are the main targets of its scientifically informed manipulation of behavior and emotion.[38]

A new development in gaming—its merger with social networking—is now taking that cynical art even deeper into children's psyches, and eliciting more compulsive and "addictive" play.

Kristian Segerstrale, who fondly recalls a childhood roaming around the forests of his native Finland ("I think all kids should have that," he says), nonetheless knows that making money off kids is easier when they are roaming around virtual worlds—like the one he and his company, Playfish, created in *Pet Society*, "the most obsessive game we have," he says. Part of the game's success is its typical (of pet sites) "avoidance schedule" setup—"kids don't like to abandon pets so they keep logging in to keep their pet happy."[39] But what makes the game stickier than even its stickiest pet-site competitors—it had 20 million registered players and 2 billion monthly player minutes just three months after coming online in 2008, and it now boasts 12 million monthly active users—is the fact it is *social*. Players play with their Facebook friends. "The real meat of the game in *Pet Society* is that all your real-world friends live in the same village as your pets, so the pet sort of becomes a virtual representation of you," says Segerstrale. "The game becomes what's happening between you and your real-world friends."[40]

25

And it is that "real world status," Segerstrale says—the fact the game has consequences in players' real lives—that makes *Pet Society* and other social games so compelling. Taking care of a friend's pet, buying it gifts (with virtual cash bought or earned at the site), having your pet hug or kiss or flirt with that pet means something in your outside-the-game relationship with that friend. "You can get people to come back to that kind of game play at a completely different level" than in a nonsocial game, says Segerstrale. "Things like love, friendship, competition, and envy among friends are far more powerful than the emotions between you and just a game."[41]

By tapping into people's real emotions and relationships, social gaming adds a new, and intensely compelling, dimension to gaming. The widely popular *Mafia Wars*, offered on Facebook by Playfish competitor Zynga games, is another example. While *Pet Society* occupies the *love* end of Lindstrom's emotional spectrum, *Mafia Wars* is firmly embedded at the *fear* end. Players "start a Mafia family with [their] friends, run a criminal empire and fight to be the most powerful family" in a game of back alley beatings, drive-by shootings, robberies, brutal muggings, and heists.[42] Warnings of "sex, drug use, violence and other subject matter that some parents may consider inappropriate for audiences under 18 years of age" likely only help entice tweens and teens, who are among the game's most avid players.[43]

Again, it is the fact players play with their actual Facebook friends—creating mob "families" with them, competing against other "families," planning heists together, and so on—that makes the game so compelling. There is a seamless interplay between players' real friendships, cliques, grudges, and alliances and what goes on within the game. As Zynga proudly boasts on its website, its games allow players to "express themselves and form deep social connections with their friends."[44]

Both *Pet Society* and *Mafia Wars* make money by selling virtual goods to players, and also by luring players with virtual cash to the sites of third-party advertisers (who, in turn, pay Playfish and Zynga for each player visit). It is a highly profitable monetization model. "There's no cost to produce one hundred machine guns and there's no inventory costs," boasts *Mafia Wars*' Scott Koenigsberg of the easy money made by selling virtual goods. "The only limit is our brains and what people think is cool."[45] As one industry insider describes it, social games are about "get[ting] users in the door to play for free and then monetiz[ing] the hell out of them once they're hooked."[46] Given that many of those users are children, even a real Mafioso might find it all a bit distasteful.

Segerstrale, who recently sold Playfish to gaming giant Electronic Arts for $300 million, says he plans to develop new social games that are even more engaging, addictive, and sticky than those currently available, and that penetrate even deeper into kids' social and emotional lives. "The most exciting area of innovation," he says, is "when players can use a friend's data as part of the game play even though that friend is not playing. They can pull that friend's name and photos as part of the game play."[47] Lika Games's *Friends for Sale* is an example of this new kind of game, says Segerstrale. The game has players bid against each other using virtual cash, which they purchase from the site with real cash, to buy and own mutual Facebook friends. "Buy people and make them your pets!" the site proclaims. "You can make your pets poke, send gifts, or just show off for you. Make money as a shrewd pet investor or as a hot commodity!"[48] The mutual friend has no idea he or she is being bought and sold, unless so informed by one of the players, but for the players involved, says Segerstrale, the buying and selling of the mutual friend "is worth something, it means something in the real world."[49]

"We've only scratched the surface of what's possible in this type of game play," Segerstrale says. What lies beneath that surface may be exciting for Segerstrale and his gaming industry friends, but it should be worrying for parents.

* * *

Our thirteen-year-old daughter was unusually upset one day. We asked her what was wrong and she told us, after a bit of prodding, that one of her Facebook friends had been making nasty comments about her, anonymously, for months, on an application called Honesty Box.[50] Launched in 2007, and currently catering to millions, Honesty Box allows users to send, receive, and reply to anonymous messages from Facebook friends. "Flirt with your crushes," the application promises. "Discover what people really think of you." Anonymity is guaranteed, and users are warned that once a message is sent, it can never be removed.[51] The site is "extremely sticky," according to its developer Dan Peguine, and has, he says, quickly become one that, like Facebook itself, people feel compelled to check each morning and return to throughout the day.[52]

The insults on Honesty Box had been particularly hurtful for our daughter that day, and there was no sign, she said, that the virtual harassment would stop anytime soon. We told her to delete the application immediately from her Facebook page, but that only made her more despondent. "I have to be on Honesty Box," she said. "Otherwise I won't know what people are saying about me."

Honesty Box makes money by brilliantly, though diabolically, exploiting the emotional turbulence of peer-obsessed adolescence. Users are invited to try to discover who has been anonymously talking to and about them, but they must pay. "Use [HB] points to 'bribe' your friends," to disclose who they are, the site declares. "More points mean you can have more negotiation power." HB points can be bought online for eleven cents each, in batches of 110, 183, 455 and 911, with credit cards, PayPal accounts, or cell phone numbers (charges appear on monthly bills, usually parents'); or they can be earned by clicking on the sites of third-party advertisers (who pay Honesty Box for each hit).[53]

Honesty Box is not all that our daughter, and a majority of teenage kids around the world, are doing on Facebook, however. Facebook itself has become a central hub of social life for most teens, a place where they spend hours each day chatting, planning, flirting, gossiping, and looking at and sharing pictures and videos. With more than 500 million members worldwide, including a full third of the population of the English-speaking world, and more than half of all teens in the United States, Facebook is the leader among a growing array of social networks—some sponsored by brands (iCoke, for example), others unique to particular regions, languages, or demographics, and still others, such as YouTube and Flikr, focused on media sharing—that is radically changing the way children and teens engage with media.[54]

Unlike traditional media—television, movies, and even traditional games and virtual worlds—where content is composed of *other* lives and landscapes (whether fictitious or real), social networks make kids the stars and stories of their own shows. Their friends, crushes, gossip, ideas, angst, pictures, and videos become the "content" of an intoxicating and all-consuming mix of real life and entertainment—that is, the ultimate "reality show"—that is simply irresistible to a demographic already obsessed with peers, celebrity, and themselves.[55]

What the rapid rise of social networks suggests, and what kid marketers are now coming to understand, is that the lives and dramas of kids themselves are likely the stickiest content of all.

The Panopticon (which means "all-seeing") is a model prison devised by British philosopher and legal reformer Jeremy Bentham in the late eighteenth century. Its structure, a radial configuration with observation posts in the center, and inmates' cells and common areas around the periphery, was designed to ensure guards could always see inmates but never be seen by them. As a result, inmates had to presume guards might be watching them at any given moment, which meant, according to Bentham, that they would have to behave *as if* they were being watched all of the time. In this way, the Panopticon, by its very structure, created the effect of total surveillance, whilst allowing for actual surveillance to be intermittent, and even absent.

29

The Panopticon was never built,[56] but Bentham's idea was revived by French philosopher Michel Foucault two centuries later to illustrate what he called the "perfection of power." Power was perfected within the Panopticon, Foucault argued, because it did not have to be exercised by guards and prison authorities. Inmates "themselves [became] the bearers of power" within a structure that had the effect of "creating and sustaining a power relation independent of the person who exercises it."[57]

The Panopticon is helpful for understanding the new power and possibilities of social media for kid marketers. On social media, "people influence people," according to Mark Zuckerberg, founder and CEO of Facebook. "It's no longer just about messages . . . broadcasted out by companies, but increasingly about information . . . shared between friends."[58] Social network friends market to each other, in other words, as "viral" tactics (also known as "word-of-mouth" and "buzz" tactics) seamlessly weave brands and commercial messages into communications among them. Users become "fans" and "friends" of brands, and get their friends to do the same; they share across their networks branded contests, quizzes, games, applications, and "widgets" (mini-applications whose viral power makes them, according to one industry insider, possibly the highest expression so far of online marketing in the post-advertising age");[59] they create branded videos, songs, stories, poems, and photographs at company websites and virally distribute them to friends.[60] These are just a few of a huge and growing array of viral strategies.

Marketing *as* marketing disappears within the viral networks of social media platforms. Boundaries are broken down between marketers and kids (as kids market to each other); between content and advertising (as advertising now infuses, rather than interrupts, content); and between kids' lives and entertainment (as their lives now become the content of that entertainment). It is truly the "perfection of [marketers'] power." Kids, like the prisoners in the Panopticon, now bear the power marketing holds over them, and the marketers, like the

Panopticon's guards, drop from view, their power now automatic and self-executing, all the greater for its invisibility.[61]

The Panopticon effect inevitably will define all media, and every domain of children's lives, as traditional media converge with social networks, and the entire media package goes mobile. In the very near future, television will be fully converged with social media;[62] most, if not all, marketing will be social or have significant social elements; all media and marketing will be accessible from mobile devices; and more and more children, at ever-younger ages, will have ready access to mobile devices. Soon, in other words, there will be no escape from the Panopticon of kid marketing.

That is a frightening prospect, not only because social media magnify the power of marketing, as already discussed, but also because such media grant marketers new and insidious powers of surveillance over children's lives. Like the guards in the Panopticon, social media enable marketers to quietly and invisibly observe every move, even the most intimate and private rituals, of those they watch.[63] "In social media," as Joel Rubinson, chief research officer at the Advertising Research Foundation, states, "people talk about their needs, lifestyles, and brand preferences in their own words. So we refer to this form of research as 'listening.'"[64]

Sophisticated algorithms analyze keystrokes and mouse-clicks from pages visited, searches conducted, ads clicked on, information shared at social sites, and products bought online to create richly complex profiles of individuals. These "social graphs," as they are called,[65] are then relied upon by marketers to target individuals in the most effective ways. As a result, states a recent JP Morgan report, while marketers "used to pay for audiences on websites [they] will now start to pay for specific users."[66] Marketing is shifting, in other words, from targeting groups on the basis of anonymous demographics to target individuals on the basis of personal psychographics.

Indeed, it is all going in a quite creepy "Big Brother" tion, especially when one considers that children an primary targets. Recently, for example, Mindset Media announced a new service that "enables brand advertisers to target consumers with specific personality traits that drive buyer behavior and brand affinity" (there are twenty-one such traits, including extroversion, modesty, pugnaciousness, dogmatism, pragmatism, altruism, and assertiveness).[67] Facebook is currently researching a "sentiment engine" that will determine if a person is having a good or bad day and thus how and when it is psychologically best to approach him or her with marketing pitches.[68] "Measurement," according to BuzzLogic, a company that trolls through blog conversations and the links connecting them to determine exactly where and what kinds of ads should be placed, "is no longer about eyeballs and page views—it's about relationships, conversations, and the degree to which they are influencing consumers."[69]

Welcome to the Panopticon of kid marketing.

Chapter Three

The New Curriculum of Childhood

In a scene from Denys Arcand's film *Days of Darkness*, a father driving a car with his two daughters asks the girls, "What's happening in school?" The older one, a teenager, buried in conversation on her cell phone, is oblivious to the question; the younger one, about eight years old, unaware her father is talking, gyrates back and forth to music playing in her headphones. Resigned, the father drives on in silence, his daughters isolated in their digital worlds, a picture of dystopian disconnection deftly deployed by Arcand, alongside surreal images of medieval barbarities, to illustrate his thesis that we are entering a new Dark Age.

It may seem odd, depicting the bright screens and flashy gadgets of digital media, harbingers of progress and possibility for so many, as signs of descent into darkness. But when I sit in a room with my kids, and they are a million miles away, absorbed by the titillating roil of social life on Facebook, or the addictive pulls of games and virtual worlds, or their own narcissism, as they stare endlessly at videos and pictures of themselves and their friends, it does feel like something is off the rails. They seem altogether somewhere else, their presence sucked right out of their bodies as they obsessively navigate the ether. Not even the ambient blathering of a family television set is shared among us.

Arcand's image of the father, alienated from his two daughters by digital gadgetry, rings disturbingly true (as does his larger message that we may be slipping into a new dark age as our relationships to gadgets displace our ability to connect humanly with others). Digital media push parents to the margins of children's lives, as kids become immersed in the endless enticements of worlds that not only exclude us but also deliberately undermine our values and concerns as parents.[1] In these ways, however, digital media only perfect a strategy that kid marketers have been using and refining for decades—namely, targeting children separately from parents with content uniquely enticing to them and often deliberately designed to wedge them away from their parents.

James McNeal, the founder and first guru of kid marketing, was a graduate student at the University of Texas in the early 1960s when he first realized that, with television now a fixture in every American home, and marketers thus able to access children directly, kids were poised to become a large and lucrative consumer market. No longer just candy munchers and toy users, he reported in his first seminal piece, *The Child Consumer: A New Market*, kids were evolving into powerful consumers with their own money to spend, and substantial influence over their parents' spending.[2]

But kids were not just miniature adults, McNeal insisted. Special marketing principles applied to them. Chief among these was meeting the "need for kids to be kids." The task for kid marketers, he counseled, was to discover, through careful observation and psychological testing, what *kids* wanted (as opposed to what their parents wanted for them), and then to design campaigns and products that responded to those wants. McNeal's ideas, laid out in numerous books and articles over the years, with the scientific rigor and precision one would expect from a leading scholar (he was a professor of marketing at the University of Texas), quickly became gospel among marketers, and a bedrock for the emerging field of kid marketing.

Through the 1960s, kid marketing grew into a mainstay on commercial television, with broadcasters creating special slots for children's programs (remember Saturday morning cartoons?), and toy, food, and beverage companies buying spots to pitch their goods. Momentum slowed slightly during the 1970s when federal regulators stepped in to impose restrictions on advertising aimed at children.[3] But those restrictions were short-lived.

In 1981 President Reagan appointed Mark Fowler, a broadcast industry attorney and Reagan fundraiser, to head the Federal Communications Commission. For Fowler, television was "just another appliance, a toaster with pictures," as he called it. Broadcast corporations, like toaster manufacturers, had no grander mission than to "determine the wants of their audiences through the normal mechanisms of the market," he believed. They were businesspeople, not "community trustees," he argued, which meant there was no case for imposing special public interest restrictions and requirements upon them.[4] Fowler used his tenure as head of the FCC to deregulate children's television. He and his commission repealed requirements that stations broadcast "educational and informational" programs, as well as limits on how much time they could devote to commercials during children's programs. The FCC stripped the Federal Trade Commission of authority to rule on unfair advertising (at a time when that commission was considering deeming all children's advertising "unfair," and banning it on that basis), and defined the regulatory term "public interest" to mean little more than "commercially successful," thus clearing the way for toy-based programs (such as *Teenage Mutant Ninja Turtles* and *Mighty Morphin Power Rangers*) to meet that standard.[5]

Around the same time, the early 1980s, cable TV was making its way into American homes, a huge boost for kid marketing as it was now possible for an entire network to be devoted to children's programming. Nickelodeon was the first company to do this, establishing an exclusively children's network in 1979. From the outset,

35

the company's explicit aim was to create a place where kids could play and feel empowered, have the kind of fun *they* wanted to have, and escape the clean-up-your-room-do-your-homework drudgery of their parents' regimes. Nickelodeon would, in its own words, "let kids be kids," become an ally and trusted friend of children that understood, cared about, and delivered what they really wanted. The network would be like the "naughty aunt or uncle who's the most fun to have in a family,"[6] as Geraldine Laybourne, its chief architect, once described it.[7]

Laybourne's big idea at Nickelodeon—to "let kids be kids" (which was essentially what McNeal had been advocating for two decades)—was executed with calculated rigor. Under her leadership, the company pioneered new and creative ways to get into kids' psyches and to understand their unique desires and drives. In the mid-1980s, for example, it co-created, with consumer research firm Yankelovich, the Nickelodeon/Yankelovich Youth Monitor to research the wants and attitudes of children and teenagers. It continued with such initiatives after Laybourne left the company in 1992, organizing weekend retreats through the 1990s, where researchers would study and observe children over days of slumber parties and play, and also creating the Nickelodeon Kid Panel, an internet network of kids monitored by expert researchers.[8]

By the time Laybourne left Nickelodeon, the company had become large and profitable, a darling of Wall Street. Continuing to work from her playbook under subsequent chiefs, it became increasingly proficient at catering to kids' own desires and senses of fun and adventure, in contrast, and sometimes contradiction, to what parents wanted for them (as, for example, with the aforementioned *Whack Your Soul Mate* and *Boneless Girl*).[9] The company became a model for other children's networks and marketers over the years, and today, due in no small part to its considerable influence, those who market to children and teenagers routinely design campaigns and content in ways that amplify children's natural and normal desires to rebel against parents, and push kids' loyalties, emotions, and affections away from parents and toward brands, gadgets, websites, characters, and avatars. It is hard for parents to compete. As our kids become immersed, ever more deeply, in a culture that works to pry them loose from us, we become less able to find the connection, respect, authority, and credibility we need to keep them safe, healthy, and in the long-term happy.

Psychologist Gordon Neufeld and physician Gabor Mate state in their book *Hold Onto Your Kids* that children and teens need strong bonds with their parents (and others who play parental roles in their lives) in order to develop self-esteem, independence, and identity. Parents, they say, provide children and teens "unconditional love and acceptance . . . [and] the willingness to sacrifice for the growth and development of the other," which are essential for their healthy emotional development.[10] When parent-child bonds are breached, Neufeld and Mate warn, children are put at risk of serious behavioral and emotional difficulties. The weakening of such bonds in modern society, they say, is part of the reason "children are becoming more difficult to parent, students are harder to teach, aggression and violence among children are escalating, adolescents are failing to mature, bullying is on the rise, children are becoming desensitized and insolence and defiance are increasing."[11]

Yet kid marketers make an art of breaching bonds between children and parents. While genuine commitment to the "let kids be kids" credo should require respecting and cultivating the most crucial bonds in kids' lives, marketers instead target and undermine those bonds for the sake of easy profits. The real credo of kid marketers—the one that truly explains their ambitions and behaviour—is not "let kids be kids," but rather "let us get at your kids." And the reasons for outrage only mount when we consider what kid marketers do with, and to, kids once they have them within their grasp.

*   *   *

No one thought fifteen-year-old Brandon Crisp was the type of kid who would run away from home, but on the cold autumn day his father took away his Xbox he jumped on his bike and disappeared. "It's every parent's worst nightmare," said his mother, Angelika Crisp, from her suburban home in Barrie, Ontario at the time. "He's always been a great kid, good at school, loves sports, or he used to love sports before he got obsessed with playing that game *Call of Duty 4: Modern Warfare*." Brandon's father had taken away his Xbox because he believed *Call of Duty* was consuming the boy's life. Brandon would get up in the middle of the night to play the game; he had retreated from family and off-line friends, fallen behind at school, and stopped playing sports. He was becoming distant and removed. When he refused to leave his room and join his family on Thanksgiving Day, so that he could keep playing the game, his father felt compelled to act.[12]

Two weeks after he disappeared, Brandon's body was found in the woods outside Barrie. An autopsy revealed he had died from falling out of a tree he had climbed. Foul play was not suspected.

Brandon's story is one in a long line of similar tragedies dating back at least a decade to the highly publicized suicide of twenty-one-year-old Shawn Woolley, who shot himself in the head while playing *EverQuest* (dubbed "EverCrack" and "NeverRest" by players). He too had become completely absorbed in the game, quitting his job so he could play all day, and losing contact with his family and friends.[13] Other gaming abuse stories are equally tragic—players dropping dead from blood clots, starvation, and exhaustion as a result of sitting and playing for excessive hours; a South Korean couple who continually left their three-month-old daughter alone in an apartment while they went to play *World of WarCraft* at a nearby internet café, returning one twelve-hour session later, to find her dead from malnutrition.[14]

The previous chapter examined how and why "addiction" has become a goal and source of profitability for the gaming industry. Here I am concerned with the other side of the issue—how and why such addiction can cause children harm.

There is an ongoing and heated debate among medical and mental health experts about whether gaming and internet addictions are *true* addictions; whether they should be treated similarly to alcohol, tobacco, and drug addictions. Some mental health experts and practitioners believe the two types of addiction are linked. Oxford neuroscientist Susan Greenfield, for example, says of gaming that

> the sheer compulsion of reliable and almost immediate reward is being linked to similar chemical systems in the brain that may also play a part in drug addiction. So we should not underestimate the "pleasure" of interacting with a screen when we puzzle over why it seems so appealing to young people.[15]

Greenfield's allusion to brain chemistry is supported by a recent study published in the *Journal of Psychiatric Research*.[16] Researchers compared ten participants with online gaming addiction problems to ten without such problems. When gaming stimuli were presented to all participants, only members of the former group showed brain activity in "regions [that] have been reported to contribute to the craving in substance dependence," the researchers state. What that means, they continue, is "that the gaming urge/craving in online gaming addiction and craving in substance dependence might share the same neurobiological mechanism."

Still, both the American Medical Association and the American Psychiatric Association currently reject the comparison between gaming and substance addiction, and refuse to recognize the former as a disorder. Whatever the final outcome of the debate about whether gaming addiction is a *true* addiction, however, what cannot be doubted is that compulsive gaming and internet use are problems in the lives of many children and teens today.[17] "A number, and it's not a small number, of people show behaviors that are the same types of behaviors they show when they are addicted to a substance," says psychologist Dr. Gentile of children and teens who play video and online games.

They become grumpy, agitated, and depressed when they are denied access. Their lives get out of balance as they withdraw from family and friends, and lose interest in school and other activities once important to them. They describe themselves as being addicted. "These kids know they should do their homework," says Gentile, "but they can't stop. They know they should go to sleep, but they have to keep going a little bit more." [18]

Gentile acknowledges this may not be exactly the same thing as addiction to a substance—"it's not a mutant substance you're ingesting," he says; "crack basically hooks everyone, games don't" [19]—but it is a serious health concern nonetheless, an impulse control disorder akin, for example, to pathological gambling. A growing literature confirms Gentile's concerns demonstrating that gaming "addiction" can harm and damage those who suffer from it, even ruin their lives. And the problem is only escalating, according to Gentile, as new technologies and increasingly aggressive marketing tactics combine to make games more enticing, compelling, and available to children and teens.

Like traditional digital gaming, social networks (along with the social games and applications they carry) promote obsessive engagement among children and teens, but arguably in different ways and with different results. When, for example, our daughter said she *needed* to be on Honesty Box, it was not so much a statement of addiction as one of social survival. For most teens today, identity and status among peers are defined largely online, which means that *being* and managing one's online self becomes essential to establishing and maintaining a place in the real world of social relations. As Sherry Turkle, an MIT professor, and founder and director of the MIT Initiative on Technology and Self, describes it, "The anxiety that teens report when they are without their cell phones or their link to the internet may not speak so much to missing the easy sociability with others but of missing the self that is constituted in these relationships." This is something greater, or at least different, than addiction, says Turkle. "The term addiction has been used to describe this state but this way of thinking is limited in its usefulness. More useful is thinking about a new state of self, one that is extended in a communications artefact." Yet, the effects are equally unhealthy, if not more so. Not only are teens compulsively engaged with the medium, but also, through obsessive chatting in the "shorthand of emoticon emotions," says Turkle, they come to depend on constant, though flattened and lifeless, affirmation to "shore up their fragile selves." This, in turn, fuels narcissism, and limits opportunities for them to "learn empathetic skills, to manage and express feelings, and to handle being alone," she says.[20]

Most children and teens spend hours each day engaged with digital games and social media, removed from other dimensions and relationships in their lives—family, school, sports, sleep, and so on—and schooled in compulsion and narcissism. The effects can be unhealthy, addictive, and devastating for some children, even if they currently fall short of indicating officially recognized disorders. Yet, as the previous chapter showed, "addiction" is deliberately and callously cultivated by producers of kid culture, who aim to hook kids on their creations for the sole purpose of wringing profit from them.

A recent study of youth in ten countries on five continents confirmed just "how 'addicted' they are to [digital media]," as the study described its findings. Conducted by the University of Maryland's International Center for Media and the Public Agenda in partnership with the Salzburg Academy on Media and Global Change, the study asked 1,000 college students to go completely unplugged for twenty-four hours. At the end of the twenty-four hours, the students were asked to write about their experiences. Among other things, the study found that (as summarized at www.theworldunplugged.wordpress.com):

- Students' "addiction" to media may not be clinically diagnosed, but the cravings sure seem real—as do the anxiety and depression;
- Students report that media—especially their mobile phones— have literally become an extension of themselves. Going without

41

media, therefore, made it seem like they had lost a part of themselves;

- Students around the world reported that being tethered to digital technology 24/7 is not just a habit, it is essential to the way they contruct their friendships and social lives;
- For many students, going without media for twenty-four hours ripped back the curtain on their hidden loneliness;
- Many students, from all continents, literally couldn't imagine how to fill up their empty hours without media.

Media violence is another area of concern (also touched upon in the previous chapter). While no one doubts it is increasing, in both quantity and intensity, consensus breaks down on the question of whether it causes harm. Debates tend to oscillate between extreme positions, with some arguing for catastrophic effects—kids, "programmed with this massive [media] violence overdose [become] the mass murderers of tomorrow," according to Dr. Phil commenting in the wake of the Virginia Tech shootings;[21] and others claiming it is just harmless fun—"I'm not walking up to someone with a pistol and shooting them; I'm shooting pixels on a screen," says Kedrick Kenerly, founder of Christian Gamers Online.[22]

The truth, as revealed by hundreds of studies on media violence conducted over the last forty years, lies somewhere in between. Exposure to media violence does not, on its own, turn children into mass murderers, though it can have a range of negative effects, including desensitization to real violence, cultivation of the belief violence resolves conflict, and an increase in violent and aggressive thoughts and actions. These effects, moreover, are heightened by interactive media, such as video and online games, which allow players to identify with aggressors, actively participate in aggression sequences, and gain rewards for increasingly aggressive behaviour.[23]

Gentile, a leading expert on media violence as well as on gaming addiction, finds it perplexing that "the same parents who take great pains to keep children from witnessing violence in the home and neighborhood," knowing intuitively that it is bad for them, "often do little to keep them from viewing large quantities of violence on television, in movies, and in video games." Part of the reason for this, he believes, is that the industry does such a good job of stifling concern. "The minute I release a study showing that violent video games do in fact increase aggression," Gentile says, "I get threatened to be sued by the video game industry." It's a knee-jerk reaction, he says, by an industry bent on neutralizing any threat to its profits.[24]

Child development expert Nancy Carlsson-Paige worries that, "Constant depictions of violence, aggression, and disrespect toward others are immersing kids in a world where 'might makes right.'"[25] With violence now at the core of the "central curriculum of childhood,"[26] as one commentator describes today's youth media culture, it seems reasonable to fear children are learning the wrong lessons about life and themselves—namely, that violence is fun, especially when it is cruel and sexualized; that it is glamorous, cool, and the solution to conflict; that justice, freedom, and heroism are achieved with a gun, or a knife or a bomb; and that, as human beings, we are naturally prone to be violent and brutal.

Media sexualization, primarily of girls, is another subject in the new curriculum of childhood. Marketers today peddle lace lingerie, padded and push-up bras, and thong underwear (sometimes emblazoned with Playboy logos, or sexual messages such as "too many boys, too little time") to girls as young as five, and routinely target girls with sexualized games, online activities, movies, television shows, books, magazines, and toys (such as the infamous Bratz dolls). As the American Psychological Association (APA) recently observed, "Throughout U.S. culture and particularly in mainstream media women and girls are depicted in a sexualizing manner,"[27] one in which a person's value comes only from his or her sexual appeal or behavior, to the exclusion of other characteristics;

a person is held to a standard that equates physical attractiveness (narrowly defined) to being sexy;

a person is sexually objectified—that is, made into a thing for others' sexual use, rather than seen as a person with the capacity for independent action and decision making;

sexuality is inappropriately imposed upon a person (especially relevant for children).[28]

Sexualization sells, which is why kid marketers and corporations use it. It taps deep feelings and emerging curiosities, plays on the "mirror effect," as Lindstrom describes kids' natural desire to be and seem older, and promotes obsessive concern with physical appearance, all of which helps sell products (cosmetics, clothes, accessories, personal care products, and so on), and draw kids to media (TV shows, games, movies, and so on).

But there are costs. A growing body of psychological research, summarized in the APA's report, links media sexualization to a series of tangible harms to girls: lack of confidence in and comfort with their bodies, eating disorders, low self-esteem, depression, distraction, shame, anxiety, self-disgust, unhealthy sexual attitudes and practices, and sexual problems in adulthood.[29] For psychologist Diane Levin, the problem is not "the fact that children are learning about sex when they are young. The problem is what today's sexualized environment is teaching them."

> They are learning about objectified sex that occurs in relationships that are often devoid of emotions, emotional attachments or consequences. They are learning about sex that is the defining activity in intimate sexual relationships to the exclusion of other vital aspects of healthy relationships. They are learning about sex that is often linked to violence and hurting others. And they are learning to link physical

appearance and buying the right, expensive products that make you look physically attractive and sexy with being successful as a person. Such lessons cannot help but have a big impact on who children become as functioning adult males or females or on the sexual relationships they have as adults.[30]

Beyond the issues of sexualization, addiction, and media violence, a large and more general lesson children and teens learn from the new "central curriculum of childhood" is that life (its meaning and purpose), and people (our identities, worth, happiness, and connections to others) are dependent on relationships to things. Research has linked overly materialist attitudes in both children and adults to unhappiness, anxiety and depression, weakened emotional attachments, less ability to empathize and cooperate with others, and narcissistic, manipulative, and antisocial behavior.[31]

These effects are harmful not only for kids and their families, according to psychologist Tim Kasser, but also for society as a whole. "To be a consumer has a very different set of implications than to be a citizen," says Kasser.

> We know that materialism and consumerism in research is associated with behaving in less cooperative and more competitive ways and less empathetic and more manipulative ways and less pro social and more anti social ways. What all that suggests is that when push comes to shove, and there are significant problems that we face, we will have lost some of the interpersonal, social skills and community skills that are really needed in order to come together as a group and solve the problems.[32]

In addition to psychological and social harms, kid marketing can also cause physical harm to children. Enticing children and teens with unhealthy products is among kid marketers' more pernicious, albeit common, practices. Food and beverage industries, for example, spend nearly $2 billion each year marketing and advertising "junk food" to children—soda pop, fast-food, sugary breakfast cereals, and numerous other unhealthy products. Children's consumption of these products has increased substantially since the early 1980s when such marketing efforts began in earnest. Over that same period, obesity and weight problems have increased threefold among American children with nearly 20 percent of all children in the United States now overweight, and thus at higher risk for type 2 diabetes and cardiovascular disease, among other problems.[33]

Food and beverage marketers are not the only ones promoting unhealthy products to youth, however. Tobacco companies, notorious in the past for preying on children, redoubled their efforts in the early 2000s with candy- and fruit-flavored cigarettes, hip-hop themed marketing campaigns, cartoon packaging, and scratch and sniff promotions (though by the mid-2000s state regulators had begun to take action, and in 2009 the FDA banned candy- and fruit-flavored cigarettes).[34] They are joined by other industries seeking to expand markets by enticing children to want the unhealthy and inappropriate products they pitch to them—fun flavored coffees and youth-oriented energy drinks hook kids on caffeine at ever younger ages; sodalike alcoholic beverages are made and marketed to appeal to teens; and online gambling sites aim advertising at kids on television and on the web.[35]

A final kind of kid marketing harm is specific to schools.[36] Over the last three decades marketing and advertising, in a variety of different forms, much of it for unhealthy food and beverages, has become ubiquitous in schools.[37] Companies plaster their ads, logos, and messages on classroom, cafeteria, and gym walls, textbook covers, screen savers, bulletin boards, scoreboards, the sides and insides of school buses, rooftops, and so on. They pay schools for exclusive rights to sell their products (mainly soda); sponsor educational materials, such as workbooks, websites, and curriculum units; and mount events and fundraising campaigns that feature and sell their products.[38]

In addition to extending the reach of advertising, and thus the scope of the kinds of harms already discussed, advertising in schools takes students' time and attention away from learning, targets a captive audience, bolsters consumerist messages with the implied authority and blessings of school officials, and arguably undermines the role of education in promoting critical thought and intelligent reflection. With respect to the latter point, a recent report on commercialism in schools notes that "advertisements are inherently *mis*-educative in that they present biased information and discourage rational thought, and thus promote unreflective consumption."[39]

Addiction, media violence, sexualization, hyperconsumerism, and unhealthy products are the core subjects of the "new curriculum of childhood." For the corporate creators of that curriculum, vaunted into positions of unprecedented power and influence over children and childhood over the last half century, profit is the only legitimate goal. From their self-interested perspectives childhood vulnerabilities that should demand protection—tender and turbulent emotions, forming intellects, inexperience, and lack of guile—instead are targeted for easy exploitation.

It is commonly argued that concerns about resulting harms are unfounded and overblown. There is no *definitive* proof of such harm, it is said; the scientific evidence of ill effects from addiction, violence, sexualization, and hyperconsumerism is lacking, or it is incomplete or disputed. We should wait for proof of harm before becoming worried and taking action, the argument goes.

Such sanguinity can seem a comfort for concerned parents (not to mention a convenient defense for implicated industries, and governments that fail to act), but it is misguided. Though the science may be incomplete and disputed, there is, as recounted earlier, strong support, both empirical and theoretical, for a range of subtle and not-so-subtle harms in all the areas discussed. Demanding *definitive* proof of such harm is unrealistic in light of the inherent complexities of the issues, and the inevitable vagaries of social (and physical) science. Moreover, scientific studies tend to focus on *single* issues when, in their actual lives, children and teens are bombarded with violent, sexualizing, and consumerist messages and images, along with compulsive and addictive enticements, all at once, all the time, and everywhere. It is the cumulative, and mutually reinforcing effect of all of this that is the real concern.

In short, if we wait for definitive proof of harm before taking action—whether as parents or as a society—we will wait for a very long time. It is telling that even courts have not always required such proof. In the U.S. Supreme Court's 1968 decision in *Ginsberg v. New York*, for example, a New York statute prohibiting the sale of "girlie" magazines (such as *Playboy* and *Penthouse*) to minors was held to be valid despite claims it violated the First Amendment's right to free speech. Though Justice William J. Brennan believed it "very doubtful that [it was] an accepted scientific fact" such magazines caused harm to teens, he and the Court nonetheless upheld the statute on the ground it aimed to protect minors from harm. "It was not irrational for the legislature to find that exposure to material condemned by the statute is harmful to minors," even in the absence of scientific evidence, the Court stated.[40]

In similar spirit, an even broader law in the province of Quebec— one that banned nearly all commercial advertising aimed at children under thirteen years old—was found by the Supreme Court of Canada in a 1989 case to comport with free-speech guarantees, again despite there being no definitive proof of harm. "Where the legislature mediates between the competing claims of different groups in the community," the court stated, it will inevitably be called upon to draw a line marking where one set of claims legitimately begins and the other fades away without access to complete knowledge as to its precise location. If the legislature has made a reasonable assessment as to where the line is most properly drawn, especially if that assessment involves weighing conflicting scientific evidence and allocating scarce resources on that basis, it is not for the courts to second guess. That would only be to substitute one estimate for another.[41]

Both the U.S. and Canadian supreme courts acknowledge, in other words, that definitive proof of harm is an unrealistically high standard for governments to meet when they act to protect children. That is one retort to the demand for such proof.

A second and related retort is that the demand misses the true point of the debate about harm. In 1973, social scientist Ithiel de Sola Pool testified before Congress on the effects of television violence on children. He was asked by Senator John Pastore (D-RI) for a definitive answer— did the science demonstrate harm? The answer he gave is instructive:

Too often scientists pontificate on public policy as if their science has given them answers when their answers come from their personal values. As to what needs to be done, I would rather say as a citizen than a scientist, because that is a civic question, not a scientific question.[42]

Many questions about harm to children, and especially those raised by the issues addressed in this and the previous chapter, are at least as much about values as they are about science. They concern our individual and collective senses of what is appropriate for children at different ages; what is good for them and what is not; what they should be taught; how they should spend their time (what activities they miss out on, for example, when they spend hours each day on screens); and what kinds of people we want them to become.

49

Imagine for a moment that the new "central curriculum of childhood" was an actual school curriculum—that for five hours each day kids were placed in front of screens to be taught that boys and men are, and should be, brutally violent, and girls and women sexual objects; that identity, self-worth, happiness, and good fortune are defined by what people buy and own; that parents are stodgy and uncool, useful only for getting the things you want; that obsessive and compulsive behavior is normal and right. Parents would be up in arms. We would consider this a disaster for children and childhood. But with the new curriculum of childhood taking up so much of kids' time and attention—even more than school itself—is that disaster not in fact upon us?

Even some of the leading lights of kid marketing believe that it is.

James McNeal (the founder and *eminence grise* of kid marketing) was in no mood to brag about his many achievements when he was interviewed for this book. Holed up in a hotel room in Oklahoma, where he was working on a new book, a semi-autobiographical novel called *Marketing Man,* he recounted how his earlier belief that marketing to kids could help them "have a better life and make better decisions" had soured into cynicism as he watched marketers twist his principles for ill ends. "Over the years," he said, "I developed basic marketing principles, and they were gradually recognized, acknowledged, and adhered to by business. But that doesn't mean it was done in an honest fashion." Kid marketing has degenerated into a deceptive practice, he said, one that exploits children's developing emotions and causes them harm.[43]

The heart of the problem, according to McNeal, is the fact kid marketers now pitch as "fun" anything that might excite or entice children into wanting or watching something, regardless of whether it is healthy or appropriate for them. "Bad things, bad values, and bad ideas are sold to kids as 'fun,'" he says. "Violence is fun, lying, stealing, revenge and greed are fun; isn't it fun to kill more people each day in a video game?"[44] As a result, kid marketing is now "injurious to children and their parents,"[45] McNeal believes. "Too many children [are] taking risks, getting fat, becoming unhealthy, not studying enough, not sleeping enough, and, in general, endangering themselves through over-consumption."[46] "We should be worried," he says about the monster he helped create. "I don't know many people that aren't."[47]

Then there is Alex Bogusky, a creative genius by all accounts. Widely credited with having invented viral marketing, among numerous other accomplishments, he is considered to be among the top youth marketers in the world. Bogusky has been showered with honors and awards, graced the cover of most major business and marketing magazines, and in 2009 was named Adweek's Creative Director of the Decade. A founding partner and longtime creative director at Crispin Porter and Bogusky, he steered the agency to winning awards in all five categories at the Cannes International Lions Advertising Festival over the years, and to being named Interactive Agency of the Year in 2010.[48]

Yet, at the relatively young age of forty-seven, Bogusky surprised everyone when, after penning a scathing manifesto against kid marketing—calling it a "destructive" practice that has no "redeeming value"—he abruptly quit the industry. Children are "incapable of protecting and defending themselves from a message that probably doesn't have their very best interests at heart," Bogusky stated, and because it is "the duty of adults in society . . . to protect . . . children," they should demand that corporations and marketers stop "spending billions to influence our innocent and defenseless offspring."[49]

Kid marketing wiz Martin Lindstrom is similarly concerned. According to him, children's constant and deepening exposure to marketing is leading to a "disaster in terms of kids and their futures." It's "very unhealthy, and it's just the beginning we're seeing now," he says, as kids "are being led to expect everything to be customized around them, including parents and schools, and if it's not, they lose patience and move on to something else." Kid marketing also destroys children's imaginations and creative capacities, he believes. "One of the biggest scares in the future is going to be lack of creative people," he says, as kids' digital and increasingly prefabricated play options (video games, virtual worlds, and so on) leave little room for true imagination.

> We're forcing the brain in the wrong direction, killing all creativity and fantasy. . . . The tween generation seems to be losing its creativity. . . . Young people once spent hours outside playing in local parks and friends' backyards. They invented games, created rules, shot a few hoops, batted a few balls and rode bikes with cards pegged to the wheels. Kids were once creative directors in neighbourhood fantasies. No more. These days, kids rarely leave their bedrooms.[50]

Lindstrom's pronouncements on the state of childhood are sobering (though somewhat perplexing in light of his own continuing involvement in the industry). "At the end of the day," he says, "it's sad, but unfortunately true, that although this is the most affluent generation to walk the planet, it also has the dubious distinction of being the most insecure and depressed. And whatever faith [kids] seem to have, it's all invested in the power of the brand."[51]

The problems are fairly clear. Even kid marketing gurus are concerned. The question, of course, is what do we do?

"Parents have *some* ability today to protect children from the risks of electronic media use,"[52] as the FCC recently stated. But that ability is diminished, as we have seen, by both marketers' deliberate strategies to wedge children away from parents and the inevitable difficulties of monitoring digital and mobile media.

Still, to the extent we have *some* power, we should use it. The American Academy of Pediatrics has recommendations for parents:

1. Limit children's total media time (with entertainment media) to no more than one to two hours of quality programming per day.
2. Remove television sets from children's bedrooms.
3. Discourage television viewing for children younger than two years, and encourage more interactive activities that will promote proper brain development, such as talking, playing, singing, and reading together.
4. Monitor the shows children and adolescents are viewing. Most programs should be informational, educational, and nonviolent.[53]

Though for most parents these targets may seem unrealistic (especially 1 and 4, and even more so if digital and mobile media are included), trying at least to narrow the gap, currently large, between them and reality would be worthwhile.

Today, 43 percent of U.S. children under the age of two watch television on a daily basis; 26 percent of them have TVs in their rooms. Ninety percent of children aged four to six are on-screen for at least two hours a day; more than 40 percent of that age group have TV sets in their rooms, and large numbers of them own portable DVD players and gaming consoles. Tweens and teens spend, on average, nearly eight hours a day consuming ten hours of media (the extra two hours is due to their using different platforms simultaneously), most of it distinctly noneducational and much of it violent. Seven out of ten tweens and teens have television sets in their bedrooms, half of them have video game consoles, and large and growing numbers own computers, internet-ready cell phones, MP3 players, and portable gaming devices.[54] With another hour per day spent texting and talking on cell phones, tweens and teens are engaged with media each day, on average, for nearly twice as long as they attend school. Only *two hours a day* remain when they are not on media, at school, or asleep.[55]

Household rules about how, when, and how much children can use media are effective in reducing total media time. In households that have such rules, tweens and teens spend an average of three fewer

53

hours engaged with media. Only a third of all households have such rules, however, making this an area where parents could perhaps do more to reduce the ill effects of media use on children and teens. Parents can also exercise the "power of the purse," refusing to buy TVs, computers, and gaming consoles for bedrooms, or to pay for internet services on cell phones, or to buy subscriptions to virtual worlds and the like. Blocking technologies, such as the V-chip, can also be used by them to help screen out inappropriate content.[56]

In general, according to child development expert Nancy Carlsson-Paige, it is important for parents to counter the ill effects of pervasive and toxic media by cultivating in their children the things that tend to be denied by media—creative play, security, and positive relationships. In her book *Taking Back Childhood*, Carlsson-Paige offers excellent advice on how to do this, and therefore on how to offset some of the corrosive effects of kid marketing and media on children and childhood.[57] At the same time, however, protecting children from these corrosive effects cannot be the responsibility of parents alone. There are limits to what we can do as parents, especially when our kids are surrounded everywhere and all the time, often out of our sight, by media and marketing. Society must also play a role, which raises the thorny question—should governments regulate children's marketing and media more robustly, and, if so, how should they do it?

On November 2, 2010, the board of supervisors of San Francisco voted by an 8 to 3 margin to ban fast-food restaurants from giving away toys with most children's meals.[58] The ban, which, among other things, made the sale of McDonald's Happy Meals illegal, was lobbied for, initiated, and justified as a measure to promote healthy eating habits and fight childhood obesity. It was "a tremendous victory for our children's health," stated San Francisco Supervisor Eric Mar, the law's sponsor. "Our children are sick. Rates of obesity in San Francisco are disturbingly high, especially among children of color."[59]

On November 5, three days after the board's vote, San Francisco's mayor at the time, Gavin Newsom, announced he would veto the law, which he did a week later (two weeks after that the veto was overturned by the board of supervisors). The law, said Newson went "way too far in inserting government to try to be the decision-maker in someone's life as opposed to parents."[60] In similar spirit, McDonald's spokesperson Danya Proud complained that "parents tell us it's their right and responsibility, not the government's, to choose what's right for their children."[61]

Focusing exclusively on *parents'* rights and responsibilities, as did the mayor and Proud, is a typical food industry strategy. By making parental choice the key issue, the strategy implicitly exonerates fast food companies of blame for childhood obesity and other ill health effects. The strategy is "disingenuous," as the Yale University Rudd Center for Food Policy and Obesity describes it in a recent report, for conveniently ignoring the substantial efforts industry makes to incite kids' desires for unhealthy food.[62] To wit, according to the report,

- In 2009, the fast food industry spent more than $4.2 billion on advertising; during that year, the average preschooler saw 2.8 TV ads for fast food every day, a 21 percent increase from 2003; older children saw 3.5 ads, a 34 percent increase; and teens saw 4.7 ads, a 39 percent increase.
- McDonald's web-based marketing starts with children as young as two at Ronald.com; McDonald's and Burger King offer children numerous sophisticated websites with 60 to 100 pages of advergames and virtual worlds (McWorld.com, HappyMeal.com, and ClubBK.com, for example); McDonald's thirteen websites attracted 365,000 unique child visitors on average each month in 2009; nine fast food restaurant Facebook pages had more than one million fans each as of July 2010, and Starbucks boasted more than 11.3 million fans; Smartphone apps were available for eight fast food chains.

- Hispanic preschoolers saw 290 Spanish-language fast food TV ads in 2009 and McDonald's was responsible for one-quarter of young people's exposure to Spanish-language fast food advertising; African American children and teens saw at least 50 percent more fast food ads on TV than did their white peers; the figure was 75 percent for McDonald's and KFC which specifically target African American youth with TV advertising, websites, and banner ads.

While it is true that parents make choices about what their children eat, and should bear responsibility for those choices, it is equally true that (a) parents' choices are heavily influenced by what children want, ask, and nag for (and by corollary, parents' desires to avoid unhappy children and family strife); and (b) the things children want, ask, and nag for are heavily influenced by marketers' relentless campaigns to get them to desire unhealthy food.[63] In the end, parents make choices about what their children should eat, but they do so in conditions strategically engineered, with billions of dollars worth of effort, to pressure them toward choices that favor industry's interests at the expense of children's health.

San Francisco's new law can be understood as an attempt to undo some of that pressure, and thus to *expand*, rather than diminish, parents' freedom of choice. By denying corporations a powerful channel through which to manipulate children's emotions and influence their desires for unhealthy food, the law boosts parents' power to choose healthy food. It frees them from the grip of children's marketing-stoked appetites and thus better enables them to protect their kids' health.

Regulating children's media and marketing can help parents promote their children's best interests, as the San Francisco law arguably demonstrates. But the larger question remains—how far should regulation go, and what exactly should it target.[64]

* * *

When Senator Jay Rockefeller (D-WV) recently screened clips of violent television scenes to a group of his senatorial colleagues, trying to convince them that something needed to be done about media violence, he was frustrated by their quick dismissal. "There was an automatic mind-set that because the First Amendment exists, you cannot even be talking about this so don't waste my time," said the senator. "I was furious."[65]

Regulators and policy makers, though concerned about the harmful effects of children's media today, nonetheless feel powerless to act, largely because of that "automatic mind-set." The FCC, for example, recently expressed concern about the risks to children of "exposure to exploitative advertising; exposure to inappropriate content (such as offensive language, sexual content, violence, or hate speech); impact on health (for example, childhood obesity, tobacco use, sexual behavior or drug and alcohol use); impact on behavior (in particular, exposure to violence leading to aggressive behaviour)."[66] But the agency shied away from regulation as a solution, preferring instead to focus on encouraging media literacy, parental controls, and self-regulation out of concern that government action be "consistent with the First Amendment."[67]

The FTC, though also attentive to the risks posed to children by, among other things, media violence and junk food marketing, is similarly wary of regulation (despite its explicit legislative mandate to prohibit deceptive and unfair trade practices). "Because of the possible First Amendment considerations in addressing each of these areas [of possible harm to children]," it recently stated, "the Commission has recognized the importance of focusing on self-regulatory efforts."[68]

If self-regulation were an adequate substitute for regulation, that might be an appropriate solution. In reality, however, self-regulation tends to be ineffective. It "hasn't really worked in any industry," according to Ellen Fried of the Rudd Center. "A watchdog won't bite the hand that feeds it."[69] Self-regulation has not worked, for example, in the video game industry, where industry rating systems for video games are often ignored by retailers. Nor has it worked in the film industry, where marketers of PG-13 movies regularly flout FTC warnings and market those movies to children as young as two years old, using ads on children's television shows and toy tie-ins at fast-food restaurants ("When it comes to the film industry and children's well-being," notes Susan Linn, director of the Campaign for a Commercial-Free Childhood, "it's clear that self-regulation has failed").[70]

Nor has self-regulation worked in the food and beverage industry. In 2006 that industry, in partnership with the Better Business Bureau, created the Children's Food and Beverage Advertising Initiative (CFBAI), "a voluntary self-regulation program . . . designed to shift the mix of advertising messaging to children to encourage healthier dietary choices and healthy lifestyles," according to its preamble. Most major food companies that market to children joined the initiative, including McDonald's, Burger King, Coca-Cola, Pepsico, Mars, and Kellogg (though McDonald's and Burger King were the only two of roughly a dozen major fast food chains).[71]

The initiative's core principle—that "participants will commit that all advertising primarily directed to children under twelve will be for healthy dietary choices, or better-for-you products, in accordance with company-developed standards that are consistent with established scientific and/or government standards"[72]—though promising in the abstract, has had little real impact. It "has been completely ineffective in shifting the landscape of food marketing to children away from its overwhelming emphasis on non-nutritious products that place children at risk of becoming obese," according to a recent report by the children's advocacy organization Children Now.[73] Evidence of ineffectiveness can be found in the fact that more than 99 percent of advertising by member companies continues despite the initiative, to be for products deemed by the U.S. Department of Health and Human Services to be of either poor (68.5 percent)[74] or moderate (31 percent) nutritional value.[75]

The behavior of McDonald's since joining the initiative in 2006 is indicative. Between that year and 2009, the company increased by roughly a quarter its TV advertising directed at children, and created numerous child-oriented websites.[76] The content of its child-directed advertising changed little in the meantime, neither highlighting nor encouraging consumption of "better-for-you" foods, and continuing to focus on building brand loyalty and toy giveaways. As well, in-store menus and promotions continued to feature unhealthy meal combinations for kids, and neglected the limited range of healthy alternatives available.[77]

The CFBAI was originally created in response to a 2006 report by the Institute of Medicine (IOM) of the National Academies. That report, commissioned by Congress in 2004, reviewed all existing literature on childhood obesity and concluded that "food and beverage marketing practices geared to children and youth are out of balance with healthful diets, and contribute to an environment that puts their health at risk." The report recommended that industry voluntarily shift its marketing practices toward healthy products and away from unhealthy ones (as the CFBAI purports to do). Importantly, the report also stated that if industry failed to make that shift on its own, *Congress should legally require it to do so.*[78]

Children Now believes that, with the CFBAI's patent failure, the time has come for government action:

> Public health officials and policymakers need to seriously consider regulatory intervention to achieve more stringent reductions in the advertising of nutritionally deficient food products to children. . . . With the current childhood obesity crisis approaching the number one threat to our nation's public health, it is clear that the failure to act strongly and swiftly holds serious adverse implications for generations of America's children. Bold strides, rather than tiny steps, will be required to reverse the long-standing predominance of unhealthy food products in the children's advertising environment.[79]

To similar effect, Michelle Obama's White House Task Force on Childhood Obesity, which issued its report in May 2010, proposes that regulation "may be helpful or even necessary to fully address the childhood obesity epidemic." Self-regulation initiatives, such as the CFBAI, are unlikely to succeed, it states, unless there is a real possibility that Congress will "promulgate laws and regulations when [such initiatives] prove insufficient." According to the task force,

> Effective voluntary reform will only occur if companies are presented with sufficient reasons to comply. The prospect of regulation of legislation has often served as a catalyst for driving meaningful reform in other industries and may do so on the context of food marketing as well.

The task force states that, unless "within three years [by May, 2013] the majority of food and beverage advertisements directed to children promote healthy foods," regulators should step in.[80]

The task force's recommendations follow the contours of what has come to be known as "co-regulation," a model used by many European countries to govern children's and other media.[81] Within this model, regulators establish policy objectives for a regime, along with benchmarks and timelines for meeting those objectives, while industry creates and administers specific norms and standards. Importantly, regulators maintain authority to monitor and influence a regime's operation and to evaluate whether it is meeting its objectives. In the event a regime fails, regulators can either try to fix the problem or step in to regulate themselves.

The "automatic mind-set" has served over the years to frustrate most attempts to regulate children's media and marketing. Yet the actual law of the First Amendment may be more open to such regulation than that mind-set suggests. The U.S. Supreme Court has recognized, for example, that children's unique vulnerabilities are an important consideration in First Amendment cases. According to Newton Minow and Craig LaMay,

> If the dozens of Supreme Court cases that make up the "child's First Amendment" tell us anything . . . they tell us that where free speech is concerned, children are a special case under our constitution and a reason for caution. . . . No matter what the medium . . . considerations arise where children are involved that do not arise with adults. Those considerations do not always carry the day, but they are always present, always will be, and cannot be belittled or dismissed, no matter what the medium.[82]

The Court itself has stated that "there is a compelling interest in protecting the physical and psychological well-being of minors" and that regulations do not infringe the First Amendment if they are the least restrictive means available for protecting that interest.[83] Despite that, courts have tended to strike down restrictions on children's media. In nearly a dozen cases, for example, state courts have struck down legislatures' attempts to restrict children's access to violent video games, reasoning that harm from such games has not been proven and that the restrictions are overbroad and vague.

Critics of these decisions argue they underestimate the degree of harm caused by violent video games, and overestimate the vagueness and overbreadth of the laws.[84] Gentile et al., for example, state that the types of harm caused by violent video games are not properly recognized by courts as a result of certain features of the judicial process. "There are no clear rules or guidelines in the public domain about what constitutes an expert," and that makes it "relatively easy for the entertainment industries to hire "experts" to refute . . . scientific findings." Because "*none* of the video game industry 'experts' in the cases to date would be considered by the scientific community as real experts on media violence," when courts give credence to their testimony, the scientific evidence on media violence is inevitably discounted.[85]

The problem is compounded by the fact "courts use different standards of causality than most social scientists." They want evidence of "immediate harm from video games" before harm is proven and are "less concerned about cumulative long-term effects" (though, as noted earlier, they sometimes take less stringent approaches to evidence of harm). Because the science on media violence tends to focus on the latter type of harm, and not so much the former, courts end up predisposed to finding no harmful effects.[86]

Courts have also consistently held that laws restricting violent video games are too vague and overbroad—that they risk, as one commentator describes it, encompassing "virtually every M-for-Mature-rated game and many T-for-Teen rated games as well"[87]—and therefore that they are not "least restrictive" as First Amendment law requires. Though the laws challenged in some of the earlier video game cases were less than precise in their definitions of "violent video game," it should be noted that the California law currently before the U.S. Supreme Court does not suffer from lack of detail.[88]

A violent video game, according to that law, which bans renting and selling such games to minors, "means a video game in which the range of options available to a player includes killing, maiming, dismembering, or sexually assaulting an image of a human being," but *only if* those acts are depicted in a manner that meets either of these two criteria:

1) "A reasonable person, considering the game as a whole, would find [that the manner of depiction] appeals to a deviant or morbid interest of minors; is patently offensive to prevailing standards in the community as to what is suitable for minors; and causes the game, as a whole, to lack serious literary, artistic, political, or scientific value for minors; or,

2) "[The manner of depiction] enables the player to virtually inflict serious injury upon images of human beings or characters with substantially human characteristics in a manner which is especially

heinous, cruel, or depraved in that it involves torture or serious physical abuse to the victim."

For further clarity, the law defines in detail the various terms it uses to articulate the above criteria: *cruel* means that the player intends to virtually inflict a high degree of pain by torture or serious physical abuse on the victim in addition to killing the victim; *depraved* means that the player relishes the virtual killing or shows indifference to the suffering of the victim, as evidenced by torture or serious physical abuse of the victim; *heinous* means shockingly atrocious, and involving additional acts of torture or serious physical abuse of the victim as set apart from other killings; *serious physical abuse* means a significant or considerable amount of injury or damage to the victim's body which involves a substantial risk of death, unconsciousness, extreme physical pain, substantial disfigurement, or substantial impairment of the function of a bodily member, organ, or mental faculty (serious physical abuse, unlike torture, does not require that the victim be conscious of the abuse at the time it is inflicted; however, the player must specifically intend the abuse apart from the killing); *torture* includes mental as well as physical abuse of the victim (in either case, the virtual victim must be conscious of the abuse at the time it is inflicted; and the player must specifically intend to virtually inflict severe mental or physical pain or suffering upon the victim, apart from killing the victim).

For even further clarity, the law states: "Pertinent factors in determining whether a killing depicted in a video game is especially heinous, cruel, or depraved include infliction of gratuitous violence upon the victim beyond that necessary to commit the killing, needless mutilation of the victim's body, and helplessness of the victim."

Taking all of these elements together, California's law encompasses a subset of games that are extreme, exceptionally egregious, and highly inappropriate for minors. It would likely permit many games that the industry itself deems unsuitable for minors through its own rating system.

While it may leave room for discretion and interpretation by decision-makers (as is true of any law on a complex issue), it cannot be denied that the legislature has attempted to craft a law that is "carefully tailored," and arguably the "least restrictive" alternative for meeting the compelling state objective of protecting minors, as First Amendment law requires. If the Supreme Court upholds California's law on these bases, it will have opened the door to more robust regulation of media violence, and other potentially harmful elements of kids' media culture. The more likely result, however, based upon previous case law, is that the court will rule against the law.

Such a decision would provide further reason to consider *co-regulation* (such as the scheme prescribed by the White House Task Force for food marketing) for regulating children's media, including violent media. The fact is that co-regulation regimes are more likely to survive First Amendment challenges than are traditional regulations (such as California's violent-video game law). If self-regulation, on its own, has proven ineffective, the addition of government monitoring, enforcement, and goal-setting, so as to ensure effectiveness, as co-regulation envisions, is arguably the next logical step in the search for least restrictive—and *effective*—alternatives. The same logic would apply to carefully tailored traditional regulations brought in *after* co-regulation had been tried and failed. At that point, such regulations would, again, arguably be the next least restrictive *effective* alternative, and thus permissible under the First Amendment.

The idea of co-regulation can thus be seen as a way through the First Amendment thicket in the area of children's media. Co-regulation moves beyond the "automatic mind-set" against regulation, but still acknowledges that traditional regulatory measures, especially broad ones, are likely to run afoul of the First Amendment. Again, if the U.S. Supreme Court follows the judicial trend and nullifies California's violent-video-game law, co-regulation should be considered in this area and others. Many questions remain unanswered, of course. The White House Task Force provides one example of co-regulation in a single area. What others would look like in other areas of kid marketing and media, and how they would be crafted to avoid First Amendment problems, remain open questions. My aim here is simply to put those questions, and thus the possibility of some form of effective regulation, on the table. Though regulation is no panacea, and will not solve all of the problems raised in this and the previous chapter, it may help solve some of them.

Chapter Four

Prescriptions for Profit

When our daughter was having problems in math, she announced "I must have ADHD." When our son described how a classmate got into trouble at school, he said it was because the kid "forgot to take his meds." Mental disorders and pharmaceutical drugs are unremarkable parts of childhood today. When children become difficult, behave badly, get moody or bratty, or flag at school, parents increasingly rush them to doctors who, in turn, are more and more likely to find mental disorders and prescribe psychotropic drugs. As a result, growing numbers of children, some of them very young, are labeled mentally ill each year and placed on pharmaceutical regimes.

Kyle Warren was one such child. He was prescribed the antipsychotic drug Risperdal when he was eighteen months old after a doctor's five-minute assessment resulted in a diagnosis of autism. A neurologist reevaluated him and pronounced he had oppositional defiant disorder. A child psychiatrist took over from the neurologist and diagnosed him with bipolar disorder. By the time he was three years old, Kyle was taking Risperdal, Prozac, and two sleeping medications. He was overweight, sedated, and prone to drooling, all side effects of the drugs. He had become "a medicated little boy," according to his mother, Brandy Warren. "I didn't have my son. It's like, you'd look into his eyes and you would just see blankness. . . . His shell was there, but he wasn't there."

Fortunately for Kyle and his mother, the boy was referred to child psychiatrist Mary Gleason, who weaned him off the drugs, worked with the Warren family, and arranged for social and mental health support services. Once off the drugs, Kyle lost weight, his behavior improved, and by six years old he was a thriving kindergarten student. Dr. Gleason found Kyle's case "disturbing," she said, as there were, in her view, no valid reasons for giving the boy (or any two-year-old) antipsychotic drugs.

Kyle's story, though not atypical today, would have been unimaginable just thirty years ago. Then it was almost unheard of for a child to be diagnosed with a mental disorder and treated with drugs. But things began to change in 1980, the year attention deficit disorder (ADD, renamed attention deficit and hyperactivity disorder, ADHD, in 1987) became an official psychiatric diagnosis. By 1990 ADHD numbers had skyrocketed, and over the next decade the number of children prescribed drugs, mainly Ritalin, to treat the disorder increased fivefold. In the meantime, through the 1990s and 2000s, new childhood disorders (such as pediatric bipolar disorder) were making their way into child psychiatry, as were new and powerful drugs (mainly selective serotonin reputake inhibitors—SSRIs).[1]

The resulting explosion of diagnoses and drug treatments of childhood mental disorders—a jump from almost nothing in 1980 tens of millions of children diagnosed and treated today—is usually attributed to two causes: a greater number of children becoming mentally ill, and more sophisticated methods for detecting and diagnosing childhood mental illness. There is, however, a third factor as well, and one likely at least as impactful as the other two: the pharmaceutical industry's growing influence over medical science and practice. Pharmaceutical companies have strategically expanded and deployed their influence over the last three decades to broaden the scope and range of pediatric mental disorders, promote the benefits of psychotropic drugs, and downplay those drugs' dangerous side effects. Child psychiatry has become a profitable enterprise for the industry as a result. But there have been costs, as Kyle Warren's story demonstrates. And sometimes there are tragedies.

On December 13, 2006, after responding to a 911 call, police in Hull, Massachusetts, found a four-year-old girl, Rebecca Riley, lying dead in her parents' bedroom, her body sprawled across a stuffed brown bear. The autopsy revealed she had died from a drug overdose. The drug that killed Rebecca, clonidine, was part of a trio of drugs prescribed by a child psychiatrist a year earlier when the girl's mother, Carolyn Riley, complained she was having difficulty sleeping and was hyperactive. The psychiatrist diagnosed Rebecca with bipolar disorder among other things.

On the night Rebecca died, her father had directed Carolyn Riley to increase her dose of clonidine in order to suppress a cough—"it was getting really annoying," he later told police, "she was keeping everybody awake." This was typical. The father would often tell Carolyn to give Rebecca and her siblings more "happy medicine" or "sleep medicine," as they called clonidine, to quiet them down when they were "acting up." Under the influence of these drugs, Rebecca often slept through the day, getting up only to eat.

The day before she died, Rebecca's uncle, who lived with the family, had worried that she was "out of it," sick, and disoriented. When he heard her gurgling in her room, and found her choking on vomit, he yelled at the parents to take her to the hospital. Instead, Carolyn Riley gave her another half tablet of clonidine and went back to bed.

Rebecca had had a difficult life. Her father had recently been charged with the attempted rape of her thirteen-year-old sister; the sister had been removed from the house and placed in foster care; the father was under a restraining order, which he routinely ignored, to stay away from the family home. Yet the child psychiatrist who treated Rebecca appears to have focused mainly on faulty brain chemistry, the purported basis of bipolar disorder, and prescribed drugs on that basis. That psychiatrist, along with Rebecca's parents, who were charged with murder for intentionally overdosing their child (the father, Michael Riley, was convicted[2]), undoubtedly played roles in Rebecca's tragic death.[3]

But there is another person as well who bears responsibility for her death, according to Dr. Lawrence Diller, a physician who specializes in children's behavioral and developmental problems. He is Dr. Joseph Biederman, the Harvard child psychiatrist who created the diagnosis of pediatric bipolar disorder.[4] In the early 1990s, Biederman challenged the well-established view among psychiatrists that bipolar disorder only afflicted adults because children rarely presented with its key symptom of euphoria. He argued that excess energy and irritability in kids were the diagnostic parallels of euphoria in adults, and that the disorder therefore had a pediatric equivalent. The psychiatric establishment quickly followed Biederman, who, most agree, is the single most influential child psychiatrist in the world ("If he breathes a drug at a conference, there will be ten thousand kids on it; if he publishes something it will be sent, courtesy of the drug companies, to every doctor who has anything to do with children," says Diller).[5] Once his findings were made public, diagnoses and treatment of pediatric bipolar disorder rose rapidly, increasing a dramatic fortyfold over the next decade.[6] Today, many experts believe the disorder, which recently did not officially exist, afflicts one of every hundred children.[7]

But others, Diller among them, believe children are being too quickly and too frequently diagnosed with the disorder. As a result, they argue, dangerous drugs are unnecessarily prescribed for kids, and other possible causes of their difficulties—dysfunctional homes, abuse, learning difficulties, problems at school or in the neighborhood, poor nutrition, allergies, or a variety of other disorders, such as dyslexia, speech delay, and autism—are neglected.[8] "The diagnosis is made with no understanding of the context of [kids' lives]," according to one prominent psychiatrist. "Then they're put on these devastating medications and condemned to a life as a psychiatric patient."[9]

When Diller learned of Rebecca Riley's death and the circumstances surrounding it, "something snapped," he says. Her treatment was "absurd, obscene, ridiculous," he believed. "I didn't want to get into trouble, I didn't want to make people unhappy with me, but to go home at night and to be quiet about this would bother me way more than getting into trouble with the Harvard group." So he did something "you don't do in medicine," he says—he named names, publicly holding Biederman morally responsible for Rebecca's death in a *Boston Globe* opinion piece.[10]

Biederman, for his part, claims he has positively "influenced the field of child psychiatry as regards to the diagnosis and treatment of pediatric bipolar disorder," defending his work as "impactful because of the strength of its science."[11] Biederman's science has recently come under a cloud, however, as a result of his close ties to pharmaceutical companies. Between 2000 and 2007 Biederman was paid $1.8 million by pharmaceutical companies (Eli Lilly, Johnson & Johnson, and Janssen), earning as much as $3,000 a day for consulting on their behalf and giving speeches that favored their products. He inadequately reported most of that income ($1.6 million of it) to his university, and thus likely flouted federal and university conflict of interest rules, according to media reports.[12] Even more damning, Biederman is alleged in these reports to have promised his corporate sponsors, in advance, that some of his research would achieve favorable results for them. Before conducting studies on the drug risperidone, for example, he apparently told its manufacturer, Johnson & Johnson, that the studies' results would "help clarify the competitive advantages of risperidone vs. other atypical neuroleptics," and "support the safety and effectiveness of risperidone in [preschoolers]."[13]

But Biederman's alleged transgressions are just one small part of a much larger and systemic problem affecting child psychiatry, and hence children and their families—the blurring of the line between medical science and pharmaceutical company marketing. The story of how that line became blurred begins with the man who almost single-handedly created the field of child psychiatry, Dr. Robert Spitzer.

Robert Spitzer, a fifteen-year-old boy intelligent beyond his years, sat in a large iron box, about the size of a telephone booth, in a psychoanalyst's office on New York City's Lower East Side. It was 1947 and the box, an "orgone accumulator," was an invention of Austrian psychoanalyst Wilhelm Reich, who claimed it could cure patients of emotional ills by exposing them to "orgone energy." Spitzer had been assigned to the box to help him quell intense anxiety and overpowering emotions that he neither understood nor could express. But the orgone accumulator did nothing for him, and after several sessions he gave up on it.[14]

A few years later in 1954, when the Food and Drug Administration sought a court order to stop Reich from fraudulently claiming his orgone accumulator had therapeutic value, the agency relied for support of its case on a devastating critique of Reich and his machine. The critique had been penned by a young college student named Robert Spitzer. Perhaps it was the machine's failure to help him that inspired Spitzer's later and lifelong mission, as a leading and highly respected Columbia University psychiatrist, to rout from psychiatry the dubious therapies and theories that had sullied its reputation.[15] By the early 1970s Spitzer had become a leading critic of psychoanalysis, which he lambasted for lacking rigor, and an advocate for the view that psychiatry should be transformed into a true medical science of well-defined disorders presumptively rooted in biological causes.[16] In 1973 the American Psychiatric Association, the field's official governing body, signaled it agreed with Spitzer by asking him to rewrite psychiatry's authoritative compilation of disorders and diagnoses, the *Diagnostic and Statistical Manual* (DSM).[17]

71

Over the next seven years Spitzer worked to produce the manual's third edition, the DSM-III, with the aid of a handpicked group of psychiatrists who shared his view that psychiatry needed to become a true science. But "there was just one problem with this utopian vision of better psychiatry through science," according to Alex Spiegel, a chronicler of Spitzer's life and work. "The science hadn't yet been done." There was little data about the nature and biological bases of abnormal behavior for Spitzer and his colleagues to draw upon, and what did exist was ambiguous and inconsistent. By necessity, Spitzer and his "data-oriented people," as committee members came to be called, proceeded without solid data, speculating, hypothesizing, and theorizing about how best to define and explain psychiatric disorders.[18]

Meetings of Spitzer's committee were, according to reports from those involved, haphazard and chaotic. Committee members would talk over one another, shout out possible definitions and criteria for disorders, and vie for Spitzer's attention. Ideas would be thrown around the room, some falling away, while others prevailed for no apparent reason, according to one participant, "except that someone just decided all of a sudden to run with it." Despite the chaos, at the end of each session a list of diagnoses with detailed descriptions and checklists of symptoms would emerge from Spitzer's typewriter. "It would usually be some combination of the accepted wisdom of the group, as interpreted by Bob, with a little added weight to the people he respected most, and a little bit to whoever got there last," according to participant Allen Frances (who would later preside over creating the next edition of the manual, DSM-IV). As a result, says participant Michael First, who also worked on subsequent editions of the manual, "a lot of what's in DSM represents what Bob thinks is right. He really saw this as his book, and if he thought [a diagnosis] was right he would push very hard to get it in."

Spitzer's DSM-III created the modern field of child psychiatry. Though children's mental health had been an issue of mounting concern through the postwar years, DSM-III was the first time it gained full recognition by official psychiatry. Earlier versions of the manual had said little about children. DSM-I (1952), for example, lacked any reference at all to childhood disorders; DSM-II (1968) spent a scant two pages on them. DSM-III (1980), in contrast, devoted sixty-five pages to childhood disorders, the most dramatic expansion of any section in the new volume. Five pages alone were devoted to ADD, compared to just one short paragraph in DSM-II (where it was called "hyperkinetic reaction"), a change that had an immediate impact. Between 1980 and 1990 diagnoses of ADD and ADHD jumped from 400,000 to 900,000, and the frequency of treatment with drugs from 28 percent of cases to 86 percent.[19] As ADHD numbers continued to escalate through the 1990s, diagnoses of other pediatric disorders—bipolar disorder, pediatric depression, social anxiety disorder, oppositional defiance disorder—along with treatment by powerful new SSRI drugs, rose dramatically as well, trends that have continued to this day.

Spitzer's DSM-III triggered all of these developments. By effectively creating ADD, expanding the list of other childhood mental disorders, and articulating detailed diagnostic criteria for all the disorders listed, the new manual set the stage for drugs becoming the first-line treatment for kids' emotional and behavioral problems. Its many pages of new, well-defined, and presumptively biological disorders gave pharmaceutical companies the targets they needed to develop and market new drugs, and psychiatrists the purportedly scientific reasons they needed to prescribe them.[20]

But something else happened in 1980 that also contributed to the dramatic increase in psychotropic drugs being used to treat children—the enactment by Congress of the Bayh-Dole Act.

By the late 1970s, the United States had lost its position as the world's technological leader. Innovation—the process of creating new technologies to increase productivity and wealth—had, like the economy itself, come to a halt, and with Ronald Reagan on his way to the White House, and neoliberalism the emerging economic orthodoxy, pundits and policy makers were blaming "big government." In particular, they argued, the federal government's insistence on owning every scientific discovery it funded was robbing scientists of any incentive to transform their discoveries into marketable inventions, and that was causing valuable discoveries to sit dormant on scientists' shelves.

The Bayh-Dole Act was the proposed solution.[21] The act, still in force today, and emulated by most industrialized nations, grants scientists and institutions ownership over the discoveries they make. That, in turn, enables them to sell those discoveries, which they do, sometimes for millions of dollars, to corporations that are ready and willing to develop them into profitable products.

The act fundamentally changed the way medical research is done. Before Bayh-Dole, such research was conducted mainly in public institutions (universities and hospitals), funded by public agencies, and run by academic physicians who were largely shielded from market incentives and their potentially corrupting influences. Bayh-Dole, with its explicit mandate "to promote collaboration between commercial concerns and . . . universities,"[22] effectively tore down the "invisible wall," as one commentator has described it, that separated research from industry.[23] Soon after its enactment, pharmaceutical money poured into medical research. Companies began buying up discoveries, scientists became entrepreneurs, universities set up "spin-off" firms and "industry liaison" offices to help broker deals, and companies became increasingly involved in the conduct and dissemination of the studies they now funded.

By the 1990s few traces were left of the "invisible wall," and medical science had become, and remains today, a culture of cooperation and collaboration between scientists and their corporate partners.[24]

The problem with this setup is that the main aim of pharmaceutical companies is to make money, not to advance scientific knowledge or promote patients' health. They *invest* in research, and as such *expect* returns. One of Bayh-Dole's legacies has been to expose medical science to the corrupting influence of that expectation. With the "invisible wall" gone, companies are able to march unimpeded into every area of medical research, including child psychiatry, and wield their influence to advance their interests. The very integrity of medical science has thus been put at risk, as has its mission to promote health through the discovery of truth.[25]

With respect to children, Bayh Dole's removal of the "invisible wall," combined with the DSM-III's expansion and elaboration of childhood mental disorders, has created the perfect storm for more children to take more drugs more often.

"I would like to introduce you to my daughter, Caitlin Elizabeth McIntosh," Glenn McIntosh announced to a panel of Food and Drug Administration (FDA) officials, a picture of Caitlin in hand, at a special meeting held in the winter of 2004. "Well, it's actually just a two-dimensional image of her, but it's all I have left."[26]

Four years earlier, Caitlin, a twelve-year-old sixth grader, died when she hung herself with a pair of shoelaces in the girl's bathroom at her school. The normally happy straight-A student, a talented musician, artist, and poet, had started taking Paxil, an antidepressant, two months earlier. The drug was prescribed by her family doctor after Caitlin's worried parents reported she was having trouble sleeping and, more generally, coping with school and the onset of adolescence. When Caitlin responded badly to Paxil, the doctor took her off the drug and referred her to a child psychiatrist. The psychiatrist prescribed Zoloft, another antidepressant. While on the drug, Caitlin began to have suicidal thoughts, hallucinations, and severe agitation. She was admitted to a psychiatric hospital where different dosages were tried and new drugs added. When she came home from the hospital her personality had completely changed, her father says. "It was the beginning of the end; the downward spiral continued until . . . she hung herself."

It is now known that SSRIs such as Paxil and Zoloft can substantially increase the risk of suicidal behavior in youth, but neither McIntosh nor Caitlin's doctors knew that in the weeks leading up to her death. "We were told that antidepressants like Paxil and Zoloft were 'wonder drugs' and that they were safe and effective for children," says McIntosh. Doctors, such as Caitlin's, were routinely prescribing the drugs to children, confident and encouraged by published reports that they were effective and largely free of adverse side effects. But the drugs' manufacturers knew otherwise. During the 1990s, company-run clinical trials had revealed the drugs could induce suicidal thoughts and behavior (suicidality, as it is called) in kids. Paxil studies, for example, showed that while the drug was ineffective for treating children and teens with major depression, it increased harmful outcomes, including episodes of self-harm and suicidality, by as much as threefold.[27]

Rather than raising an alarm and informing the medical community, the companies concealed the studies and continued to publicize only those findings that presented their drugs in a favorable light.[28] "We were lied to," McIntosh told the FDA officials at the meeting. "The pharmaceutical companies have known for years that these drugs could cause suicide in some patients. Why didn't we?" More stories like Caitlin's began to emerge in the early 2000s causing a media stir, and prompting regulators and courts to force the secret studies into public view. Shortly thereafter, in fall 2003, Britain banned the use of all SSRIs (except Prozac) for treating children and teens. A few months after that, on the heels of the meeting where Glenn McIntosh recounted Caitlin's tragic story, the FDA mandated "black box" warnings on SSRI pill bottle labels about the risk of suicidality for youths taking the drugs.[29]

To this day no law requires drug companies to publish results from clinical trials in the medical literature. Studies must be filed with the FDA (which is legally obliged to keep them confidential to ensure companies' proprietary information is protected), and since 2007 (due to a change in the law described below) they must also be registered and filed in a web-based registry. Beyond that, companies can do what they want with the studies they sponsor and conduct. Not surprisingly they routinely publish and publicize positive results and keep as quiet as they can about the negative ones. As a result, according to a 2008 survey published in the *New England Journal of Medicine*, while only half of the total number of trials conducted on antidepressants yield positive results, nearly *all* of the trials published in medical journals are positive.[30] In other words, the published medical literature that doctors rely upon to help them decide when and whether to medicate children and what drugs to use is heavily and systematically biased in favor of happy news.

Going back to the early 2000s, the sad fact is that if Glenn McIntosh and Caitlin's doctors had known what was contained in the secret studies at the time, things might have turned out differently for Caitlin. And beyond Caitlin's tragedy, one can only suspect that others might have been averted if the suppressed data had been made public when the companies first knew of it. Dr. David Healy, a professor of psychiatry at the University of Wales, and a former secretary of the British Association of Psychopharmacology, estimates that hundreds of kids' lives might have been saved "if people had been aware of the evidence from the trials and seen the risks." Healy finds it appalling, but not surprising, that the companies covered up. Caitlin's story is endemic, he says, of the dangerous secrecy and manipulation that result from pharmaceutical industry control over research.[31]

But the larger story behind the tragedy, says Healy, is the demise of medical science itself, including that related to children's mental health.

Healy, once a darling of the drug companies, confesses to having enjoyed the lavish meals and entertainment that companies offered him at conferences and meetings, as well as the attention of "extremely bright, very, very attractive women" hired by companies to chaperone him around. "It's seductive," he says of the life of a researcher courted by drug companies. "You have people who are hanging on every word that you say, and who think that the things you say are clever and interesting and smart." [32] But two things began to nag at him as, in meeting after meeting, he listened to his fellow researchers, most of them on drug company payrolls, extol the virtues of the latest wonder drug. First, he says, "we knew extremely little about what the pills actually did"; and second, he was starting to realize that "the pharmaceutical industry was a much bigger player than it was actually supposed to be in a scientific field." [33]

When, in the 1990s, Healy began noticing that some of his patients were becoming suicidal after taking Prozac, an antidepressant manufactured by Eli Lilly, his suspicions were further aroused. In 2000—the same year Caitlin committed suicide—Healy published a short article, *Good Science or Good Business*, in the *Hastings Review*, a bioethics journal. The article questioned the therapeutic value of Prozac and documented how its popularity among physicians had been fueled by questionable tactics on the part of its manufacturer, including burying adverse data, and paying academics to put their names on articles written by company officials. Shortly after the article was published, Lilly pulled its funding from the journal's publisher, the Hastings Center.

A few months later, in July 2000, Healy presented a paper at the annual meeting of the British Association for Pharmacology. There he reported evidence of a link between SSRI drugs, like Prozac, and suicidality, and he again questioned pharmaceutical industry tactics. Charles Nemeroff, a highly influential psychiatrist attending the meeting—"the most powerful man in psychiatry . . . the 'boss of bosses,'" according to the psychiatric journal *Ten*—responded by denouncing Healy's work as having no place at an academic meeting, Healy recalled in an account of the meeting. Later that day, Healy says, Nemeroff confronted him in the hallway and warned him that the kind of work he was doing would harm his career, and that he, Nemeroff, had been approached to get involved in legal action against him.[34] Nemeroff, who according to the *Washington Monthly*, may "hold some sort of record among academic clinicians for the most conflicts of interest,"[35] earned more than $2.8 million in consulting fees from pharmaceutical companies and device makers between 2000 and 2007. One of the companies he received substantial sums from was Lilly.[36]

But for Healy, the larger issue is that medical science as a whole has been corrupted by industry influence. "Industry has manipulated the clinical trials that they've done, they depend on doctors not to be able to read particulars all that well, and they control the literature that ought to get published," he says. "And through means like this, that have nothing to do with what people usually think of as being marketing, they are able to get the field generally to do the things that they want."[37] As a result, says Healy, "medicine has lost its way." The marketing departments of pharmaceutical companies, among "the most potent cultural forces in our world," have taken over and corrupted psychiatric science, he says, and they use their influence to turn "life's vicissitudes and variations" into medical disorders requiring pharmaceutical treatment.[38] This "degradation of the scientific and academic base of medicine" is most troubling in child psychiatry, he says. "There's no good science" is how he describes both the diagnosis and treatment regimes around pediatric bipolar disorder, the disorder Rebecca Riley was alleged to have suffered from. "There's nothing that up to a few years ago would have actually been called science."[39]

In 2003 Healy conducted a review of every medical journal article written and published to that point on the antidepressant drug Zoloft (the one twelve-year-old Caitlin McIntosh had been taking when she hung herself in 2000). He found that more than half the articles—fifty-five out of ninety-six—had been penned by "medical communications" companies hired by the drug's manufacturer, Pfizer. Moreover, he discovered, the physicians listed as authors had had little or nothing to do with writing the articles nor with conducting the research they were based upon. In exchange for payment from Pfizer, those physicians had permitted the company to list them as "authors."[40] Ghostwriting—the term used to describe the practice by drug companies of writing articles (usually with the help of medical communications firms) and hiring physicians to appear as "authors"—is rife throughout the medical literature. Though clearly a form of deception, because it presents company-sponsored research as though it is independent, companies routinely produce papers in this way, and journals, usually unwittingly, publish them.[41]

Ghostwriting is not the only way companies leverage the credibility of respected academic physicians to promote their products, however. They also hire physicians, such as Biederman and Nemeroff, to give speeches and consultations touting their latest drugs to colleagues at meetings and seminars, hospital rounds, and various other physician gatherings, often sponsored by companies and held at lavish restaurants and resorts, even on luxury cruises. Lilly alone spent $22 million in the first three months of 2009 hiring 3,400 doctors to give speeches and provide consultations.[42] Lilly is not unique, however. All major pharmaceutical companies invest heavily in speeches and consultations, and they do so for the same reason they ghostwrite articles—to imbue research that is sponsored and spun by companies with the credibility of independent science, and thus to help persuade physicians to prescribe their drugs. "The only reason companies hire doctors is to increase sales," as Harvard medical professor Eric Campbell describes it. "They call it education and the doctors call it education, but it's about making money. The focus may get away from what is best for patients."[43]

Even more worrying, however, is the increasing influence of pharmaceutical companies at the very heart of medical science—the design and conduct of clinical trials. Clinical trials play the crucial role in medicine of evaluating the efficacy and possible side effects of new drugs. Because test tubes, petri dishes, and animal studies provide only limited information about drugs, clinical trials are necessary. A clinical trial compares outcomes for patients treated with a new drug to outcomes for those treated with a different drug or given a placebo. Regulators routinely rely on these trials to decide whether a drug should be approved, and physicians depend upon them to decide which drugs to use to treat their patients.

But clinical trials, by their very nature, are plagued with ambiguities and uncertainties, and thus vulnerable to manipulation. In a clinical trial, "you can control what data you look at, control the analysis, and then shade your interpretation of the results," says Dr. Marcia Angell, a former editor-in-chief of the *New England Journal of Medicine*. "You can design studies to come out the way you want them to."[44] To have integrity, and to be reliable, clinical trials must therefore be designed, conducted, and analyzed by researchers who have no preference for particular results and are under no pressure to obtain them. Such purity is difficult to achieve in the post-Bayh-Dole world, however, because companies, with very strong preferences for particular results, now control much of the clinical trial process.[45] And with profit the overriding goal of pharmaceutical companies, and millions, even billions, of dollars at stake in any given series of trials, it is naïve to expect those companies *not* to work ambiguities and uncertainties to their advantage.

Richard Smith, a former editor of the *British Medical Journal*, says it took him "almost a quarter of a century to wake up to what was happening"—namely, that pharmaceutical companies "get the results they want not by diddling the results, which would be far too crude and possibly detectable by peer review, but rather by asking the 'right' questions." A company-sponsored clinical trial might, for example, compare a new drug to a drug known to be ineffective, thus exaggerating the first drug's positive effects; or it might test the drug against too low a dose of a comparator drug, thus again favoring the first drug; or it might test that drug against too *high* a dose of another drug, thus exaggerating the latter's adverse side effects.[46]

81

In light of such techniques—just a sampling—it is not surprising that, as several recent surveys have revealed, clinical trials sponsored by pharmaceutical companies yield positive results significantly more often than those conducted independently. As one such survey concludes, "the results of clinical trials that are funded by pharmaceutical companies or whose authors have financial conflicts of interest are favourable to the products of the sponsoring company far more frequently than studies whose funding comes from other sources."[47]

Universities and hospitals try to lower the risk of clinical trial manipulation by strengthening rules governing research, but such measures can backfire by driving companies to less-regulated environments. According to John Hepburn, vice president of research at the University of British Columbia, "Industry complains about the complicated process with university bureaucracy, especially contract negotiations and ethical review," and as a result, he says, "drug companies are working more with private firms and offshore."[48] The private firms Hepburn refers to are contract research organizations (CROs), for-profit companies in the business of conducting clinical trials for pharmaceutical companies. Currently running thirty thousand trials worldwide and collecting more than $15 billion a year in revenue, the industry has continued to grow mainly by scooping clinical trial business away from universities and hospitals. Hepburn worries that "the level of scrutiny [over research] isn't as high with these [CRO] trials as at universities." Or as former UBC dean of medicine Dr. Graydon Meneilly describes it, "The pharmaceutical industry doesn't want the scrutiny that comes with partnering with academic centers. It's easier to work with a clinical trial factory in the middle of nowhere."[49]

All of which, of course, only makes the already shaky clinical trial ground that much shakier.

Even the DSM process appears to have been tainted by pharmaceutical company influence. "Pharmaceutical companies have a vested interest in what mental disorders are included in the DSM," state the authors of a recent study revealing that every member of DSM-IV panels responsible for creating the manual's entries for mood disorders, schizophrenia, and other psychotic disorders had ties to at least one pharmaceutical company. "In light of the extreme profitability of the psychotropic drug market," the authors conclude, "the connections found in this study between the DSM and the pharmaceutical industry are cause for concern."[50]

Robert Spitzer, the original creator of the modern DSM system (and also, as noted earlier, the founder of child psychiatry), along with his colleague Allen Frances, who oversaw the making of DSM-IV, now worry that they may have unwittingly created a monster. The two psychiatrists believe DSM-V, scheduled for release in 2013, could push psychiatry even deeper into the arms of the pharmaceutical industry by including, as it likely will, *subthreshold* (such as *mild* depression) and *premorbid* (such as *pre*psychotic) categories.[51]

"The APA might well be accused of a conflict of interest in fashioning DSM-V to create new patients for psychiatrists and new customers for the pharmaceutical companies," say Frances and Spitzer. "Tens of millions of newly diagnosed 'patients'—the majority of whom would likely be false positives subjected to needless side effects and expense of treatment," will, in their view, be the inevitable consequence of adding the new categories.[52] Frances, who believes the proposed changes are "reckless" and "potentially disastrous," predicts they will trigger "a wholesale imperial medicalization of normality that will trivialize mental disorder and lead to a deluge of unneeded medication treatments—a bonanza for the pharmaceutical industry but at a huge cost to the new false-positive patients caught in the excessively wide DSM-V net."[53]

Taken together the various tactics pharmaceutical companies deploy— ghostwriting, sponsored speeches and seminars, control of clinical trials, suppression of negative research findings, and influence within the DSM process—work to broaden the diagnostic brackets of children's behavioral and emotional disorders and to make powerful drugs the first-line treatments for those disorders. The use of such tactics is "all about bypassing science," according to Dr. Drummond Rennie, a former editor of the *Journal of the American Medical Association* who believes they are having the effect of turning medicine into "a sort of Cloud Cuckoo Land, where doctors don't know what papers they can trust in the journals, and the public doesn't know what to believe." [54]

Left unchecked, pharmaceutical industry influence over science will continue to favor the creation and diagnosis of more childhood disorders and the use of more drugs more often to treat them. As a result, increasing numbers of children will end up taking dangerous drugs unnecessarily, suffering harmful side effects, taking the wrong drugs in the wrong doses, and being deprived of nonpharmaceutical interventions that might better help them and their parents address their difficulties.

It is not only the research and data that are being unduly influenced by pharmaceutical companies, however. The physicians who diagnose and treat children for behavioral and emotional problems are also targets, as the next chapter reveals.

Chapter Five

Pom-Poms for Pills

"They don't ask what the major is," says University of Kentucky cheerleading coach Mr. T. Lynn Williamson of the drug companies that come knocking on his door to recruit sales representatives. "They want the best cheerleaders—exaggerated motions, exaggerated smiles, exaggerated enthusiasm. Girls who can get people to do what they want." [1]

Hundreds of former college cheerleaders, many of whom continue to cheerlead part-time for NFL and NBA teams, are now working for pharmaceutical companies as "drug reps." There is Jennifer at Novartis, for example, and Kimberley at Bayer, just two among many former cheerleaders placed in their jobs by Spirited Sales Leaders, an agency specializing in matching cheerleaders to drug companies. [2] Cheerleaders "bring a unique combination of peer leadership and community interaction experiences along with the all-around people skills necessary to build successful relationships in any business endeavor," the company promises potential employers. [3]

Armed with free drug samples, and the persuasive power of good looks and charm, drug reps (not all of whom are former cheerleaders) visit doctors' offices with offers of friendship, gifts, free lunches, dinners, and trips—even sexual favors and kickbacks, according to recent allegations[4]—all the while motivated by the prospect of handsome rewards and bonuses for boosting prescriptions. The best reps prepare diligently for their visits, collecting information about a doctor's personal life and avocations to help them develop an intimate rapport, and tracking doctors' prescribing practices. By all accounts, drug reps help drug companies sell drugs. "I'd like to give doctors credit," says surgeon Dan Foster, who is also a member of the West Virginia senate, "but I know from personal experience that these 'detailers,' as we call them . . . can be very convincing. It's like everything else in life. If they're physically attractive, they have an advantage."[5]

Sharam Ahari, a former drug rep who promoted Eli Lilly's top-selling drug, the antipsychotic Zyprexa, to child psychiatrists among others, understands why pharmaceutical companies hire cheerleaders. Good looks, a "physical iconic appeal," is the "primary commonality that you see among drug reps," he says (admitting, with no false modesty, that he fits the bill).[6] Ahari, a science graduate, unlike most of his drug rep colleagues, began his career enthusiastically representing Zyprexa. But just a week into his new job, when a doctor asked him, point blank, "with quite a bit of concern in his eyes and his voice," he recalls, why his patients on Zyprexa were gaining weight and getting diabetes (side effects of the drug), Ahari began to have doubts. He was taken aback by the question, he says, and could not provide an answer. "I retreated from the conversation," he says, assuring the doctor that he would raise the issue with the company. Similar complaints from other doctors began to mount—they "seemed to haunt Zyprexa wherever I would go, whether to a new territory or a new physician," he says—but when he voiced concerns to the company, answers were not forthcoming. Instead, he received missives from the marketing department instructing him on tactics he could use to derail doctors' concerns and complaints.

One of his more dubious practices, says Ahari, was unlawfully promoting Zyprexa to treat children. Zyprexa is not approved by the FDA for pediatric use, which makes it illegal for companies to market it for such use. Despite that, Ahari says, Lilly instructed its sales force to visit child psychiatrists and leave them with free samples of the drug, prepackaged in small doses specifically designed for kids, hoping that would encourage them to prescribe it "off-label." "When the studies began to show that kids were getting diabetes from Zyprexa, I wasn't surprised," he says.

Ahari, who initially, he says, naïvely "drank the Kool-aid out of sales school," believing that "Zyprexa would benefit millions of patients," began to worry his job was not really about helping doctors help patients, but rather about manipulating and deceiving them to prescribe his drug. "I had many misgivings," he says. "You're swaying these doctors to prescribe not necessarily what's best for patients, but what's best economically for company shareholders. It gnawed at my conscience." As he became better at his job—earning a reputation as a "safecracker," someone who could get in to see doctors who refused to see other reps—Ahari began to worry he was becoming worse as a person. "It was very disconcerting to see how manipulative I had become by virtue of my job, by virtue of my training and, arguably, by virtue of my character," he says. "I began to use that approach in my personal life, with my family and my girlfriend. When I was with Lilly I was completely bought."

Ahari quit his job two years after he started at Lilly.[7] Still, he says, the problems in the industry run much deeper than drug reps. Companies use numerous other questionable marketing tactics to boost prescriptions and profits, and because "laws are weak and penalties nominal," he says, it is "a no brainer" for them to flout the law to serve their bottom lines.

When, in 2000, Enron collapsed in a flurry of greed and crime, Hank McKinnell, then CEO of Pfizer, the world's largest pharmaceutical company, dismissed it as a "very isolated incident." Good corporate citizenship was the norm, he insisted, and some companies, his own included, went beyond that to being truly stellar. "Pfizer can be the company which does more good for more people than any other company on the planet," he said, boasting of his company's free drug programs in Africa, its rebuilding of inner city neighborhoods, and its partnerships with schools.[8]

Yet, even as McKinnell was speaking, his company was committing crimes that, by the end of the decade, would earn it a place, alongside Enron, as one of the world's worst corporate criminals. Pfizer had tangled with the law before, but the things it got up to during the 2000s made its earlier crimes look like small-town heists. By the end of the decade, the company and its subsidiary, Pharmacia & Upjohn, would plead guilty to a felony violation for promoting the sale of arthritis drug Bextra for uses and dosages that the FDA had specifically deemed dangerous and declined to approve. On September 2, 2009, Pfizer was fined $1.3 billion for its transgressions, the largest criminal fine in history.[9]

That doubled the previous record—$615 million—which had been set, just months earlier, by Pfizer's competitor and Ahari's former employer, Eli Lilly. Lilly was finally caught for campaigning (with the help of sales reps like Ahari) to expand markets for Zyprexa beyond the drug's FDA approved uses.[10] In addition to targeting children, it had illegally touted the drug for dementia, Alzheimer's, and agitation in the elderly, as well as for common complaints such as sleep problems and mild depression in the general population.[11] Its campaign, dubbed "Viva Zyprexa," had been a spectacular success. Sales soared and the drug became the company's top seller as doctors jumped on the bandwagon. In each of 2009 and 2010 Zyprexa sales were more than $1.2 billion, representing close to a quarter of the company's revenue for those years.[12] Over its lifetime, the drug has earned more than $50 billion, a significant share of that likely from "off-label" prescribing encouraged by illegal marketing.[13] In short, the $615 million criminal fine was a paltry sum when compared to the company's gains from the drug. Crime paid for Eli Lilly, and it paid well.

Lilly's case demonstrates just how difficult it is to penalize large companies *effectively*, in any industry, for unlawful behavior. Fines, no matter how large, tend be fractions of the benefits companies reap from illegal activities, and they can easily be dismissed as mere costs of doing business.[14] Moreover, despite the fact the unprecedented fines to Pfizer and Lilly placed those companies atop history's "most wanted" list of corporate criminals, they are not alone in the Big Pharma rogue's gallery; they are not just a couple of bad apples in an otherwise good barrel. Indeed, crime is pervasive throughout the pharmaceutical industry, as the following "rap sheet" of major company offenses over the last fifteen years demonstrates:

Dey Pharma, Abbott, Roxanne, and Braun, 2010: Each of the four companies agreed to pay, in total, more than $700 million to settle claims that they engaged in schemes to report false and substantially inflated prices for numerous pharmaceutical products, knowing that federal health care programs relied on those reported prices to set payment rates.[15]

Biovail, 2008: Agreed to plead guilty to kickback and conspiracy charges for paying physicians and other health care providers to prescribe and recommend its drug Cardizem and to pay a $22 million criminal fine.[16]

Merck, 2008: Agreed to pay over $650 million to settle allegations that it failed to pay rebates to Medicaid and that it offered kickbacks to physicians to induce them to use its drugs.[17]

Cephalon Inc., 2008: Agreed to plead guilty to the illegal promotion of three of its drugs—Actiq, Gabitril, and Provigil—and to pay $425 million to settle criminal and civil charges.[18]

Pharmacia & Upjohn (Pfizer), 2007: Agreed to plead guilty to offering kickbacks to physicians and pay a criminal fine of $19.68 million.[19]

Bristol-Myers Squibb, 2007: Agreed to pay $515 million to settle civil claims for wrongful drug marketing and pricing practices, including promoting its drug Abilify for off-label treatment of children and the elderly.[20]

Purdue, 2007: Agreed to pay $600 million to settle criminal and civil claims for fraudulently marketing and promoting its drug OxyContin as less addictive and less subject to abuse and diversion than it actually is.[21]

Aventis, 2007: Paid $190 million to resolve allegations it fraudulently inflated prices for its drug Anzemet knowing government reimbursements would be based on those prices.[22]

InterMune, 2007: Paid $36.9 million to settle claims it had marketed its drug, Actimmune, for unapproved purposes for which it had failed to demonstrate efficacy.[23]

Serono Labs, 2006: Agreed to plead guilty to conspiracy and kickback charges in relation to its AIDS drug Serostim, and to pay $704 million to resolve civil and criminal claims.[24]

Eli Lilly, 2006: Agreed to plead guilty to illegal promotion of its drug Evista and to pay a total of $36 million to settle criminal and civil charges.[25]

Dey Inc. (Merck), 2003: Agreed to pay $18.5 million to settle allegations the company had submitted false pricing information and caused health care providers to submit inflated reimbursement claims to Medicaid programs.[26]

Abbott Labs, 2003: Agreed to pay a $382 million fine after an undercover investigation by the FBI and other agencies (called "Operation Headwaters") revealed the company and its subsidiary Ross were offering kickbacks and instructing potential purchasers on how to defraud the government. Another Abbott subsidiary paid $200 million in criminal fines.[27]

AstraZeneca Pharmaceuticals, 2003: Agreed to plead guilty to a conspiracy to cause payment claims to be submitted to governments for free samples of its drug Zoladex and to pay a $64 million criminal fine, as well as nearly $300 million in civil penalties and damages.[28]

Bayer Corp., 2003: Agreed to plead guilty to one criminal count of Medicare fraud for a scheme that concealed and then avoided obligations to pay rebates to Medicaid, and to pay a $5.5 million criminal fine, and over $250 million to settle civil allegations.[29]

Pfizer Inc., 2002: Agreed to pay $49 million to settle allegations under the False Claims Act that the company and its subsidiaries, Warner Lambert and Parke, fraudulently avoided paying rebates to governments in respect to sales of its cholesterol lowering drug Lipitor.[30]

TAP Pharmaceutical Products, Inc. 2001: Agreed to plead guilty to a conspiracy to violate the Prescription Drug Marketing Act, and to pay a $290 million criminal fine, the largest criminal fine at the time in a health care fraud prosecution, and close to $600 million in civil fines.[31]

LifeScan (Johnson & Johnson), 2000: Agreed to plead guilty to criminal charges for misbranding a device (a home glucose monitor for diabetes), failing to notify the FDA, and submitting false reports to the FDA, and to pay $29.4 million in criminal fines, as well as $30.6 million in civil penalties, damages, attorneys fees, and restitution.[32]

F. Hoffmann-La Roche Ltd., 1999: Agreed to plead guilty to a worldwide conspiracy to raise and fix prices and allocate market shares for certain vitamins sold in the United States and elsewhere, and to pay a $500 million criminal fine—the highest criminal fine ever at the time.[33]

Hoechst AG, 1999: Agreed to plead guilty to participating in a seventeen-year international conspiracy to fix prices and allocate market shares on the sale of sorbates in the United States and elsewhere, and to pay a $36 million criminal fine.[34]

Genentech Inc., 1999: Agreed to plead guilty to marketing to doctors one of its most lucrative prescription drugs, Protropin, for uses which had not been approved by the FDA, and to pay a $30 million criminal fine.[35]

Pfizer Inc., 1999: Agreed to plead guilty to participating in two international price fixing conspiracies in the food additives industry and to pay criminal fines totaling $20 million.[36]

Copley Pharmaceutical, Inc., 1997: Agreed to plead guilty to one count of conspiracy to defraud the FDA, and to pay a $10.65 million criminal fine.[37]

Haarmann & Reimer Corp. (subsidiary of Bayer AG), 1997: Agreed to plead guilty to participating in an international conspiracy to fix prices and allocate sales in the citric acid market worldwide, and to pay a $50 million criminal fine.[38]

None of these are victimless crimes. Behind the convictions, guilty pleas, and civil penalties lie tragic stories of illness, injury, death, ruined lives, shattered families, conspiracies, and frauds against governments and consumers. It is hard to choose the worst offender, but any short list would have to include Purdue Pharma's crimes around its popular and highly profitable opiate-based painkiller, OxyContin.

Today, one out of every five teens in the United States abuses prescription drugs, sometimes with devastating effects, and OxyContin is their drug of choice. The only drug more used unlawfully by youth is marijuana. As early as 2001 the National Drug Intelligence Center warned that the "pharmacological effects of OxyContin make it a suitable substitute for heroin."[39]

Anthony Fernandez, a Staten Island youth now in his twenties, began experimenting with OxyContin when he was fourteen. He quickly became addicted to the drug, often referred to as "hillbilly heroin," but managed to shake the addiction in his later teens. "I've gotten that phone call about eleven times," he says of the calls announcing friends' deaths from overdosing on OxyContin. "I've been to more wakes than I've been to birthday parties."[40]

OxyContin abuse is fueled by two factors, in addition to the euphoric high it creates. First, teens tend to believe the drug is "controllable" and "safe" when compared to illicit drugs. Second, it is easy to obtain—even easier, teens report, than buying beer. The drug is readily supplied to teens by friends, snuck from parents' medicine cabinets, and easily bought online or from illicit dealers. "The streets, the schools, all you've got to do is make a call," says one Staten Island youth. "Everybody has an unlimited amount of connections. You get more popular, make more money, and everybody knows your name [if you sell it]." [41]

Purdue, OxyContin's maker, has surely profited from the widespread abuse of its drug by teenagers, but that alone does not justify criminal charges. What got the company into trouble was the fact it consciously and strategically cultivated OxyContin abuse. For the first five years of the drug's life, 1996 to 2001, the company waged a marketing campaign that deliberately and illegally downplayed the drug's potential to addict and be abused. "In the process," according to John Brownlee, a Virginia United States Attorney who helped prosecute the case against Purdue, "scores died as a result of OxyContin abuse and an even greater number of people became addicted to OxyContin." [42]

Purdue paid more than half a billion dollars in criminal fines and civil penalties after pleading guilty to the federal charge that "certain Purdue supervisors and employees, with the intent to defraud or mislead, marketed and promoted OxyContin as less addictive, less subject to abuse and diversion, and less likely to cause tolerance and withdrawal than other pain medications." Three executives also entered personal guilty pleas but were spared imprisonment when they agreed to pay $34.5 million in penalties. [43]

The larger and unsettling lesson to be learned from the OxyContin story, together with the numerous other stories of pharmaceutical industry crime and corruption, is that the companies now driving the science and practice of children's mental health are so compelled by their penchant for profit that they will break the law, time and time again, in pursuit of it. More generally, the fact is that physicians, along with the body of knowledge they rely upon to treat children for emotional and behavioral problems, are currently under the influence of self-interested, often unscrupulous, and sometimes criminal corporations concerned mainly to create markets for their products, and not necessarily to discover scientific truth or promote children's health.

No doubt, some children's lives are improved by being treated for mental and emotional disorders with psychotropic drugs. But that does not deny the large, tangible, and growing threat to children's health and well-being from overdiagnosis and overmedication. Pharmaceutical industry influence over the science and practice of pediatric mental health is at the root of that threat, as I have argued. The question is what to do about it.

When our kids become difficult or unusually moody, or a teacher sends home a note suggesting they might have ADHD, or a checklist survey at school "diagnoses" them with anxiety or depression, or they say they feel sad and depressed, we may feel inclined to take them to a doctor or a child psychiatrist. The latter may, in turn, diagnose a mental or behavioral disorder and prescribe a powerful and potentially dangerous psychotropic drug or cocktail of drugs. This is a difficult place to be as a parent.

Child psychiatrist Elizabeth Roberts provides some concrete advice to parents on what to do in these circumstances in her book, *Should You Medicate Your Child's Mind?* Though "the current trend in psychiatry [is] to overdiagnose and overmedicate children, to use the strongest and most dangerous medications available even in the youngest children," she says, parents can take steps to protect their children from the harmful effects of this trend. Dr. Roberts helpfully elaborates what these steps are and provides useful insights into "exactly which behaviors constitute the basis of a psychiatric diagnosis, which behaviors and conditions in children do not need medication and which do." [44]

At the same time, however, parents should not be saddled with the entire burden of protecting children from a threat that emanates largely from the self-interested behavior of pharmaceutical companies. Governments must also be accountable, and called upon to curb, by passing laws and regulations if necessary, the ability of companies to drive the overdiagnosis and overmedication trend. Currently, only the most flagrant transgressions of pharmaceutical companies—such as the ones described in the "rap sheet" above—are legally prohibited: defrauding governments, deliberately misleading doctors and consumers, fixing prices, providing kickbacks to doctors, and marketing drugs for unapproved ("off-label") uses. Other questionable tactics—such as those canvassed in this and the previous chapter—have been left largely untouched.

Recently regulators have begun to address some of these issues, albeit with modest measures of uncertain effect. Suppressing negative results from clinical trials is one area where some action has been taken. In 2007, several years after the hidden-data scandals and Caitlin McIntosh's tragic death, Congress enacted legislation requiring all clinical trials and results to be registered at the web-based registry ClinicalTrials.gov.[45] The new law is a positive step, though not sufficient on its own to solve the problems it targets. To begin with, it only applies to trials conducted after 2007, meaning that most drugs currently on the market are not covered. Next, while "the degree of positive change will depend on the quality of information submitted to registries," as one expert states [46] there are no guarantees the information registered will be of sufficient quality to reveal anything of substance. There is the further concern that physicians—trained as they are to rely upon medical journals for their information—will shy away from using the registry, thus undercutting its potential role in countering suppression-based biases in the published medical literature. Finally, there is the problem of enforcement. Reporting requirements, such as those in the 2007 law, are notoriously underenforced by regulators, a problem magnified by the difficulty of detecting suppressed data, especially when trials are conducted offshore by private clinical research organizations (CROs). For the law to truly have an impact, according to regulation experts Thomas McGarity and Wendy Wagner, Congress must "expand agency enforcement resources and require the agencies to conduct a specific number of unannounced inspections of research facilities and research contractors each year."[47] There are currently no signs of this happening.[48]

Conflict of interest is another area where legal bolstering could help curb the overdiagnosis and overmedication of children. Though most medical journals and the FDA demand researchers disclose funding sources, affiliations, and financial relationships, these standards are not well enforced, and are narrow in scope. The standards do not, for example, demand disclosure of the roles of CROs, medical communications firms, and other subcontractors in conducting studies, analyzing data, and writing up reports and articles. Nor do they apply beyond clinical trials and medical publications to include other kinds of scientific information and dissemination that play important roles in regulatory and judicial processes (such as unpublished critiques, analyses, and reports).[49] Well-enforced laws requiring mandatory disclosure of all relevant information in all scientific reporting contexts would certainly be an advance. Ghostwriting could also be targeted in such laws by requiring primary authors to declare formally that they were actually substantially involved in the conduct of studies with their names on them. They would have to verify that they had access to and knowledge of all relevant data, and that they controlled decisions about whether to submit the work for publication.[50]

Even broader and better-enforced disclosure laws would not attack the root problem in medical science, however—the subtle, not-so-subtle, and routine manipulation of research that results, inevitably, from too-close ties between scientists and the pharmaceutical industry. Disclosure laws *manage* conflict of interest, but they do not eliminate it. They therefore do not go far enough, according to epidemiologist David Michaels (speaking as an academic scientist, before he became head of the federal Occupational Safety and Health Administration). "Too much is at stake," he says. "Data interpretation requires independent judgment; the public needs assurance that the opinions expressed in these settings are unbiased by commercial interest."[51] The solution, according to Michaels (and some others), is to separate medical research from commercial interests—to rebuild, albeit in a different spot, the "invisible wall" that was torn down by the Bayh-Dole Act. "Any study desired by (or required of) industry would be paid for by the industry but conducted by independent researchers, under federal auspices," he proposes and subsequent publication would be completely independent of the sponsoring corporations."[52] This is a proposal worthy of serious consideration for its potential to restore some of the integrity in medical science that has been lost to industry influence.

A final area in need of regulatory attention is the range of questionable tactics used by pharmaceutical companies to persuade physicians to prescribe their drugs, often for "off-label" uses. Companies spend a staggering $20 billion each year (in total) sponsoring lavish dinners, golf club seminars, lectures and consultations, grand rounds at hospitals, gifts and perks from drug reps, and so on.[53] Such practices risk incentivizing, among other things, overdiagnoses and overmedication of children. Doctors on company payrolls might be inclined to give speeches and conduct consultations touting drugs and diagnoses in ways that serve sponsors', rather than patients', interests; doctors receiving gifts and perks might be more inclined to prescribe donor companies' drugs. Concerns about such practices have been growing, especially as high-profile cases, such as Dr. Joseph Biederman's, come to light. "The interest is exponentially more now than it was five years ago, which was exponentially more than it was five years before that," states Richard Krugman, dean of the University of Colorado School of Medicine.[54] As a result, federal law will soon require disclosure by all drug companies of how much they pay individual doctors, either directly or in the form of gifts, dinners, and perks.[55] Beyond such mandatory disclosure laws, however, there are currently no checks or restrictions on practices that risk compromising the care of patients.

Chapter Six

A Dangerous and Unnatural Experiment

On a recent visit to Sydney, Nova Scotia, where I had been invited to give a lecture at Cape Breton University, my host John MacKinnon, dean of the university's business school, wanted to show me something. Throughout the day, MacKinnon had excitedly shared with me his "new economy" plans for the Cape, a region reeling from deindustrialization—"see those empty runways," he proudly proclaimed at the airport, "not many planes come in these days; so we're creating an international flight training school for pilots from developing countries"—but he was oddly subdued as we began the drive back to my hotel after the talk. "Have you seen the tar ponds?" he finally asked, his tone hushed and reluctant, as though he had something shameful to confess. "No," I said, "I haven't." MacKinnon quickly changed lanes, took an exit, and made some turns. As we approached a brightly lit bridge he slowed down and pointed a finger past my face and out the passenger-side window. "There they are," he said. I nodded somberly, as if I could see something more profound than the blackness of night.

But I knew what was out there. Muggah Creek, a once pristine estuary, flowed just beneath us into the Sydney harbor. A century of steelmaking on its banks had polluted it, along with the silt and mud beneath it, to a depth of 24 meters, with 700,000 tons of toxic sludge.[1] Over the years the creek had become the infamous tar ponds, and "the paradise of this part of the world," as one chronicler had described Sydney in 1859, was transformed into an environmental disaster without equal in North America.[2] The ponds' toxic brew was composed mainly of runoff from the coke ovens that had turned coal into fuel to run the mill for nearly a century. Those ovens, now dormant, lay just behind us and off to the left, parallel to Frederick Street and its row of now-abandoned wooden houses.

It was a resident of one of those houses, Debbie Ouellette, who ten years earlier had noticed a yellow-orange ooze seeping out of the rail bed adjacent to her property. She was having intense migraine-like headaches at the time, and when, by chance, two neighbors mentioned similar headaches, Debbie realized the yellow-orange ooze—which, as it turned out, was laced with arsenic and other poisonous chemicals—might be the cause.[3] But it was not just the headaches. Debbie, a nurse by training, began to consider other strange things happening on her street. Her last pregnancy had been difficult, and her son had almost died during childbirth. As he grew up, he suffered frequent and serious ear infections, asthma, and behavioral problems. Her older son had found a strangely deformed dead mouse, with huge ears and froglike hind legs, on Frederick Street, and every dog on the street had died of cancer. A neighbor's son had been born with deformed genitals. A healthy two-year-old child, Larissa Boone, became seriously ill after moving to Frederick Street—ear infections, fluid-filled lungs, an eye swollen shut with pus—only to become healthy again, almost immediately, once she and her family moved away.[4]

Asthma, birth deformities, behavioral disorders, and cancer seemed to plague residents of Frederick Street, and of Sydney more generally, in unusually high numbers. Citizens complained, and federally mandated studies confirmed what they already knew—their environment was severely contaminated with a toxic brew of poisons, and they were getting sick and dying (from cancer in particular) in unusually high numbers.[5] Yet industry and local governments denied (and still do) that the levels of illness and death were linked to the toxic environment. Rather, they argued, the likely cause was Sydney citizens' propensities to eat too much salt and fat and not enough fiber, and to smoke and drink too much.[6] The provincial government commissioned its own studies and trumpeted results—later discredited, as we shall see below—that exonerated the toxic environment, and those who had made it so.[7]

There are many Sydneys in the world, places where abnormally high concentrations of illness and death exist alongside unusually high levels of environmental contaminants. It is most often poor and minority communities that suffer such fates. The "clusters" of illness—often the exact illnesses known to be associated with the chemicals pervasive in the environment—are acknowledged to exist by governments and industry, who nonetheless insist the pollutants have not been proven to *cause* the illness and that therefore no one is to blame, and nothing need be done.

That same logic—a presumption of innocence for industrial chemicals and pollutants until they are proven, beyond a doubt, to be guilty—has, with the help of vociferous industry lobbying and influence, come to define the regulation of *all* chemicals, not only those found at cluster sites. Corporations, as a result, are now permitted to use and release into the environment vast quantities of thousands of different chemicals, 99.8 percent of which have not been proven to be safe, and many of which are known carcinogens, neurotoxins, and hormone disruptors.[8] The dangers have only mounted as pollution, once mainly "out there" in the external environment, has become embedded within, and is now emitted from, the products we use and consume every day—food, soaps, cleaners, carpets, mattresses, toys, garden hoses, and just about everything else. Our households—indeed our very bodies, as we shall see—have become, in effect, miniature Sydneys, and as was true of Sydney itself, children are the main victims.

101

*   *   *

Over the last several decades, children's chronic health problems rose dramatically as more and more chemicals, in increasing amounts, infused their environments. Asthma rates in the United States jumped nearly 50 percent (so that the disease now affects one out of every ten children and is the leading cause of childhood hospitalizations and school absences).[9] Childhood leukemia and brain cancer (the most common childhood cancers) increased by more than 40 percent.[10] Autism rates grew by 1,000 percent.[11] Babies were born on average a week earlier, and 30 percent more of them were born premature.[12] Girls reached puberty at significantly earlier ages, and the number of boys born with serious genital abnormalities doubled.[13] Developmental disorders—mental disabilities, and learning and behavioral problems chief among them—rose as well during this period.[14]

"We are the humans in a dangerous and unnatural experiment in the United States, and I think it's unconscionable," states Dr. Leo Trasande of New York City's Mount Sinai Hospital. Trasande links the current epidemic of childhood chronic illness to the 7,500 percent increase in industrial chemicals in the environment over the last few decades, and the fact 26,000 new such chemicals have come into use during that time.[15]

In 2005 Rowan Holland, then one year old, made history by becoming the youngest person ever to be tested for industrial chemicals in his body. His parents, Jeremiah Holland and Michele Hammond, had volunteered the family to take part in the testing as part of an investigation by a local newspaper.[16] Rowan's levels of industrial chemicals were up to seven times higher than those of his parents. Polybrominated diphenyl ethers (PBDEs), to take one example, coursed through Rowan's veins at twice the level known to cause thyroid failure in rats. Testing of other children, thousands since Rowan was tested, reveals that his results were not unusual. It is a sad and alarming truth that for each successive generation, children carry more and greater amounts of industrial chemicals in their bodies than do their parents.

Yet, little is being done to protect children and that, says Trasande, is because regulators and industry continue to rely upon scientific models that ignore children's unique vulnerabilities to chemical exposure. Traditional toxicology, the basis of current regulatory regimes, is guided by the presumption that "the dose makes the poison," as Paracelsus, the sixteenth-century founder of the field, first described it. "Safe" levels of exposure are thus designated at the point below which a particular chemical has been proven to cause immediate and tangible ill effects. The model is limited by its inability to capture differences between adults and children; in particular, the different effects of chemical exposures on *developing*, as distinct from developed, biological systems. "The more we look," says Trasande, "the more we realize that the paradigm from the world of toxicology does not fit the universe of experience." While a substantial exposure to some chemical might have no ill effects on adults, a very small exposure could cause "profound and lifelong consequences" for infants, children, teens, and especially if it occurs during the prenatal period. These "extremely vulnerable windows," as Trasande describes them, are the moments when organ systems are developing, and thus easily and irreparably, damaged.[17]

The limitations of current toxicological models, and the regulatory system based upon them, are illustrated by the government's treatment of the chemical Bisphenol A (BPA). BPA production jumped almost 15,000 percent in the United States over the last few decades as the chemical became a key ingredient in food and drink containers (including baby bottles), plastic wraps, and the lining of cans (including those containing infant formula). BPA leaches into food and drinks from all these products, especially when they are heated.[18] The current government "fact sheet" on BPA, issued by the U.S. Department of Health and Human Services, reflects traditional toxicology's presumption that low doses are harmless. "There are small amounts of BPA in liquid infant formulas sold in cans," it states. "Infant formula in this packaging can offer important health advantages for some infants, and the proven benefit of good nutrition outweighs the potential risk of BPA exposure." It is simply presumed, following "the dose makes the poison" logic, that the "potential risk" from small doses of BPA is minimal, a presumption which may turn out to be horribly wrong.[19]

A growing body of evidence suggests BPA can in fact work ill effects at even very low levels of exposure. Typically in these studies, rodents are exposed to doses of BPA that approximate those humans are normally exposed to in the environment. These can be thousands of times smaller than the doses deemed "safe" by regulatory agencies, and millions of times smaller than the doses normally used in toxicological studies.[20] Even at these very low levels of exposure, worrying effects have been found, including insulin resistance (which in roughly 25 percent of cases leads to type II diabetes); altered mammary gland development; adverse effects on the prostate gland; altered sexual differentiation in brain and behavior; adverse effects on the female reproductive tract; suppressed sperm count; obesity; heart disease; and premature sexual development.[21] According to a recent report authored by thirty-eight of the world's top independent BPA researchers: "The whole range of adverse effects of low doses of BPA in laboratory animals exposed both during development and in adulthood is a great cause for concern with regard to the potential for similar adverse effects in humans." [22]

Scientists are only beginning to understand the precise mechanisms through which low-dose exposure to chemicals such as BPA affect developing biological systems. Timing and hormones appear to be crucial elements. For biological systems to mature and function properly it is necessary that billions of intricate cell divisions occur, without interruption, during gestation and childhood. The genes responsible for a system's growth must be turned on and off at exactly the right times, meaning the hormones that flip the on/off switches must be released in precisely the right sequences.[23]

Many chemicals, BPA among them, disrupt or mimic hormonal processes (which is the reason why BPA was proposed as a hormone replacement therapy in the 1930s). They turn genes on and off at the wrong times, and thus potentially interfere with the development of biological systems. A variety of adverse outcomes can result: birth defects (from *in utero* exposure), childhood disorders and difficulties (asthma, autism, allergies, cancer, intelligence deficiencies, behavioral problems, vulnerability to infections), and diseases later in life (cancer, dementia, heart disease).[24]

The importance of timing of exposure to a chemical is illustrated by the well-known thalidomide tragedy. Thalidomide, a sedative introduced in 1957, was marketed as a treatment for morning sickness in pregnant women. Four years later, after tens of thousands of children had been born with serious limb deformities to mothers who had taken the drug during their pregnancies, it was pulled from the market. That is the part of the story people know. Less well known is the fact the deformities occurred only in babies whose mothers took the drug during days 20 to 24 of the first month of their pregnancies. Over those five days, the complicated cell-division processes necessary for healthy limb formation were uniquely susceptible to interruption by even small doses of the drug. Outside that window—before those processes began, and after they were completed—the drug was harmless.[25]

But timing and hormones are not the only factors governing the likely impact of chemical exposures. Important as well are interactions among different toxic exposures, and between toxins and genetic or congenital dispositions. Every child falling ill with acute lymphoblastic leukemia (ALL), for example, has a particular chromosomal defect, either inherited or a result of prenatal exposure to a chemical toxicant. Yet, because most children with that chromosomal defect do not get the disease, it is believed subsequent exposure to some toxicant is necessary for leukemia to develop in those children who have the defect. To similar effect, recent studies on asthma suggest that, at least in some cases, the disease is caused by exposure to environmental toxicants, but only in children with particular genetic predispositions. A child exposed to tobacco in utero, for example, is at increased risk for asthma only if he or she has a GSTM1 null genotype as part of his or her genetic makeup.[26]

Chemicals can cause harm in numerous different ways. Disruption of hormones is a particularly worrying one for children because of the ubiquity of hormone-disrupting chemicals in their environments and the fact that their developing biological systems are uniquely susceptible to them. Chemicals in the family of compounds known as phthalates, for example, interfere with hormonal processes necessary for normal development of reproductive systems, particularly in males, and are linked to a series of abnormalities in animals and humans. The male offspring of pregnant mothers (both human and animal) exposed to certain phthalates have been shown to be at risk for a group of "demasculization" disorders—undescended testicles, a shorter distance between anus and genitals, hypospadias,[27] and testicular tumors later in life.[28] Scientists also suspect phthalates may be linked to declining sperm counts in adult males and diminishing birth weight differentials between boys and girls (male hormones are responsible for boys being heavier) as both trends began around the time (the 1970s) these chemicals were first released into the environment. A recent study found that boys born to mothers exposed to high levels of phthalates were more likely to exhibit feminized behavior, further supporting the theory that phthalates interfere with the processes responsible for sexual differentiation.[29]

Phthalates are pervasive in children's environments. They are found, for example, in:

Toys (especially soft and rubbery toys, such as balls, pucks, action figures, and bath toys)
Screen prints on children's clothing (often in combination with lead and arsenic that help stabilize the plastic—my favorite example is a

baby jumpsuit emblazoned with "green baby" and an image of the recycling logo; the screen print is laden with phthalates and also contains lead at nearly five times the U.S. permissible limit and arsenic at nearly twice the level considered safe)[30]

Kitchen floors, where young children commonly play (floor tiles, once made of relatively nontoxic linoleum, are now typically made of polyvinyl chloride, which in turn contains high levels of phthalates, as well as various chlorinated compounds, some of which, such as vinyl chloride, are known to be carcinogenic)

School backpacks, pencil cases, lunchboxes, and reusable lunch bags (a Dora the Explorer Activity Tote, for example, contains high levels of phthalates and also lead at a staggering twenty times the U.S. permissible level)[31]

Children's shoes, flip-flops, plastic sandals, and clogs[32]

Electronic gadgets and equipment

Household infrastructure, such as shower curtains, window frames, doors, and blinds

Personal care products, especially those with scent ("parfum" on the ingredient list usually indicates phthalates), including soaps, shampoos, deodorants, cosmetics, and skin softeners.[33]

PBDEs are also hormone disruptors. Commonly used as flame retardants, they are found in (and leach out from) sofas, mattresses, curtains, computer and television casings, kitchen and small appliances (hair dryers, fans, heaters), mobile phones, fax machines, remote controls, printers, and wall coverings. The chemicals end up in house dust which children then ingest when they put their hands, toys, and various other things in their mouths.

Perfluorochemicals (PFCs) are found in Teflon and other no-stick products, as well as in anti-stain and waterproofing products, and carpets and carpet cleaners ("children are particularly susceptible to exposure from inhalation of PFC off-gassing," according to the Environmental Protection Agency (EPA), because "they are lying, crawling and spending large amounts of time playing on the carpet"). These chemicals are known to disrupt hormonal processes and also to be carcinogenic.[34]

Various pesticides and herbicides (atrazine, endosulfan, DDT, dioxins, HCH, and many others), fungicides (such as vinclozolin), along with preservatives and antibacterial agents (such as triclosan, an ingredient in a wide variety of personal care products, household items, and even garden hoses) are all specifically designed to disrupt hormonal processes—that is how they do their jobs of killing weeds, bugs, fungi, and bacteria.

Perchlorate, a hormone disruptor used to make rocket fuel and fireworks, is pervasive throughout the environment. It is found in high concentrations in women's breast milk—high enough, according to one recent study, to risk suppressing thyroid hormone production in infants (especially those with low levels of the nutrient iodide), and thus exposing them to the risk of permanent neurological damage.[35]

Numerous other chemicals in children's daily lives are potentially toxic. To give a sense of the scope of the problem, I cross-referenced chemicals starting with the letters A, B, or C against government-compiled lists of known carcinogenic compounds in common household products. Even this quite conservative filter produced worrying results.[36] Hair products (conditioners, sprays, and gels) and body washes may contain acetamide, acrylonitrile; glue, including school glue, and glue remover, may contain acetaldehyde, carbon tetrachloride, chloroform; paint may contain amiline, benzene, butyl benzyl phthalate, cadmium, carbon black, chlorothanonil; pesticides and anti-flea and tick products for pets may contain acetochlor, alachlor, captan, carbaryl, chlorothanonil; printer cartridges contain carbon black; and batteries may contain cobalt.[37]

Children sop up, like sponges, all of these chemicals, along with BPA, PBDEs, PFCs, perchlorates, and untold numbers of others among the approximately 86,000 chemicals currently in commercial use. They are in fact perfectly put together to accumulate and store chemicals in their bodies, as Rowan Holland's story suggests. They live close to the ground, spend much of their time on the floor, where they are exposed to chemical-laden household dust, [38] and outside on the chemically saturated lawn. They put things in their mouths, are in constant contact with plastics, and their small size means that, pound for pound, they are exposed to chemicals in higher proportions than are adults. Their still-developing bodies are less efficient at metabolizing and eliminating toxins; and when they are born, their bodies are already saturated with hundreds of industrial chemicals as a result of being exposed to them *in utero* (a recent study of ten babies' umbilical cord blood found in each sample an average of two hundred industrial chemicals, many of them carcinogenic, neurotoxic, or linked to birth defects and abnormal development).[39]

Moreover, certain chemicals, such as PBDEs and PFCs, "persist and bioaccumulate in humans," as the EPA describes it, meaning that "comparatively low exposures can result in large body burdens."[40] As well, persistence and accumulation of such chemicals in the environment leads to each generation beginning life at higher levels of exposure than previous ones did—the likely reason why Rowan Holland's levels of PBDEs were so much higher than his parents'. PBDE levels in humans have in fact doubled every five years since the chemical entered the market, to the point where they are now 100 times higher than they were in the early 1980s.[41]

Despite all of that, industry and governments insist everything is fine. According to Elizabeth Whelan, president of the industry-backed American Council on Science and Health, "the mere ability to detect chemicals is [not] the same as proving a hazard, that if you have this chemical, you are at risk of a disease."[42] The government Centers for Disease Control and Prevention echoes her view. "The presence of an environmental chemical in people's blood or urine does not mean that it will cause effects or disease," it states. "Small amounts may be of no health consequence, whereas larger amounts may cause adverse health effects."[43]

For Dr. Bruce Lanphear, a leading expert on children's environmental health, such comments symbolize an inexcusable and far-reaching failure by governments to protect the public, and particularly children, from the effects of exposure to industrial chemicals. "One of the most disturbing things for me," says Lanphear, "is that we know that environmental chemicals have the potential to be toxic at very low doses yet we fail to recognize that." In order to protect children's health, he says, we need to assume there are likely to be ill effects from chemical exposure even at the lowest measureable levels. "Yet that's not how we regulate these chemicals," he says, and as a result current regulations "are so obsolete right now that we can't trust them."[44]

Why is this so? Why does Paracelsus's sixteenth-century notion that the "dose makes the poison" persist despite mounting evidence that, in many instances, it is wrong? Why, more generally, are we as a society failing so badly to protect children from profound threats to their health and well-being?

The next chapter provides some answers.

Chapter Seven

Precautionary Tales

U nder our free institutions anybody can poison himself that wants
to," Samuel Clemens (aka Mark Twain) blithely remarked in his
autobiography. But purveyors of possible poisons know that people
generally prefer not to poison themselves, which is why industries
work so hard to repress, discredit, and counter indications that their
products might cause harm.

On May 28, 2009, at one of Clemens's favorite haunts, the vaunted
Cosmos Club of Washington, D.C., representatives from Coca-Cola,
Del Monte, Alcoa, the Grocery Manufacturers Association, and the
American Chemistry Council gathered together for a secret meeting.
United by their fear of a growing public backlash against the use of
BPA as a metal can liner, they aimed to "develop potential commu-
nication/media strategies around BPA."[1] Even the misanthropic Clemens would likely have been surprised by the cynicism of the ideas
they canvassed. Threaten consumers with baby food scarcities and
high food prices if BPA is banned, they proposed. Explain how African American and Hispanic minorities, along with poor people more
generally, would be hit hardest by a ban. Appeal to young mothers
and mothers-to-be by finding a "pregnant young mother who would
be willing to speak around the country about the benefits of BPA"

(the "holy grail" of spokespersons for BPA, according to attendees). Keep up the work of "befriending people that are able to manipulate the legislative process."[2] And if the battle for BPA is lost, do not stop fighting. "It does not matter what the next material is," the meeting's minutes reported, "there will be issues with it, and the committee wants to work to make people feel more comfortable with BPA and 'BPA2' or whatever chemical comes next."[3]

Recent efforts by industry to "make people feel more comfortable with BPA" have included launching websites purporting to offer consumers expert and neutral advice about the chemical. Search "BPA safety" and many such sites pop up. Factsaboutbpa.org points out that "scientists and regulatory agencies around the world have found BPA to be safe for use in current food contact applications," and also that "products made with BPA contribute to the health and safety of people." Bisphenol-A.org states that "in the forty plus years since its first commercial use, BPA's safety has been confirmed by numerous tests designed to evaluate potential health effects and by government assessments of those tests." Plasticsinfo.org notes that "extensive safety data on BPA show that polycarbonate plastic can be used safely in consumer products."[4]

The legions of studies revealing concerns about exposure to low doses of BPA are quickly dismissed if mentioned at all on these websites. There is no acknowledgment that BPA could have any ill effects whatsoever on human health, and governments, such as Canada's, that have imposed or are considering restrictions on the chemical are tagged as overzealous and irrational. The websites are remarkably similar in their messages. Or perhaps it is not so remarkable, given that *all* of the sites are hosted by the American Chemistry Council. The appearance of numerous different organizations, each seemingly neutral and independent, delivering the same good news is a complete sham—clever public relations, perhaps, but decidedly unhelpful for anyone seeking to understand the truth about BPA.

The distorting influences of such campaigns is regrettable, as are the cynical deceptions hatched at meetings like that at the Cosmos Club. But even deeper and more insidious assaults on truth are the result today of science being commandeered by corporate self-interest.

"Scholarship and independence are essential elements in the search for answers to complex questions, such as understanding the health risks from environmental agents," according to the prestigious University of Michigan Risk Science Center.[5] In July 2008, the acting head of that center, Martin Philbert, a University of Michigan professor of toxicology, was appointed by the FDA to chair its subcommittee on BPA, a result of growing pressure on the agency to investigate the chemical. A month after assuming his new post, Philbert and his committee—five of the eight members of which had been appointed by Philbert—issued a report declaring BPA to be safe for all uses.[6]

Around the time Philbert assumed his new post, Charles Gelman, a retired industrialist who had made his considerable fortune manufacturing medical supplies (in which BPA is a key ingredient), donated $5 million to the Risk Science Center, an amount twenty-five times the organization's annual budget of $210,000. Gelman believes BPA is "perfectly safe," and that concerns about the chemical have been overblown by "mothers' groups and others who don't know the science."[7] As for the $5 million gift, Gelman says his motivation was to "help inform the public about how to properly assess the benefits and hazards posed by technology, chemicals in particular."[8] Gelman's gift raised concerns. Not only was the timing suspect, but Gelman had admitted he had informed Philbert of his views on BPA in "several conversations." "He [Philbert] knows where I stand," he is reported to have said. For his part, Philbert admitted to being aware of Gelman's views, but insisted that he was "not open to any undue influence."[9] The FDA agreed, finding Philbert was not in a conflict of interest as a result of Gelman's gift to the center.[10] Still, the Gelman-Philbert connection is troubling.[11]

Even more troubling, however, is the broader influence the chemical industry appears to have over BPA science and public policy. In the years leading up to the creation of Philbert's committee, FDA officials had been in constant contact with chemical industry lobbyists about BPA.[12] In glaring contrast, not one independent scientist—and therefore no one from the growing number of researchers whose work has revealed BPA's possible dangers—was canvassed by the FDA for opinions on the chemical. Making matters worse, attempts by some of those independent scientists to share their views with the FDA were actively rebuffed. "Appalling," is how Fred vom Saal, one the world's top BPA researchers, describes it. "These people [FDA officials] are really now, and have obviously been for a long time, in industry's pocket."[13]

Philbert's report was itself based almost entirely on material submitted by industry groups, chiefly ICF International, a consulting firm whose clients include the American Chemistry Council, the American Petroleum Institute, the American Plastics Council (a branch of the American Chemistry Council), and industry lobbyist Steven Hentges (who is also executive director of the BPA group at the American Chemistry Council). ICF International's material, which, not surprisingly, downplayed and discredited concerns about BPA's safety, was so heavily relied upon by Philbert and his committee that one newspaper story described the final report as having been "written largely by the plastics industry and others with a financial stake in the controversial chemical."[14]

Industry was able to strengthen its influence in the process by producing its own research, tailored to its self-interested purposes. Four industry-funded rodent studies formed the backbone of ICF International's submissions to Philbert's committee. Each concluded that exposure to BPA had no adverse health effects. Yet those four studies were, taken together, "flawed," "antiquated," "invalid," "not appropriate for use in setting health standards," and likely to "jeopardize public health,"[15] according to a statement jointly authored by thirty-six top BPA researchers.[16]

The problem with science funded by, controlled by, and conducted by industry is that it risks bias in favor of industry interests (as we have already seen in relation to pharmaceuticals). A 2006 survey revealed, for example, that while BPA was found to cause adverse health effects by 90 percent of government-funded rodent studies, not one of numerous industry-funded studies reported such effects.[17] Yet industry funding is becoming the norm in environmental health research, not only in relation to BPA but across the entire field, especially as public funds dry up and academic researchers, particularly those in the junior ranks (who are under pressure from their departments to publish), turn to industry for support.[18] As a result, more and more environmental health scientists are, like their colleagues in medical and pharmaceutical sciences, tied to industry. It has now reached the point where, as scientist Bruce Lanphear points out, federal agencies such as the FDA have a difficult time finding conflict-free experts to staff their advisory committees. "It's not unusual to see up to 50 percent of an advisory committee that have some financial ties with industry," he says.[19] According to one recent report, conflict of interest threatens the entire scientific enterprise, as "powerful industrial interests . . . undermin[e] independent research on hazard and risk in Europe and North America."[20]

Compounding the problem, substantially, is the persistence and operation of the principle that regulatory restriction of a chemical is justified only once all doubt has been removed that the chemical causes harm. Take that principle away, and much of industry's power to stall protective measures disappears, which is why industry fights so hard to keep it in place.

Back in Sydney, Nova Scotia, staring at the darkness as we drove across the bridge spanning Muggah Creek, I wondered what my host, John MacKinnon, was thinking. He had offered no opinion about the tar ponds, seemingly content merely to point them out to me. So I asked

115

him—"What do you think about it all. Do you think people in Sydney are getting sick and dying because of the toxic environment?" He took a moment before answering, "I don't know. It's controversial. Nothing has really been proven one way or the other."

It is true, nothing has been proven in Sydney, at least not definitively. And most of us tend to accept, as a kind of common sense about environmental health issues—not just in Sydney but in all instances—that, without definitive proof, "nothing has been proven" (often accompanied by its corollaries, "more research is needed" and "an association or correlation is not the same thing as a cause"). The position seems reasonable—is it not *unreasonable* to allocate blame without proving fault?—and often trumps competing intuitions, particularly the intuition that exposure to toxic chemicals causes illness. In other words, we tend to side with science over our less precise and inchoate intuitions. We await and trust its pronouncements before taking action, and in the name of reason and rationality, repress our unscientific fears. That's not always a bad thing. History is replete with blunders and misguided actions, not to mention horrors, injustices, and persecutions perpetrated in the name of unfounded fears.

If our intuitions can be dangerous and imperfect, however, so too can science's immodesty, its patina of all-knowing truth. Though valuable and essential, science is also profoundly incomplete, vulnerable to distortion and abuse, and at the end of the day not worthy—at least not yet—of having us forfeit intuition. For thousands of years human beings have intuited dangers in the environment, heeded clues and cues from nature in order to survive. The residents of Frederick Street intuited that their unusual rates of illness and death had something to do with the fact they lived on the edge of a huge stew of toxic chemicals. They drew not on scientific evidence of direct causation (there was none) but rather, as Rick Smith and Bruce Lourie describe it in their book *Slow Death by Rubber Duck*, "on the kind of intuition that is hardwired in many humans but has been replaced by the mechanistic framework that has dominated modern times."[21] At the heart of that mechanistic framework is the belief that "X" does not cause "Y" unless and until it is proven beyond all doubt that it does.

Not surprisingly, corporations and their allies (including in government) preach this gospel of doubt, and funnel substantial resources into lobbying, media, public relations, think tanks, and front groups to discredit "unproven" claims of environmental harm, what they call "junk science." As one tobacco industry executive famously remarked in the wake of 1970s revelations that his industry had deviously misled the public for years about tobacco's ill effects, "Doubt is our product. It is the best means of competing with the 'body of fact' that exists in the mind of the general public."[22]

By the late 1990s the Nova Scotia government, which had taken over the old Sydney steel mill, was faced with a troubling (for it) "body of fact." Studies throughout the 1980s and 1990s had confirmed Sydney residents' belief that they got cancer and died from it more than their counterparts in other communities. Levels of coke dust and other pollutants had exceeded regulatory limits by as much as sixty times while the steel mill was in operation, it was disclosed, and in the early 1980s, federal officials had closed the lobster fishery in Sydney Harbor, into which Muggah Creek flowed, after finding dangerously high levels of toxins. Testing of soil and water samples throughout the 1990s confirmed that Sydney continued to be an extremely toxic environment, even after the steel mill had closed.[23]

With political pressure mounting, the Nova Scotia government hired Cantox, one of a new breed of for-profit research firms (staffed, in large part, by former government employees axed in the process of downsizing) that conduct risk assessments for industry and government. The business model at Cantox, and similar firms—Exponent Inc., the Weinberg Group, and ChemRisk among them—is simple. Do science, but make sure the science you do helps your client avoid liability for and regulation of its harmful products and activities.[24] "It's about putting our client's interests first," boasts Cantox on its website, and "deliver[ing] excellent value by avoiding activities . . . that won't move ahead to a successful outcome." [25]

In Sydney's case, Cantox reached a "successful outcome" for its client, concluding in its report that "No measureable health effects in local residents are predicted to result from long-term exposure to chemicals in the Frederick Street neighborhood." The report's findings were widely reported in the media upon its release and helped defuse growing opposition to the government's inaction. As it turned out, however, the report was flawed due to poor methodologies, dubious presumptions, and the fact it included already-discredited studies in formulating its analyses, according to two respected independent experts who reviewed it. [26] But Cantox had done its job.

More generally, "manufacturing doubt" about possible harms and dangers, whether with the help of firms such as Cantox, or through a range of other tactics, has become a key strategy for industries trying to avoid responsibility for harms linked to their activities and products.

The history of lead demonstrates just how effective that strategy can be.

Lead, when subject to corrosion, turns into a white powder that can be used to make paint. In the early twentieth century, lead-based paint, which was widely used in residential housing, was found to be the cause of alarmingly high rates of childhood lead poisoning. Peeling paint and household dust containing particles from paint was being ingested by children, and when their blood levels reached a certain point (around 70 μg/dl), seizure, coma, and death could result. [27] These effects, well known by the 1920s, caused some European countries (France, Belgium, and Austria) to ban lead paint in the 1930s. Yet, largely due to various industries' successful campaigns to manufacture doubt, lead paint remained legal in the United States for another forty years.

Throughout that period, the paint and lead industries worked tirelessly to discount reports of the element's harmful effects, and to thwart regulatory initiatives. They lobbied governments and public health authorities, sponsored research to counter adverse findings, and deployed public relations strategies to assuage people's fears. They argued there was no definitive evidence linking lead to ill health effects in children; that other factors were to blame, and that lead paint could actually promote good health among children.[28] Their efforts were successful. They managed to stave off regulation until the early 1970s, by which time they had found cheaper and more effective alternatives for making white paint.[29]

Leaded gasoline was another source of lead in children's environments. It was eventually phased out, but again only years after concerns were first raised about it. In the early 1920s, researchers at General Motors found that adding tetra ethyl lead (TEL) to gasoline stopped the "knocking" in new high compression engines. Pierre du Pont, who ran GM at the time, formed the Ethyl Corporation with Standard Oil to get the new product onto the market.[30] Du Pont knew TEL was toxic, writing in 1922 (to his brother, Irénée, who ran Du Pont Chemical) that the chemical was "very poisonous if absorbed through the skin, resulting in lead poisoning almost immediately." Numerous workers producing TEL died and hundreds became ill—one plant was known as the "House of Butterflies" on account of reports of hallucinating lead-exposed workers swatting at imaginary insects.

As was the case with lead paint, however, here too industry representatives vociferously denied any ill health effects. Despite warnings from health experts and government officials, they argued there was no definitive proof that lead emitted from automobile tailpipes caused harm. Lead was poisonous, they acknowledged, and huge quantities of it were ending up in the environment as a result of its use as a gasoline additive, but that did not prove it was linked to health problems, they insisted. Regulators finally took action in 1972, beginning a phase out of leaded gasoline, but it would still take another thirty-four years before the product was fully banned in the United States.

The lead saga did not end there, however. In 2006, a four-year-old boy, Jarnell Brown, died four days after being admitted to a Minneapolis hospital complaining of stomach pain. Emergency room physicians first suspected stomach flu, so they missed the small heart-shaped pendant branded with the name Reebok that lay in the boy's stomach. That pendant, part of a children's charm bracelet that had come with a pair of Reebok running shoes, was composed of a staggering 99 percent lead (federal law states that lead in children's jewelry should not exceed 0.06 percent by weight).[31] Jarnell had died of lead poisoning. Reebok issued a public apology, recalled 300,000 of the Chinese-made pendants, and paid a $1 million fine for violating the Federal Hazardous Substances Act.[32]

By 2007 toy manufacturers and retailers were pulling lead-infested toys—including Barbie, Thomas the Tank Engine, Curious George, and Winnie-the-Pooh toys, along with dozens of others—from store shelves and out of the hands of children. The companies involved (Mattel, Fisher-Price, Baby Einstein, Target, Walmart, and Toys 'R' Us, among them) were, for the most part, contrite and cooperative, accepting responsibility and promising to do better (unlike their early twentieth-century counterparts in the paint and gasoline industries). They knew that the toxicity of lead, and the need to safeguard children from it, could no longer be plausibly denied.

Products with over 300 ppm lead are now banned in the United States, a standard that may soon be dropped to 100 ppm (the current European standard). The American Academy of Pediatricians nonetheless insists that any exposure above 40 ppm can be unsafe, and most scientists agree that there really is no safe limit for lead exposure. Products still sneak through the 300 ppm regulatory net, however, such as the "Green Baby" jumpsuit and Dora Explorer Activity Pack described earlier. Dozens of lead-risk recalls are initiated by the federal Consumer Product Safety Commission each month, with recalls recently issued for, among other things, floor hockey sets, children's charm bracelets, wind chime toys, animal and action figures, sports balls, dinosaur sets, toy trucks and cars, and Disney Tinker Bell wands.[33]

The good news is that children's blood lead levels have decreased dramatically over the last forty years, largely due to the bans imposed on lead gasoline and paint. Physician and environmental health expert Bruce Lanphear nonetheless finds it hard to celebrate. For years, he says, children have died and become ill because "industry's expertly packaged arguments" swayed governments, scientists, and physicians to believe that the case against lead had not been sufficiently proven. "We chose to deny the burgeoning evidence about lead toxicity," says Lanphear, and in "our quest for scientific certainty, we inadvertently delayed the promulgation of regulations at the expense of public health."[34] In the end, says Lanphear, the victory against lead was a "pyrrhic victory," and all the more so because of "our failure to learn from the [lead poisoning] epidemic and take steps to dramatically reduce exposures to other confirmed and suspected environmental toxicants."

My father never lost his temper when I was growing up. He rarely raised his voice. But when I came home one summer day in 1967 (I was eight years old) to discover my worried family huddled around a somber-sounding radio, he was shaking with anger.

"Where the hell have you been? You could have been killed."

I had been at the top of a tree—though that's not what I told him ("a friend's house" seemed a safer response)—a tall pine with close-knit branches, perfect for climbing. A humid and muggy summer day in mid-Michigan (my family lived in East Lansing at the time) had quickly turned into a raging storm, and when the air raid siren sounded, warning that a tornado might hit, I decided to climb up the tree and watch for funnel clouds. I got soaked by the rain and my face stung from hail pellets, but there were no tornadoes to be seen, just dark and ominous storm clouds and streaks of lightning. So I climbed down the tree and went home to a tornado's worth of parental wrath.

No tornado hit East Lansing that day. No tornado hit the town before or since that day. But at least a few times each summer the air raid siren wails, the town is brought to a standstill, and everyone scurries for shelter. Someday meteorologists will be able to predict exactly when and where a tornado will hit. Using instruments and technologies that we cannot even imagine, they will collect data about temperatures, air currents, cloud formations, sun spot activity, tides in the oceans—whatever it takes—run it all through formulas and programs still uninvented, and end up with pinpoint predictions. Until that day, however, they will continue to draw reasonable inferences from the limited evidence available, preferring probable overreaction to possible (albeit not likely) devastation.

Tornado warnings are issued on the basis of what has come to be known as the "precautionary principle," the notion that full scientific certainty should not be required before taking action against threats of serious or irreversible harm. We should deploy that same principle in the area of environmental health policy, according to epidemiologist and Occupational Safety and Health Administration head Dr. David Michaels, echoing the views of most environmental health scientists. "Absolute certainty is rarely an option" in the area of environmental health, he says, and if we insist on waiting for it before taking action, "people will die, and the environment will be damaged." [35] Like meteorologists tracking tornados, environmental health scientists make pronouncements about hazards and risk by weighing available, albeit incomplete, evidence and preferring to err on the side of overreaction. "It is art rather than science; more accurately yet it is art based on science," says Michaels. "We know enough to protect the public, but only with the acknowledgment that we may be overregulating on a given issue." [36]

It is simply not possible, given current states of knowledge about complex and varied biological processes, for scientists to understand every chemical's ill effects on children's health. Infinite combinations and permutations—of timing of exposure, unique susceptibilities of different individuals (based, in turn, on age, gender, genetics, epigenetics, social circumstances, general health, and so on), dosages, routes of exposure, and interactions among different chemicals—ensure there will never, or at least not anytime soon, be complete knowledge. Some doubt will always exist, which means action will always be forestalled, as industry desires, if all doubt must be eliminated before it is taken.

Scientists may someday uncover the precise mechanisms through which different chemicals interfere with developing biological systems and cause disease, much as meteorologists may find ways to determine exactly when and where tornados will hit. But in the meantime, "We shall not invariably sit around awaiting the results of the research before deducing 'causation' and taking action," as esteemed epidemiologist Austin Bradford Hill pronounced nearly fifty years ago.[37] Science, after all, is an inherently slow and cumbersome process, especially in the area of environmental health where ethical considerations preclude human experimentation, animal research is easily dismissed as irrelevant to humans, and epidemiological studies demonstrate associations but not *definitive* causal links between chemicals and ill health. Add to that the scarcity of funding, and the fact it can take years to get one study of one chemical in relation to one potential health effect off the ground and complete—the researcher has to write a proposal, apply for funding, run the study, and submit the results for peer review and publication—and one can understand why, as Leo Trasande remarked, "It takes a thick skin to be in the field [of children's environmental health]."[38]

The ponderous pace of science is difficult to change (albeit more resources for independent research on children's environmental health would certainly help), but what can be changed is the standard that scientific research must meet before governments are prepared to act upon its findings. Though "all scientific work is incomplete," as Bradford Hill described it, "that does not confer upon us a freedom to ignore the knowledge we already have, or to postpone the action that it appears to demand at a given time."[39] The real question is, which side do we err on in the face of partial knowledge and much uncertainty? The bias of the current regulatory system—lobbied for by industry and cultivated through its influence—is to wait for full knowledge before imposing bans or restrictions on chemicals.[40] "My bias," says Bruce Lanphear, "is to err on the side of protecting children. When it comes to protecting children from environmental toxicants, it's clear we know enough." There are many reasons we might dismiss that fact, he says, whether uncertainty in science or our dependence on industry or because we feel overwhelmed by the task of cleaning up a contaminated environment. "But in the end" he says, "it is clear that many of the major diseases of industrialized society are, to a greater or lesser extent, due to industrial pollutants, airborne pollutants, environmental chemicals."[41] Insufficient evidence can no longer be an excuse for inaction, he says. The evidence is there. The problem is that we are not acting on it. "It's hard sometimes not to be bitter," he admits. "I know something that is harming millions of children and nobody will listen."[42]

The solution, according to Lanphear, and most other children's environmental health experts, is simple (at least in principle)—move from an "absolute proof" model to a "precautionary" model. More specifically, ban or restrict chemicals, such as BPA, certain phthalates, and PBDEs, where the evidence points to, albeit does not prove absolutely, adverse human health implications; undertake systematic testing of thousands of other chemicals that may be harmful; and require proactive testing of new chemicals before they are permitted to enter the market. Such government action is necessary because industry will not act on its own, and the problem is far too large for parents to handle.

We may have some ability as parents to protect our children. We can buy organic food (if we can afford to), and try to avoid, as best we can, the thousands of everyday products that might contain potentially harmful chemicals.[43] Being "smart consumers" in these ways is better than nothing—and it makes us feel better than doing nothing.

But in the end it cannot protect children from the ill effects of exposure to industrial chemicals. Our power as consumers is just too limited. How, after all, can we even know which chemicals are dangerous when the relevant science is incomplete, contradictory, and riddled with conflicts of interest? How can we shield children from exposure to chemicals that are everywhere and in everything? How do we know what are the *right* choices within the narrow range of choices we have—should we buy organic canned tomato sauce (with Bisphenol A in the lining) or nonorganic tomato sauce in a glass bottle (with pesticides in the contents)? Should we chuck our electronic gadgets and mattresses because they are likely to be off-gassing PBDEs? Should we avoid waterproof jackets because they contain PFCs?

Even Lanphear, a leading environmental health expert, says he is unable as a father to protect his children from chemical toxicants. "I feel totally ignorant about most of it," he told me. "I can't keep up with it, even if the data were out there; but the data's not out there for most of these things." Moreover, he says, kids do not necessarily listen to their parents. "Do you really need to wear toxicant-laced rouge or eye shadow?" he asks his daughters, to which they, of course, reply, "Yes." "The best I've been able to do is get them to use a nontoxic fingernail polish."[44] In the end, says Lanphear, protecting children in this area cannot be the sole responsibility of parents. "Parents can't be expected to know—they shouldn't be expected to be chemists," he says. "Some things are beyond our control." Which is why we need to establish new legal rules, and properly enforce them, he says—to regulate comprehensively the companies that manufacture, distribute, use, and emit industrial chemicals.[45]

On January 15, 2010, the FDA announced it had "some concern about the potential effects of BPA on the brain, behavior and prostate gland of fetuses, infants and children."[46] In making that announcement, the agency retreated from its earlier position (based on the

2008 Philbert committee report discussed earlier) that BPA is entirely safe. "For the first time [we are] saying we believe there is some concern about the substance's safety," principal deputy commissioner Dr. Joshua Sharfstein stated at the time. Despite that, Sharfstein added, the agency would continue to act on the presumption that the chemical is safe. "If we thought it was unsafe we would be taking strong regulatory action."[47]

Once again, regulatory action must await definitive proof that a chemical is unsafe.[48] Reasonable concern is not enough. That approach, which as noted earlier pervades the entire chemical regulatory system, is largely responsible for the system's ineffectiveness.[49] During the thirty-five-year life of the Toxic Substances Control Act, the system's foundation and centerpiece, only 200 out of a possible 86,000 chemicals in commercial use have been tested, and only five of those have been restricted. No attempts have been made to regulate a chemical under the act since 1989, the year an EPA-sponsored restriction on asbestos, a chemical known to be highly carcinogenic, was overturned by a court on the ground the substance did not pose an "unreasonable risk" as required by the act.[50] Senator Frank Lautenberg (D-NJ) recently observed that "America's system for regulating industrial chemicals is broken," and it is hard to disagree with him.[51]

Strides have been made in Europe, however, where the REACH (Registration, Evaluation, Authorization, and Restriction of Chemical Substances) system now sets rigorous and precautionary standards for industrial chemicals. Under that system, companies that manufacture or import chemicals into Europe must submit to health and safety tests of compounds sold in excess of 1 million metric tons a year. If a chemical is found to be hazardous, the manufacturer or importer must demonstrate that it can be used safely, or that no safer alternative is available.[52]

Reforms in the United States, by contrast, have been piecemeal and patchwork (though still mildly encouraging). The 2008 U.S. Consumer Product Safety Improvement Act, for example, bans or restricts certain phthalates and heavy metals in children's products; some states (Maine, California, Washington, and Minnesota, with Connecticut, Massachusetts, and New York likely to follow) have enacted even broader regimes for regulating high risk chemicals, particularly in children's products.[53]

The most sweeping and promising recent U.S. proposal for reform, however, was the Safe Chemicals Act of 2010. The bill, introduced in Congress by Senator Lautenberg, took the form of an amendment to the Toxic Substances Control Act and was designed, as the senator described it, to "breathe new life into a long-dead statute by empowering [the] EPA to get tough on toxic chemicals." It received wide support from health and environmental groups,[54] and also from EPA chief Lisa Jackson. The bill required, like Europe's REACH, that chemical manufacturers and users prove their chemicals to be safe (especially for vulnerable subpopulations, such as children) before those chemicals could enter the market—a precautionary-inspired reversal of the current system's onus on governments to prove chemicals unsafe before they can be regulated. Manufacturers were also required by the bill to submit reliable hazard and risk information to the EPA, and were restricted in their ability to shield that information from public scrutiny (as has been common practice) by declaring it "confidential business information." The bill further required the EPA to prioritize chemicals in terms of hazards and risk, and to take action against those it deemed to be of high risk, and it obliged the federal government to establish and fund programs to develop "green chemistry" and safer alternatives to chemicals of concern.[55]

Altogether, the Safe Chemicals Act of 2010 was a remarkably far-reaching bill that, had it been made law, would have significantly reduced threats to children's health and lives posed by industrial chemicals in the environment. Not surprisingly, industry lobbied heavily against the bill (it set "an impossibly high hurdle for all chemicals in commerce," according to American Chemistry Council president Cal Dooley)[56] and managed to stall it in Congress. That, along with the Republican takeover of Congress in 2010, caused the bill, like its predecessor, Lautenberg's Kid Safe Chemical Act of 2008, to languish in committee and never become law.

No doubt the Safe Chemicals Act's final fate is disheartening. But the very fact it was introduced and garnered such wide support, both within government and from outside, demonstrates the possibility of using political action to confront a major threat to children's health and well-being. Our job now as parents and citizens is to do what we can to ensure that something akin to the Safe Chemicals Act is again introduced in Congress and this time made law. In the meantime, activism at state and local levels has yielded results in several jurisdictions, as noted above, and should inspire work in others.

Chapter Eight

In Our Own Backyard

I live in Vancouver, British Columbia, one of the most beautiful cities in the world. Surrounded by mountains and ocean, the city is a paradise of beaches and gardens, parks and yoga studios; a hub of green ideas, progressive politics, and entertainment industry glitter.

But there is a dark underside to my hometown.

Vancouver is located in a province, British Columbia, that has the most astonishingly neglectful child labor laws in North America, indeed in the world. Afghanistan and Haiti have more protective laws on their books.[1] In British Columbia, a child can go to work at twelve years old, in just about any job, hazardous or not (mines, taverns, bars, and lounges are the only exceptions), and he or she can be required to work at any time of the day or night except during school hours.[2] The introduction of this regime in 2004—before which the minimum age for work was fifteen—has had the effect of increasing substantially the number of children working in the province.[3]

Business tends to favor permissive child labor laws (likely the reason British Columbia's government pronounced its new law would help make the province more "economically competitive"). Young people work for less pay than adults.[4] They are easily cajoled to work long and irregular hours without overtime pay, and to accept pay deductions

129

for transportation, uniforms, and equipment. They are more willing to take on tasks and less likely to ask questions about safety and training. They usually do not know or inquire about workplace rights, and they tend not to report abuses. They do not organize unions. None of this makes child labor right. But it does make it attractive for businesses seeking flexible and pliant workers, and for governments bent on serving those businesses' interests.

British Columbia's new regime belies any belief that child labor is solely a problem in the developing world. True, child labor is a scourge in poorer countries, where most of the world's 218 million child laborers work in harsh and unhealthy conditions, for little pay, often making the very products that fuel our own society's hyperconsumerism.[5] But most poor countries have joined forces to eradicate this kind of child exploitation. Over the last few years, 156 countries including Afghanistan and Haiti, two of the world's poorest, have signed an international treaty that bans the employment of children under the age of fifteen, and requires signatories to raise that minimum age to sixteen when conditions permit.[6] Canada and the United States, two of the world's richest countries, have refused to take part in the effort. As a result, both countries explicitly permit forms of child labor that are banned in a majority of the world's nations.

In December 2006, ten-year-old Salvador Velasquez was driving a pickup truck in a Florida orange grove when he unintentionally ran over his two-year-old brother, Ruben, and crushed him to death. Salvador had been driving the truck, and working in the grove alongside his parents, for several years. The owner of the grove, Orlampa Citrus, and the labor contractor who supplied the field workers, were together fined $3,284 for employing the ten-year-old in breach of federal labor law.[7]

Ruben's is not the only tragic death in the fields, however. Between 2005 and 2008 forty-three children and teens died from work-related injuries on farms. Among them were a twelve-year-old boy who died on an Iowa farm after being crushed between a truck and the hay wagon he was hitching to it; a fourteen-year-old boy who died on an Ohio farm after losing his balance and falling into a cattle feed grinder while dropping bales of hay into the machine with a handheld hook; and a pregnant seventeen-year-old who died from heat exposure in California after picking grapes for nine hours in 100-degree temperatures.[8]

Farm work is dangerous, with work-related fatalities at nine times the national workplace average. And children, because of their size and inexperience, are especially vulnerable.[9] But the deaths only underscore a larger national shame. Hundreds of thousands of children in the United States, some as young as five years old, mostly immigrants or sons or daughters of immigrants, many of them illegal, toil in fields, orchards, and packing sheds, usually at the mercy of unscrupulous and uncaring bosses. They work long shifts, ten hours or more a day, with few breaks, no days off, and often without provision of drinking water or access to bathrooms. They work before school, after school, all day when school is out, and often while they should be in school. Their pay is typically well below the minimum wage, and further reduced by employers' deductions for equipment and transportation. Their jobs—picking, digging, tilling, and the like—are monotonous, repetitive, physically demanding, and dangerous.

Child farm workers are killed, injured, and made ill as a result of accidents with heavy equipment and exposure to toxic pesticides, sun, extreme heat, and snake and rat bites. Safety standards are ill enforced, and training and protective gear seldom provided. Children are worn down, sexually abused, and harassed on the job. Their educations are cut short (they drop out of school at four times the national average),[10] thus denying them the means to escape the grinding poverty that keeps them in the fields. They, along with their adult co-workers, are uninformed and unaware of the meager rights they have under federal

131

and state laws, and unlikely to complain or report abuses out of fear of being fired or deported.

Much of this is perfectly legal in the United States. Federal law permits children as young as twelve, and under twelve in some instances,[11] to work in "nonhazardous" farm jobs anytime outside of school hours so long as they have written consent from one of their parents. Parental consent is not necessary for children who work on the same farms as their parents, or for those who have reached the age of fourteen. For children sixteen and older—or at any age if they work on a farm owned or run by a parent—there are no restrictions at all on types or hours of work.

Even the minimal limits of the regime are routinely flouted by farm employers. An ABC news team recently found children as young as five years old picking blueberries at Adkin Blue Ribbon Packing Company in Michigan, a supplier to Walmart (which had featured the company's owner, Randy Adkin, in a billboard campaign for "locally produced and sold blueberries").[12] Adkin is not alone, however. Farm companies regularly employ children under the age of twelve, or hire children under the age of fourteen without a parent's consent, or assign children under the age of sixteen to do hazardous work or work during school hours.[13]

The problem is that child labor laws, not only on farms but across the rest of the economy as well, are profoundly underenforced. Walmart, for example, despite its pious pronouncements in the wake of the Adkin revelations—"Walmart will not tolerate the use of child labor," a company official stated after severing business ties with Adkins—has been a major offender.[14] In the United States, fourteen is the minimum legal age for nonagricultural work, and hours and types of work are strictly limited until the age of eighteen. In the year 2000 Walmart was charged with violations of these standards in every one of its twenty stores in Maine—1,436 violations in total. The company paid $205,650 to settle the claims and vowed to prevent future violations. In 2004, an internal company audit of 128 stores in several states during a one-week period revealed 1,371 instances of minors working during school hours, too late at night, or for too many hours during the day in breach of the law. In 2005, the company settled twenty-four claims of federal child labor violations in Connecticut, Arkansas, and New Hampshire, most of them involving children under the age of eighteen operating hazardous machinery, such as chain saws and cardboard balers.[15] The Department of Labor's (DOL's) fines to Walmart in 2000 and 2005 were widely criticized as being little more than slaps on the wrist, and unlikely to have any deterrent effect. The fines reflected neither the seriousness of the offenses, nor their large number, critics charged, and were also unlikely, in light of Walmart's size and revenue, to deter the company from committing future offenses.[16]

Paltry fines and weak enforcement are typical in the area of child labor, however. A federal child labor violation draws a maximum fine of $11,000, but the average fine levied by the DOL has been under $1,000 in recent years. Adkin Blue Ribbon, to take an example of serious and flagrant breaches, was fined just $2,584 for its transgressions; in the Salvador and Ruben Velasquez tragedy, the grove owner and labor contractor were, as noted above, fined only $3,284.[17] The real problem, however, is that most violations of child labor laws are never even discovered, let alone prosecuted (Adkin's infractions were only discovered as a result of ABC's investigation; Salvador Velasquez's illegal employment only by virtue of his brother's death). There has been a "dramatic decline" in enforcement of child labor laws over the last decade, to the point where such laws are now "rarely enforced," according to a recent Human Rights Watch report,[18] a result of "too few investigators, too little attention devoted to child labor, and of those resources devoted to child labor, too little focus on agriculture."[19] The Department of Labor lost a quarter of its budget between 1992 and 2004, even while the U.S. workforce grew larger, and it now typically resorts to "soft" enforcement measures, such as pamphlets and seminars aimed at encouraging voluntary compliance, in place of inspections and prosecutions. Between 2004 and 2005 alone, child labor investigations dropped by 32 percent. Proactive investigations are now a rarity.

Complaints from vulnerable child workers and their parents are even rarer.[20] This is partly due to fears of being fired or deported, as noted above, but there is another reason too. The U.S. Government Accountability Office recently revealed that the division of the DOL responsible for enforcement of child labor laws actively discourages complaints. It provides misleading and contradictory information on how to file complaints; many offices only accept written complaints; and in a truly Kafka-esque twist, some offices require complainants to speak to an investigator before an investigation is launched, but then direct calls to voicemail and never return them.[21]

Just how pervasive child labor is in the United States, and what kinds of jobs children are working in, is a mystery. Illegal employment is under the radar, and legal employers of youth have no obligation to report their employees' ages. Estimates are that hundreds of thousands of children are working on farms, but it is less clear what the situation is in the rest of the economy. Workplace injury and death reports suggest the numbers are high, however. More than 200,000 children and teens are reported injured in workplaces each year, and nearly one hundred are killed.[22]

In 1908, a *New York Times* editorial ridiculed the "mistaken notion," advocated by century-of-the-child reformers, "that . . . children under fourteen shall not work at all and shall be compelled to attend school practically all the time."[23] The National Association of Manufacturers, and many others, agreed with the *Times*, believing it was acceptable, indeed desirable, for children to spend their days toiling in the mines, factories, fields, and sweatshops of America. Their worry was not that children were working, but that they were not working enough. Child labor instilled useful skills and attitudes among children, and helped poor families survive the woefully low pay attached to most adult jobs, they argued.[24]

Reformers, on the other hand, rejected the argument that putting children to work in exploitative and unhealthy jobs could be justified as a measure to enable families to survive their impoverished circumstances. Not only was it morally pernicious to take advantage of families' desperation in this way, they argued, but employing children in low-skill, low-paying, unsafe, and unhealthy jobs was more likely to deepen poverty than ameliorate it.[25] Children needed education, and material and emotional security, if they were to flourish and grow into healthy and productive adults and citizens, reformers argued. And child labor, to the extent it undermined fulfillment of those needs, was thus bad policy, in addition to being morally wrong, despite whatever limited and short-term economic benefits bestowed upon employers, children, and their families.[26]

The reformers ultimately prevailed in the United States, though thirty years would pass before they fully persuaded Americans that, in the words of one reformer, "When labor begins, the child ceases to be." The 1938 Fair Labor Standards Act was finally enacted after three failed attempts at similar legislation (in 1906, 1916, and 1919), and to this day it stands as one of the triumphs of century-of-the-child reformers and the humanistic ideals that inspired them.[27]

The arguments against child labor are really no different today than they were a century ago. Child labor "is a violation of fundamental human rights and has been shown to hinder children's development, potentially leading to lifelong physical or psychological damage," as the United Nations International Labour Organization (ILO) recently stated. This is so, the organization continues, because child labor uses and exploits children without adequate regard for their interests. It puts them in jobs that endanger and harm them, interferes with and denies them schooling, takes away recreational pursuits and time with family and friends, and adds heavy work and long hours to their school days.[28] Child labor is "unacceptable," states the organization, "because the children involved are too young and should be in school, or because even though they have attained the minimum age for admission to employment, the work that they do is unsuitable for a person below the age of 18."[29]

Child labor can be eliminated, however. Better laws are necessary—perhaps along the lines of the ILO Convention, with its minimum age of fifteen for work, and its various limitations and allowances—as are more effective enforcement mechanisms and stronger penalties for violations. But more far-reaching reforms are needed as well. Child labor is most often rooted in poverty, and the practice is likely to persist so long as children need to work in order to survive. Elimination of child labor therefore requires at a minimum that poor children and their families are adequately supported, and more generally that measures are taken to eradicate poverty itself. It is not enough, in other words, to deny employers the *right* to hire children. Children must also be relieved of the *need* to work.

At the same time, it bears stating that not *all* work by children should be banned as child labor. As the ILO has stated, "Helping parents around the home or earning pocket money outside school hours and during school holidays" should not be considered child labor. More generally, "When children or adolescents participate in stimulating activities, volunteering or work that does not affect their health and personal development, or interfere with their education, this is generally seen as being positive."[30] Restrictions on child labor must, and most do, make allowances for legitimate forms of work by children, ones that serve, rather than undermine their interests.

British Columbia's permissive child labor law goes well beyond that, however, as does the U.S. regime governing child labor on farms. Despite that, willful blindness continues to foster the belief that child labor is only a problem "out there," in the developing world, but not here at home. The U.S. federal government, for example, spent $26 million dollars in 2009 supporting ILO efforts to eliminate child labor in the developing world—a contribution larger than all other countries' combined—while its own laws actively promoted some of the worst forms of child labor in the world. It is important to ask what is the significance of the seeming indifference to child labor in our own backyard. Are we moving toward a wider acceptance and greater facilitation of child labor in North America? Or are lax laws and poor enforcement momentary exceptions to a growing intolerance of the practice?[31]

How these questions are answered over coming years will depend on what we, the people, believe and do about child labor. In my view, as is likely clear by now, no child should have to work in ways that are dangerous, unhealthy, and that compromise his or her schooling. The alleged benefits to business of child labor—children's pliability and credulity—should be treated as reasons to protect children, not to exploit them. Policy should be driven by the principle that it is not only wrong for a society to permit the employment of children, but also wrong to permit the existence of conditions that make it necessary for them to work in order to survive.

Moreover, as early twentieth-century reformers insisted, getting children out of the workplace is not enough. They must also be placed in schools. The movement to end child labor is, and always has been, linked to demands for universal education. "This equation is straightforward," according to the ILO. "We will not eliminate child labor without universal education and, conversely, we will not ensure every child is in school unless we bring an end to child labor."[32] The presumption that child labor squanders children's potential as human beings is matched equally by the belief that education helps them realize it. Public education cultivates children's minds, imaginations, and moral sensibilities rather than exploiting their bodies for labor; it serves their needs, and more broadly, those

Kids from the Ville and Altgeld Gardens had been warring, in gangs and otherwise, since they were forced together by the sudden closure of the Altgeld Gardens school. Ville kids, loyal to their neighborhood—"It's the neighborhood we're from, who we are, how we act, what we do," as one of them stated—resented the sudden influx of kids from Altgeld Gardens. Gang tensions mounted, punches were thrown in school hallways, and fights broke out in the streets. Safety for Altgeld Garden kids lay just beyond some rusty old train tracks near the Agape Community Center, the unofficial boundary of Ville territory.

As Truitt and his brother approached the tracks, a crowd of Ville kids began to form behind them. The two boys walked faster. "All I was thinking was 'Okay, we're getting close to the tracks, so they're going to turn around,'" Truitt later reported. But the Ville kids did not turn around. Several cars full of Altgeld Garden kids were waiting for them near the tracks, and both sides got ready to fight. Just after he crossed the tracks, near a gravel vacant lot adjacent to the Agape Community Center, Truill was hit hard across his back with an old railroad tie. He began to fall, recovered, and then turned around to fight.

Albert, in the meantime, was walking on the sidewalk next to the vacant lot, apparently minding his own business (he, like Truitt, was aligned with neither the Ville nor Altgeld Garden factions). Two members of the Ville group approached him, one struck him on the head with a wooden railroad tie, and the other punched him in the face. He fell down, seemed to lose consciousness for a moment, pulled himself away from his attackers, and tried to get up. He was then struck on the head by a member of the Altgeld Garden faction, again with a railroad tie, and another youth from that faction stomped on his head repeatedly after he fell back to the ground. Truitt, though involved in the brawl, was not among Albert's attackers. He managed to walk away, bruised and sore, but otherwise all right. Albert was not so lucky. When it was all over, he lay on the ground in the vacant gravel lot, bloodied and still. A youth worker dragged him into the community center and called for help. He died a short while later. A make-shift memorial was quickly erected by fellow students and friends at the spot where he had fallen. Two days later, it had been burned down.

Four other Chicago teens died from violence in the month Albert was killed. The numbers of youth violently killed on Chicago's streets had indeed been escalating since 2006,[2] the year Chicago's mayor, Richard Daly, and his education chief, Arne Duncan, began clos-ing down schools—dozens had been closed by 2010—as part of the city's business-backed school reform plan, Renaissance 2010. As more and more students were forced by closures to commute to schools in distant neighbourhoods, violence was fuelled by territorial resent-ments. "To make it to school," reported the *Chicago Tribune* at the time, "students crisscross streets carved up by gangs, board buses at chaotic stops and steer clear of particularly dangerous swaths of the neighborhood. . . . Gangs, guns and drugs stir neighborhood violence so routine that many of the 116,000 high school students have grown numb to it."[3]

Diane Latiker, a Ville neighborhood resident, has a wall in her house memorializing every Chicago youth who has died over the last two years as a result of being beaten, stabbed, or shot. For each fallen youth, she affixes to the wall a cut-out paper headstone. When Albert died she had already run out of room on her wall. "We have 163 stones right now, but we are 20, now 21, behind," she said.

Community leaders warned Duncan of the risks of his school-closing strategy, but when asked directly whether his policies had anything to do with Albert's murder, he flatly denied there was a con-nection.[4]

In the spring of 2008, a symposium was held at Chicago's exclusive Mid-America Club to celebrate the first three years of Renaissance 2010's operation. The name of the symposium, "Free to Choose, Free to Succeed: The New Market of Public Education," captured its animating idea that public schooling should be governed by private sector values and goals. Arne Duncan, the symposium's star attraction, delighted his audience, composed mainly of representatives from corporations, right-wing think tanks, and school privatization philanthropy and advocacy groups, with his all-business message.[5] "We're trying to blur the lines between the public and the private," he told them. "I am not a manager of six hundred schools. I'm a portfolio manager of six hundred schools and I'm trying to improve the portfolio." He might have added, as further proof of his business credentials, that he was not a school superintendent, but a chief executive officer, his official title as head of the Chicago public school system.[6]

Renaissance 2010 was created by the city's business elite, as represented by the Commercial Club of Chicago. The club's clear and stated aim was to reform Chicago's school system so as to make it run more like a business. To that end, it commissioned top business management firm A.T. Kearney to do the plan's detailed drafting. "Drawing on our program-management skills and our knowledge of best practices used across industries," A.T. Kearney would later boast of its work in Chicago, "we provided a private-sector perspective on how to address many of the complex issues that challenge . . . large urban education transformations."[7]

At the heart of Renaissance 2010's "private-sector perspective" were three fundamental ideas. First, failing schools, like failing businesses, should be closed down; second, the measure of failure (or success) should be students' performance on standardized tests; and third, new schools should be run by private organizations.[8] More than sixty schools were closed and 100 opened in their place under Renaissance 2010. The new schools were all run by private organizations—for-profit corporations among them—rather than the public district. Unlike the schools they replaced, none had unions. Chicago's business elite, once again through the auspices of the Commercial Club, was instrumental in raising funds for the transformation, as well as in deciding which schools should be closed down, what organizations should develop and run new ones, and how accountability and performance should be measured within the new schools.[9]

Renaissance 2010 transformed a quintessentially public institution—public schooling—into a market-driven partnership with business. It jettisoned unions, invited for-profit corporations to play increasingly substantial roles in schools, and destabilized, sometimes with harmful and tragic effects (such as the violence that claimed Albert's life), the lives of students, teachers, parents, and communities. Despite all of that, Renaissance 2010 did little to improve Chicago's public schools. The program's few bright spots (and even these are contested) were offset by failures, and the aggregate performance of its newly opened schools turned out to be no better than that of the schools they replaced. "Overall it wasn't the game changer that people thought it would be," according to Barbara Radford, head of De Paul University's Center for Urban Education. "In some ways it has been more harmful than good because all the attention, all the funding, all the hope was directed at Ren10 to the detriment of other effective strategies CPS [Chicago Public Schools] was developing."[10]

Yet the market-driven reforms of Renaissance 2010 now serve as a model for the entire nation. President Obama's Race to the Top, the new national education policy, incorporates most of its elements, and his new secretary of education is none other than Chicago's Arne Duncan.

Since the early 1980s, children, along with their teachers and schools, have been blamed for America's decline in the world economy. Their poor training for the global workforce was putting America at risk of becoming a second-rate nation, industry and government groups solemnly declared, and nothing short of radical reform of public education could stop the slide.

The fearful finger-pointing began in 1983 with publication of *A Nation at Risk*. Commissioned by President Reagan's secretary of education, Terrel H. Bell, the report blamed the "rising tide of mediocrity" in education for the fact that "our once unchallenged preeminence in commerce, industry, science and technological innovation is being overtaken by competitors throughout the world." Though America's education system had, from the late 1800s to the mid-twentieth century, "provided the educated workforce needed to seal the success of the Industrial Revolution and to provide the margin of victory in two world wars," it was failing badly at the end of the twentieth century. "If an unfriendly foreign power had attempted to impose on America the mediocre educational performance that exists today," the report warned, "we might well have viewed it as an act of war." [11] The proposed solution was to add rigor to education and emphasize results, do what was necessary to produce the "highly skilled workers" demanded by the new global economy. Specific recommendations included more homework, longer school days and years, time management training in early grades, standardized testing, and the coupling of teachers' pay to their performance. "We firmly believe," the report stated, "that a movement of America's schools in the direction called for by our recommendations will prepare . . . children for far more effective lives in a far stronger America." [12]

The decidedly utilitarian spirit of *A Nation at Risk*, its central claim that schools' singular purpose is to train children for lives of work, profoundly shaped education reforms over subsequent decades. George W. Bush's No Child Left Behind and President Obama's Race to the Top, along with most other recent reform proposals and initiatives, make similar calls for more rigor in education—more schooling, an earlier start to formal studies, more testing, and higher standards. Over the course of those decades, and mainly during the last of them, however, a new element has been added to that set of prescriptions. Proposed or implied by subsequent reports, and in various plans for reform (as exemplified by Chicago's Renaissance 2010) is the idea that schools should not only groom children to work in corporations, but should themselves be run like, and in many instances by, corporations.

Without the discipline of markets, it is (and was) argued, teachers and principals lack incentives to perform well, and mediocrity inevitably sets in. Part of the problem with America's public schools, in other words, is that they *are* public—that as *public* institutions, they are not governed by private-sector imperatives.

That idea now inspires and justifies reforms that are radically re-making the nation's education system. The transformation is happening quickly, deeply, without much public debate, or even awareness. Under the leadership of both Republicans and Democrats, at district, state, and federal levels, lobbied for and cheered on by leading philanthropists (chiefly the Bill and Melinda Gates foundation), right-wing think tanks, and corporate lobbies, schools are being transformed into "the new market of public education" celebrated by the symposium in Chicago. Race to the Top, President Obama and Arne Duncan's national education policy, created in 2009, is the current centerpiece of the movement. It grants federal money to states whose proposed education reforms best meet its market-driven criteria. And with most states cash-strapped and desperate for funds, it is having a profound impact on America's schools.[13]

"The lure of the market," according to Diane Ravitch, an historian and former Bush administration education mandarin (who more recently became disillusioned with the market-driven reform movement), "is the idea that freedom from government regulation is a solution all by itself."[14] That idea is at the heart of education reforms today, including those called for by Race to the Top.

America's schools are far from perfect. The system—or at least many parts of it, and especially those serving poor minority communities—is struggling. There is much to be improved. Reforms are needed. The current reform movement, however, blinded as it is by the lure of the market, conveniently ignores the perilous effects of deep and racialized poverty on teachers' abilities to teach and students'

145

to learn.[15] It blames allegedly incompetent teachers and principals, and attacks schools for not providing useful and relevant skills to their students, when the real reason many schools struggle is because they operate in conditions profoundly hostile to fulfilling their mandates and missions.

Market-driven solutions have nothing to say or do about those conditions, and more than that they work to undermine the very values of equal, broad, and liberal education that the public system is designed to embody and serve.

For my beloved aunt Ally, a master teacher in the Brooklyn public school system until she retired in the early 1990s, teaching was a passion, a calling. As much admired by colleagues as she was adored by students—she was even featured for her great teaching in an article in the *New York Post*—she touched the lives of her students, most of whom came from impoverished and minority backgrounds. She inspired many to stay in school, go to college, or to find hope in their difficult circumstances. She mentored some to places like Princeton and Yale, and guided countless others to make positive choices at definining moments in their lives (a bus driver she recently ran into, for example, a former student, thanked her for encouraging him to stay in school).

My own experience as Aunt Ally's "student" was more modest than any of that, but nonetheless memorable. I was ten years old and walking down Brooklyn's Fifty-second Street with her. As we approached Thirteenth Avenue and the heavy iron girders of the elevated B train tracks I saw scattered before us on the sidewalk at least a hundred Batman collector cards. Amazed at my good fortune—I loved Batman cards—I greedily began scooping them up. But almost immediately I felt a gentle tug on my arm. "I know how much you want those cards," my aunt said, "but somebody might have dropped them by accident, and that person would be sad to find them gone, just like you

would be if you were that person." Normally I would have been indig-
nant, argued, complained, and railed against the ridiculous injustice
of it all. Instead, I dropped the cards, gave my head a shake, and said
to my aunt, "Yeah, you're right." Something about the way she spoke,
how her words conveyed concern for the cards' rightful owner, but
also sympathy for my feelings of impending loss, reached right into
me. I sensed, but did not fully understand at the time, that I had just
been hit by great teaching.

My aunt Ally began teaching at Brooklyn's fabled Erasmus Hall
High School in 1958 (the school traces its history back to 1786 and
was the first public high school in the United States). By the 1970s,
the school's Flatbush neighborhood was struggling, and Erasmus had
begun to slide. Teaching became increasingly difficult as kids "were
coming to school from a very hard time at home," my aunt told me.
"Discipline was a problem," she said. "You would have kids wander-
ing the halls. Kids who wanted to do well were victimized, beaten,
and mugged. More and more, the focus became how do you stop kids
from exploding." [16]

The challenges only fueled her determination, however. "Coming
from where I did [a childhood of poverty] I identified with these kids,
and I remember your grandma saying to me: 'I'm so proud of you
because you teach poor black children,'" she told me. "We came from
a home where this was the kind of thing that you should be proud of,
not that you were going to go out and make a million dollars, but you
were going to help these kids better themselves." [17] Her sense of mission was typical of her generation of teachers, she said. "In my generation, teachers were idealistic. That was what you were there for, trying
to help kids feel like they meant something, to aspire to something
better than what their parents had, and to make society better." [18]

What, I asked my aunt Ally, was the key to her success as a teacher?
How did she manage to reach kids, to get them interested in the subjects she taught, American history and economics, in one of the most
difficult schools in the New York system? "You have to make kids feel

like they mean something," she told me. "You have to focus on and treat them as human beings. Give them a sense that they can make it, that they can do well, that they can aspire to go to college, that you are there with them." Her students' successes gave her great pride, she told me. "I wasn't there to point out their faults but to make them feel they were worth something," she said. "The overwhelming majority of kids really want to be treated as individuals and made to feel that you're there for them."[19]

What did she think about teaching and schools today, I wanted to know. "What's happening now," she told me, trying to describe the effects on schools of the market-driven reforms sweeping her district of New York and the nation as a whole, "is you see very little said about, you know, your human relationships with kids. The humanism has gone out of teaching."[20]

There is not much about Erasmus today that my aunt Ally would find familiar. The main entrance to the imposing Gothic-style building is locked up, the elegant college-style courtyard now a parking lot. Students enter the building through back doors where they are screened by metal detectors. In 2002 the school was broken up into three small schools as part of a city-wide movement to replace large schools with smaller ones, but those were closed in 2007 due to poor performance. Five new schools were opened in their place. The new schools too have been plagued by poor performance, low graduation rates, discipline problems, allegations of grade and ranking survey inflation, and threats of closure.[21]

All five of Erasmus's new small schools emphasize particular vocational areas. The Academy of Hospitality and Tourism is one of these, a "career academy," as such schools are known, because of their focus on training children for specific industries. It, like similar career academies across the country, is supported by and partnered with the National Academy Foundation, an organization, funded in part by the Gates Foundation, which works to "sustain a national network of career academies" and promote its "real skills for the real world" vision of what schools should provide to students.[22] The Gates foundation[23] also funneled millions of dollars into New York City schools to assist former chancellor Joel Klein in closing scores of large high schools, such as Erasmus, and replacing them with small schools. The jury is out on whether this program has been successful in improving the city's schools. A 2009 study, for example, found no improvement in dropout rates, and little to no improvement in performance when small schools were compared to their larger counterparts.[24] One result of the small school movement is unequivocal, however. It has increased the number of "career academies" in the city and thus boosted the workplace-training movement these schools represent.

Writer and teacher Jonathan Kozol tells the story [25] of a South Bronx fifth-grader, Timeka, who attended one such career academy, "The Paul Robeson School for Medical Careers and Health Professions" middle school (recently closed). The school promised in its brochure "an understanding and embracement of medical science and health," and Timeka applied because, she said, "It's a medical school. I want to be a baby doctor." But the program at the school was geared to producing low-paid nursing aides and health assistants, not doctors. From Robeson, Timeka went to a similarly themed inner-city high school called "Health Opportunities." That school promised its students the possibility of becoming "lifelong learners and providers of excellent health care." [26] Only 20 percent of the school's students made it to grade twelve. Timeka dropped out in grade eleven.

Career academies are invariably found in low-income neighborhoods, and despite their lofty names they are almost always designed to prepare students for low-skilled, low-wage jobs. They require children to make decisions about career paths at ages as young as ten years old, and close off, in terms of their educations and imagina-

149

tions, broader possibilities than those offered by their limited pro-grams. Career academies, says Kozol, deny poor minority children the same broad educations their wealthier counterparts receive, and thus represent a kind of apartheid in education. "Admittedly, the economic needs of a society are bound to be reflected to some rational degree within the policies and purposes of public schools," he says.

> But, even so, most of us are inclined to ask, there must be some-thing more to life as it is lived by six-year-olds or ten-year-olds, or by teenagers for that matter, than concerns about "successful global competition." Childhood is not merely basic training for utilitarian adulthood. It should have some claims upon our mercy, not for its future value to the economic interests of competitive societies but for its present value as a perishable piece of life itself.[27]

The "something more" of which Kozol speaks is embodied in the idea, and ideal, of liberal education, one of the major legacies of century-of-the-child reforms. The notion holds that education should be rich and multidimensioned; that it should prepare children for lives as literate, informed, and thinking citizens, not only as skilled work-ers; and that it should cultivate their full potential as human beings, not only as human resources.[28] Schools, in delivering a liberal educa-tion, must therefore ensure students understand the world they live in, appreciate what individuals and societies are capable of in science, politics, the arts and humanities, and develop the capacities for critical thought and principled action essential to democratic citizenship. "A well-educated person has a well-furnished mind, shaped by reading and thinking about history, science, literature, the arts, and politics," says Diane Ravitch. "The well-educated person has learned how to explain ideas and listen respectfully to others."[29]

Education should also, of course, be about teaching basic knowl-edge and skills that people need to be productive members of soci-ety, including within the workplace. When it is narrowed only to, or even primarily to, that purpose, however, it belies its roots and ideals. That is the problem with "career academies," and more generally, and ominously, with the entire market-driven education reform movement, from *A Nation at Risk* through President Obama's Race to the Top.[30]

Chapter Ten

Narrowing Minds

"Accountability" is a compelling concept. Like other compelling concepts, "freedom," "reasonableness," "common sense," for example, it attracts agreement to whatever it attaches to, and criticism of endeavors that fall short of its demands. Who can doubt, as the market-driven education reform movement insists, that accountability in schools is important and necessary, and that its apparent lack needs to be remedied? But pry open the lid of that proposition, even just a little bit, and three agreement-smashing questions jump out—Who should be accountable to whom? For what? And by what measure?

Reformers' demands for accountability, as enshrined most recently in President Obama's Race to the Top, presume a particular set of answers to these questions. Teachers (along with principals and schools) should be accountable to students, parents, and districts, for delivering strong performance, as measured by standardized tests. The logic is captured by a recent New York *Daily News* editorial extoling Race to the Top:

> Standards must be raised, and there can be no retreat from the drive
> to hold principals and teachers accountable for lifting achievement
> so students graduate from high school fully prepared for college or
> work. . . . Education had become complacent about mediocrity if not

failure, and hidebound in protecting interests of adults rather than kids. . . . The teachers unions have fought to maintain job protections even for classroom incompetents. . . . For the first time [with Race to the Top in place] instructors will be evaluated on improving student performance. The washouts will be let go. There is now agreement that teachers must produce measurable results.[1]

Race to the Top was indeed a triumph for the market-oriented reform movement and its particular conception of accountability. A central focus of the program is "improving teacher and principal effectiveness based on performance," and it prompts states to reward "highly effective teachers and principals" with "additional compensation" in order to achieve this.[2] By implication, *ineffective* teachers and principals should be sanctioned—"the washouts will be let go," as the *Daily News* put it—which may explain why President Obama applauded recently when Rhode Island fired the entire teaching staff of a struggling high school. Not to be outdone, Washington, D.C., recently fired two hundred teachers in the bottom tier of its evaluation system, and New York state has made it law that poorly performing teachers will be let go.[3] The get-tough-on-teachers message is clear in all instances, and it is likely no coincidence that Rhode Island, Washington, D.C., and New York were among the nine winners of Race to the Top funding in August 2010. Closing schools is another accountability measure prescribed by Race to the Top, which rewards states for developing programs that close, transform, turn around, or restart the "lowest-achieving schools."[4]

Blaming teachers, principals, and schools for struggles and failures in education—making them *accountable*—is the driving idea behind market-oriented reforms. It is an idea with surface appeal, and one that has been instrumental in selling those reforms to the public. But closer inspection reveals that the idea misses the mark, and risks fostering bad policies and unfair decisions, for being both overinclusive and underinclusive in terms of *who* it targets for accountability.

153

It is *overinclusive* because it blames individuals and institutions that often have little or no control over the circumstances contributing to schools' struggles and failures. Chronic underfunding leads to crowded classrooms, deteriorating buildings, broken-down furniture, too few teachers and staff, and outdated textbooks and materials. Poverty and its ill effects of violence, crime, drug and alcohol abuse, hunger, inadequate shelter, unavailable parents, and broken and sometimes violent homes, cause students to be distracted, depressed, poorly motivated, angry, unhealthy, and low in energy and self-esteem.[5] When schools operate in these kinds of conditions it may be impossible, or extremely difficult, for teachers to teach and students to learn. Holding teachers and principals solely or primarily accountable for underperformance thus makes little sense.

In the meantime—and here the problem is *underinclusiveness*—those who should be blamed for schools' struggles are not. Among that group would be district, city, state, and federal officials and governments, along with their supporters and friends, who push for, create, and maintain tax and economic policies that underfund schools and exacerbate and fail to remedy shameful poverty in urban communities.[6] True accountability, in other words, would have to include the individuals and organizations responsible for fostering policies that neglect schools and neighborhoods, and that therefore contribute to schools' difficulties.

No doubt some teachers and administrators are better than others. Some may contribute to failure, while others, such as my aunt Ally, manage to shine in difficult circumstances. The point is not that individual teachers and administrators bear no responsibility for bad or good outcomes. It is that they do not bear *all* of it all of the time, or even most of it most of the time. The accountability movement, with its near exclusive emphasis on blaming and rewarding teachers and administrators, inevitably targets individuals and institutions that have, in many cases, little control over schools' fates, while ignoring those that do have some control. That is accountability turned upside down. The accountability movement thus gets a poor grade for how it answers the question of *who* is accountable.

It fares no better in answering the question of *how* accountability should be measured.

Standardized tests are supposed to create accountability by providing common and objective measures of performance and comparison among students, teachers, principals, and schools. They are now at the core of American education, largely a result of policies such as No Child Left Behind and Race to the Top.[7] The former mandates that students in grades three through eight take standardized tests each year in math, reading, and science, and that high school students take at least one such test over the course of their studies. The latter rewards states that develop, in groups of significant numbers, "common, high-quality assessments" that are aligned with common "content standards . . . that are substantially identical."[8]

For the companies retained by governments and districts to create and mark standardized tests, profitability, not accountability (except to shareholders), is the goal.[9] And the key to profitability is keeping company costs low while maintaining affordable prices for cash-strapped states. Tests composed of multiple-choice questions are ideal because they can be mechanically, and thus inexpensively, marked. Through the mid-2000s many states began to rely more heavily on such tests—with some, such as Kansas and Mississippi, opting to use them exclusively—so as to meet, within the terms of their shrinking budgets, the testing requirements of No Child Left Behind. That led to a public backlash, with critics charging that No Child Left Behind was having the effect of "dumbing down" testing, and thus education. "Don't tell us that the only way to teach a child is to spend too much of the year preparing him to fill out a few bubbles in a standardized test," chided presidential hopeful Barak Obama at the time.[10] Once he became president, and was thus himself at the helm of education

155

reform, Obama put his words into action. Race to the Top strongly signals movement away from mechanical testing and calls for tests that, albeit still standardized, "measure a student's knowledge, understanding of and ability to apply, critical concepts through the use of a variety of item types and formats (e.g., open-ended, performance-based tasks)."[11]

Upgrading tests to include richer and less mechanical questions, however, only sharpens the horns of standardized testing's basic dilemma. The less mechanical the tests are, the more expensive they are to mark; and because states cannot afford to pay higher prices and testing companies refuse to accept lower profits, the only way those companies can deliver more sophisticated testing *affordably* is by keeping their marking costs low—as low (or as close to it) as the costs of mechanically marking multiple-choice questions. Companies must therefore squeeze as much marking out of as few employees for as little pay as they possibly can. And that is what they do, which, of course, creates its own problems.[12]

According to Todd Fairley, who spent fifteen years working for some of the biggest testing companies in the United States, rising to the ranks of supervisor and trainer, "[short answer and essay] tests get scored each year by a motley crew of temporary employees earning low hourly wages." Some are conscientious employees, he says, but "many end up working in test-scoring centers only because they can't get jobs elsewhere, and over the years I worked with every kind of drunk, dingbat, and dilettante."[13] The pressure of deadlines adds to the problem. "The number of tests that need to be read and scored each year is so massive that every conceivable shortcut is taken to get that job done," according to Fairley.

The testing industry works exceedingly hard to meet deadlines and get scores put on to tests, while I saw much less interest in getting the correct scores put on them. When I was a supervisor and trainer in charge of 10, 20, 100 people, the last thing I needed was for each

scorer to give a meticulous and earnest review to every student response. All I really needed was for them to quickly slap down a score
and move on to the next answer.[14]

Most damning of Fairley's accusations is that the test-scoring industry
cheats—on the qualifications of its employees, and on reliability and
validity scores. "I am guilty too," he says, "and over the years I fudged
the numbers like everyone else. Statistical tomfoolery and corporate
chicanery were the hallmark of my test-scoring career, and while I'm
not proud of that, it is a fact."[15]

In the end, Fairley says, teachers are more likely to bring accountability to evaluating students than the testing industry. "While accountability in education may be an important goal," he says, "it's
critical to realize how difficult that might be to pin down. The lesson
of my career should be that trusting massive corporations that answer
to a bottom line to make decisions about American schools is a whole
lot different than trusting those men and women who stand everyday
at the front of the classroom."[16]

The larger question about standardized testing, however, beyond
concerns about marking and costs, is whether, even assuming more
sophisticated testing can be made to work affordably, the increasingly
heavy reliance on testing in schools is consistent with the delivery of
a good education.

"When we define what matters in education only by what we can
measure," according to Diane Ravitch, "we tend to forget that schools
are responsible for shaping character, developing sound minds in
healthy bodies (*mens sana in corpore sana*), and forming citizens for
our democracy, not just for teaching basic skills." The very notion of
a "good education" slips away, according to Ravitch, as test results become a primary focus. Moreover, when we rely on those results, "with
all their limitations, as a routine means to fire educators, hand out

bonuses, and close schools, then we distort the purpose of schooling altogether." [17]

As my aunt Ally explains it, "I think something gets lost with this business of standardized testing." For her—and I believe this is true for most teachers—teaching children and teens is about more than the mechanical transmission of a standardized set of skills and knowledge for the purpose of scoring high on a test. Awakening curiosity, inspiring thought, imparting understanding of the world, building confidence, being a moral guide and role model—these are the intangible ambitions of teaching. When I asked my aunt Ally what she was trying to accomplish over the course of her long career as a teacher, it was these intangibles, not test scores, that she spoke of—the ceremony she created for her honors class ("they would come down the aisle with candles, wearing flowers; they would put on a performance and their parents would be invited; they'd be given certificates, it was a sense of pride"); the palpable awakening of civic sensibilities in her American history students; the parents who visited her between their work shifts to say "thank you" for getting their children interested in learning and wanting to stay in school. "It sounds corny," she said, "but the return is wonderful." When I asked her what had been her greatest moment as a teacher, she told me about a boy she had taught who started off in the slow-learning class and ended up an honors student and class valedictorian "He was a little guy, very quiet, soft-spoken, but brilliant," she said. In his valedictorian address he said to the graduating class, 'I want everybody to stand up,' and all these kids stood up, and then he said, 'I want you to say, thank you mother, thank you father [at this point my aunt Ally paused: "Oh sorry, Joel . . . this makes me cry"] and thank you teachers.' It was beautiful, because all these kids stood up and together thanked their parents and teachers as he had told them to do."

When experts in far-away government and corporate offices measure educational success and failure on the basis of standardized tests that they create and mark, teachers are left with little more to do than produce proficient test takers. Thus demoted from pedagogical professionals to test-proficiency technicians, they become alienated from the human and creative aspects of their work, and disconnected, as thinking and caring individuals, from their students.[18] With standardized testing, knowledge itself becomes a commodity, little more than a currency of numeric scores to cash in for various tangible rewards. What gets lost are all of learning's other and varied dimensions—intellect, curiosity, reason, criticism, beauty, compassion; all the things that help us define who we are, and what we aspire to in the world. Knowledge ends up being delivered rather than taught.

The reasons behind increasing standardization, and the movement away from liberal education, are varied and complex. One of them that cannot be ignored, however, is the simple fact the new market-driven reforms make money for big business.

Several years ago, in an interview for my earlier book *The Corporation*, Benno Schmidt, Jr., former president of Yale University and then chairman of Edison Schools, a publicly traded for-profit company in the business of running schools under contract with public systems, described as "almost unimaginably vast" the potential for growth in the education industry. "Education is bigger than defense, bigger than the whole domestic auto industry," he said. "Only health care has a larger segment of the American marketplace."[19] In another interview, education industry investor Michael Moe noted that "the classic investment opportunity is where there's a problem. The larger the problem, the larger the opportunity; there is no larger problem than how to educate our populace."[20]

Standardized testing is a profitable and growing industry.[21] No Child Left Behind created demand for 45 million tests to be produced and graded each year, and accounted for a full third of the $3 billion of revenue generated by the testing industry in 2008.[22] Standardized testing has continued to grow over the last few years, and will only grow more as states scurry to meet Race to the Top requirements.[23]

Testing companies are not the only ones lobbying for, and getting, access to new markets in education, however. Education management organizations (EMOs), companies like Edison, that contract with districts to open and run new schools and take over the management of existing ones, are also benefiting. In 2003, the Government Accountability Office observed that:

> The accountability provisions of the No Child Left Behind Act of 2001 may further increase [private companies managing poorly performing schools] because schools that continuously fail to make adequate progress toward meeting state goals are eventually subject to fundamental restructuring by the state, which may include turning the operation of the school over to a private company.[24]

The statement was prescient. EMOs are now poised to reap huge benefits as public schools across the nation risk being defunded, closed, or subjected to severe "turnaround" programs due to poor performance (as measured by standardized tests), trends fueled by both No Child Left Behind and Race to the Top.

Growth in the EMO sector has already been swift. Between 1998 and 2003 the number of public schools managed by private companies tripled, with fifty companies now managing over four hundred schools.[25] Then it doubled between 2003 and 2009 (representing a sixfold increase since 1998) with close to one hundred companies now running nearly eight hundred schools.[26] The large majority of schools run by EMOs (over 90 percent of them) are charter schools, publicly funded but privately managed. In the schools they run, EMOs are generally responsible for all operations, including hiring and remuneration of teachers (most charter schools are nonunion), curriculum, physical plant, and school policies.

Race to the Top explicitly encourages states to increase the numbers and facilitate the creation of charter schools (while placing no limit on how far such privatization can go), a spur to further growth and expansion of the EMO industry. Most states are falling into line. New York State, for example, as part of its successful bid for Race to the Top money, recently raised its charter school cap from 200 to 460, and created a state fund to help operators of high-performing charter schools build new facilities.[27]

There is no solid evidence that EMOs fulfill their promise of running schools better, and at lower costs, than public education authorities. The glossy brochures and annual reports touting better academic performance (as measured by standardized tests) and more motivated teachers (who can win cash bonuses if their students get high test scores) are belied by studies demonstrating EMO schools do no better than traditional ones, as well as by a series of scandals involving manipulation and inflation of test and evaluation results by leading EMOs.[28] One thing is clear about EMO-run schools, however. Overall, they tend to eschew the principles of liberal education and embrace more utilitarian approaches and curriculum content. Heavy reliance on testing, standardized curriculum, rigid discipline, centralized control, scripted lessons, and longer school days and years are typical.[29] It is generally taken for granted at EMO-run schools that the main purpose of education is the narrow utilitarian one of preparing children to be future workers, and that standardized tests are the appropriate measures of performance.

"Education is not the filling of a pail but the lighting of a fire," as the poet William Yeats wrote. Lighting that fire, creating thinking, informed, inspired and self-actualized individuals and citizens, is the purpose of liberal education. That ideal was embraced by democratic societies over the last century not only to help individuals reach their potentials, but also to help democracy survive and thrive. Democracy needs informed and thinking citizens as much as individuals need to be informed and thoughtful.[30] Education is not, in other words, only about what we provide for our children; it is also about what our children are likely to provide to the world. How we educate youth, how we cultivate their minds, how we guide their social and moral development—these are key parts not only of who and what they become as individuals, but also of how we, as a society, create our future and collective destiny. It may be cliché, but it is also profoundly true, that youth are our future; that "upon our children—how they are taught—rests the fate or fortune of tomorrow's world," as B. C. Forbes, the founder of *Forbes* magazine, described it.

Over the course of the twentieth century we, as a species, achieved something entirely new. We gave ourselves the power to destroy ourselves. We invented nuclear weapons that can wipe out entire cities, synthetic chemicals that poison our bodies and environments, and fossil fuel burning machines that dangerously pollute and warm the globe. Alone or in combination, these could end or at least severely strain (and arguably they already have done this) the Earth's capacity to sustain life. Especially in light of these new dangers, the question of how we educate youth is of pressing importance.

Education must be a much grander project than preparing children to succeed in the global economy. It must also prepare them to understand that global economy, to question and skeptically assess its virtues and weaknesses, to have and pursue ideals, and to work against our apparent tendency and certain capacity, as human societies, to be self-destructive.

These are the larger jobs of education.

Conclusion

Nelson Mandela's sage observation, that "there can be no keener revelation of a society's soul than the way in which it treats its children,"[1] invites concern about our own society's soul as big business ruthlessly squeezes childhood into forms and practices designed to yield profit. From the self-interested perspective of corporations, children are little more than opportunities to exploit or costs to avoid—opportunities as markets for fast food, psychotropic drugs, or standardized tests, for example; costs as reasons for regulatory restrictions on manipulative marketing, industrial chemicals, or child labor. And as corporations become dominant (if not *the* dominant) forces in children's and parents' lives, that morally myopic perspective and the practices it inspires defines more and more of what we, as a society, think and do about childhood. Our societal aspirations to manifest the *values* of childhood—caring for, nurturing, protecting, supporting, and enabling children—end up getting pushed aside by strategies devised to maximize the economic *value* of children.

This is a quite recent development. It bears repeating that for most of the twentieth century, the "century of the child," childhood was conceived in more beneficent terms. It was widely believed that societies, through their governments and public institutions, were obliged to protect children from economic exploitation and harm, and to enable

163

them to flourish, realize their potentials, and grow into engaged and productive democratic citizens. Inspired by that view, public regulatory regimes were created to limit economic practices that clashed with children's needs and interests, and public schools were built to guide their forming intellects and sensibilities. The overarching idea was that children and childhood needed the kinds of *public* protection and support that only society could offer.

Around 1980 we began to retreat from that idea, however. Childhood was reconceived as a primarily private affair, appropriately governed by parents, families, and markets, but not so much by governments. Public regulations designed to protect children were recast as illegitimate intrusions into parents' freedoms to parent and corporations' freedoms to profit, and deregulation became the new dogma and practice. Today, as a result (and by way of summary), kid marketers are free to manipulate children's emotions, credulity, and inexperience, and to pitch to them unhealthy ideas and products; pharmaceutical companies are free to pressure and co-opt scientists and physicians in order to boost pediatric sales of their psychotropic drugs; chemical manufacturers, users, and emitters are free to turn children's environments—indeed their very bodies—into toxic stews of synthetic chemicals; agricultural concerns are free to exploit the labor of impoverished and migrant children; and education companies are free to profit from school systems increasingly geared toward the narrow needs and visions of big business.

In all these areas, as we have seen, few public regulatory measures exist to protect children from economic activities that might cause them harm. Where regulations do exist, they are weakly enforced, or oriented more toward industry's needs than children's, and proposals for new regulations inevitably come up against nearly impenetrable walls of legal and political resistance.[2] As a result, children are left largely unprotected from corporations' unbridled pursuit of profit. In short we, as a society, are conflicted about what childhood is and should be. We instinctively cling to century-of-the-child ideas about childhood, believing children should be protected by society and provided the means to flourish and to develop healthfully. Yet we permit, indeed encourage, corporations to exploit and ignore children's unique needs and vulnerabilities when it is profitable for them to do so. Our instincts about childhood and children are thus profoundly belied by our practices.

The obvious solution is to narrow the gap between instincts and practices. Less obvious is how, in concrete terms, we should do that.

I have this image of my mother, a five-year-old girl, out with her two sisters, one eight, the other three. They are speeding through the streets of lower Manhattan in the open top of a double-decker bus at the dusky end of a depression-era summer day, on their way home to Brooklyn where, hours earlier, their parents (my grandparents), desperate for some peace and quiet, had kicked them out of the apartment with instructions not to return until the street lights came on. During the week, while my grandmother stitched garments and my grandfather fixed sewing machines, my mother, still five years old, would wander the streets of Brooklyn, visiting shopkeepers, sneaking into movies at the local cinema, and chatting with the prostitutes and numbers racketeers she befriended along the way.

"You'd have to be crazy to let your kids run around the city like that today," my mother used to say after telling her childhood tales (though, she said, her parents' lax ways were not unusual at the time). And most people would agree. The thought is terrifying for a parent—unless that parent happens to be New York City newspaper reporter Lenore Skenazy.

Skenazy caused a national stir when she wrote a story about how she had deliberately abandoned her nine-year-old son at Bloomingdales in Manhattan, with a $20 bill, some quarters for a phone call (he did not have a cell phone), a subway map, and a MetroCard.[3] His job, happily accepted by him, was to make his own way home. To do that he had to work out that he would have to take the Lexington Avenue subway south, and then catch a crosstown bus on Thirty-fourth Street.

Skenazy, dubbed "America's worst mom" for her efforts,[4] confessed to "a tinge" of worry, but she also knew that abductions of children and random acts of violence against them are extremely rare. She trusted that if her son needed help he would ask a stranger, and that that stranger would not decide, "Gee, I was about to catch my train home, but now I think I'll abduct this adorable child instead." Skenazy's son got home, "ecstatic with independence." But still, she says, many of her readers wanted to turn her in for child abuse, apparently believing, she says, that "keeping kids under lock and key and helmet and cell phone and nanny and surveillance is the right way to rear [them]."

I agree with Skezany's main point that we, as parents, tend to be overprotective. Too often we trust neither children's competence to navigate the world, nor the goodwill of adults they might meet along the way. We monitor children constantly, hover over them, tie ourselves into knots of worry and suspicion, and deny them the independence they need and crave.[5] So why, you may reasonably ask, would I fill the pages of this book with more and new reasons to worry? The answer is simple. While I agree with Skezany that sometimes we overprotect children, it is also true, I believe, that, at other times, we *under*protect them.

The important point here is that both overprotection and underprotection can result from corporations' and industries' strategic channelling of information to boost profits and protect interests. Overprotection occurs when parents' fears are stoked about, for example, children having mental disorders (thus justifying treatment with psychotropic drugs); or being exposed to germs and contamination (thus justifying the use of pesticides, preservatives, and antibacterial agents); or being taught by incompetent and unaccountable teachers (thus justifying market-driven reforms of the education system). Underprotection is the result when parents' fears are unduly *diminished*, for example, about the side effects of psychotropic drugs; the ill effects of chemical toxins (including those found in pesticides, preservatives, and antibacterial agents); or the narrowing of education that results from standardization. In short, corporations and industries are among the ranks of "shrewd leaders, cliques, and pressure groups [that] can make people see exaggerated dangers—or make them ignore existing danger until it is too late," as Erik Erikson describes it. The inevitable consequence, as he further states, is that "even enlightened and demo-cratic [citizens] are blunted in their capacity to fear accurately."[6]

My hope for this book is that it contributes to sharpening (or at least de-blunting) parents' capacity to fear accurately, and thus helps them—along with grandparents, uncles, aunts, and anyone else with children in their lives—make more informed choices and decisions. As I have stressed throughout the book, however, ensuring children have good and healthy childhoods is not only about parents' *individual* choices and decisions. It is also about the social *conditions* in which they make those choices and decisions—conditions, I have argued, that, today more than ever, are dictated by the self-serving maneuvers of corporations and the reluctance of governments to regulate in areas where children are especially vulnerable to harm.

Over the last thirty years public policy regarding children (and more generally) has been driven by a presumption against regulatory protec-tion. Parents should be free and responsible to parent as they see fit (without the interference or assistance of government), it is argued; and corporations, guided by market forces and their socially respon-sible sensibilities, should be trusted to refrain from causing children harm (without the compulsion of government regulation). The "old regulatory model" should therefore be abandoned, as former British Prime Minister Gordon Brown prescribed while still in office, and "the educated parent consumer [and] trust in the responsible com-pany" should be relied upon to take its place.[7] That prescription, though perhaps plausible in the abstract, is in fact wildly misguided in reality, where parents have little freedom to make choices as "educated consumers," and corporations have little capacity to be "responsible."

Parents are limited in the choices they can make, as I have emphasized throughout this book, by the conditions in which they make those choices. Sometimes they feel compelled by conditions to choose one way over another (by, for example, their children's marketing-fueled demands for unhealthy foods, or a physician's quick advice to medicate a child). At other times, they simply have no choice (about, for example, most of the chemicals children are exposed to in their environments, or the closing of a neighborhood school); or they depend, unwittingly and by necessity, upon information that is partial and distorted by industry influence (as, for example, in the cases of pharmaceutical drugs, industrial chemicals, or the effects of media violence); or they lack the time, resources, and expertise to properly digest, interpret, analyze, and act upon the information that is available. The notion that parents, as "educated consumers," can be relied upon to provide children adequate protection is, for all of these reasons, implausible.

That of "trust in the responsible company" is no more realistic. As I have been at pains to point out, here and elsewhere, corporations are ill-equipped to be responsible to anyone but themselves and their shareholders. Programmed to put self-interest above all else, and to view harms they might cause others as "externalities" (and thus beyond their concern and responsibility), they are prone to exploit and neglect others, despite whatever good intentions their employees might have. Corporations simply cannot be trusted (any more than can the human psychopaths they resemble) to regulate their behavior, and to act responsibly toward others.[8]

Even Alan Greenspan, chief architect of deregulation in the financial sector through the 2000s, realized after the 2008 economic collapse that he had been wrong about the abilities of companies to act responsibly when they are not being regulated. "I made a mistake," he told a congressional committee, "in presuming that the self-interests of organizations, specifically banks and others, [would lead them to protect] their own shareholders and their equity in firms."[9] It is an equal, if not greater, mistake to presume self-interested organizations will act out of concern for those—children in this case—who they tap and neglect in their pursuit of profit. They may *purport* to be concerned, in order to mollify adverse public opinion, or ward off the (unlikely) prospect of regulation, but acting out of *genuine* concern for others' interests is not something corporations, as currently constituted, can do. That is why they need to be regulated, and why self-regulation has proven ineffective as a replacement for the "old regulatory model." As Willem Buiter, chief economist at Citigroup, astutely observes, "self-regulation stands in relation to regulation the way self-importance stands in relation to importance and self-righteousness to righteousness."[10]

In the end, governments, whatever else may be said of them, are the only institutions in our society that have sufficient authority, legitimacy, and mandate to set and enforce rules and standards effective for protecting children from corporate-created threats to their health and well-being. They are alone in being able, through the enactment of laws and regulations, to change, for the better, the conditions in which parents make choices for their children. In saying this, I am not suggesting regulation is the answer to every childhood problem; nor that other measures should not be pursued; nor that traditional "command and control" models of regulation are always best.[11]

What I am suggesting, however, is that the ideologically driven view that regulation is never, or at least very rarely, appropriate is wrong, and that it has served over the last thirty years to forestall measures that could have improved children's lives, health, and well-being. Regulation is not government against the people, as its critics suggest, but rather a mechanism through which the people, as citizens, can protect their, and their children's, interests. No doubt the regulatory system falls short of such ideals in its actual operations, but that is a reason to work to make it better, not to abandon it.

Earlier chapters provided ideas and suggestions on how to improve regulatory regimes in particular areas—children's media and marketing, psychotropic drugs, environmental toxins, and child labor. More generally, a number of global reforms would help the system as a whole come closer to realizing the principles it is supposed to serve. To begin with, measures must be taken to reduce big business's influence over government. Corporate lobbying, electoral campaign financing, and the "revolving door" between industry and agencies need to be addressed, as do the insufficient funding and staff shortages currently afflicting most regulatory agencies and eroding their abilities to do their jobs.[12] Next, embracing the precautionary principle—which, as discussed in earlier chapters, commands regulatory action where good reasons exist to believe an activity is harmful even though definitive proof of harm is absent—would be an important reform, especially in areas where science is uncertain and possible harms are serious. Even with the precautionary principle in place, however (and certainly without it), creating and operating effective regulatory regimes in most areas requires reliable scientific information. Today, the priorities, questions, methodologies, and results of scientific research are increasingly dictated by the needs of corporations, as public funding for research is replaced by self-interested corporate support and previously bright lines between science and commerce are blurred. More public institutional and financial support needs to be dedicated to creating and disseminating genuinely independent information about what needs to be done to protect children in light of their unique vulnerabilities.

In addition to reaching lawmakers with such information, parents and other key players in children's lives need to be informed. Media campaigns by governments and public health authorities can be used to create public awareness around the kinds of issues addressed in this book. Education too can be used in this way. Health practitioners, for example, in their initial degree programs and in subsequent training, can be made aware of the pitfalls of pharmaceutical industry influence over medical practice and science, or taught the basics of children's environmental health issues (environmental health expert Leo Trasande told me that, currently, "the amount of time on average in a medical school that's devoted to environmental health is less than that spent on one heart bypass surgery case; it's a very small sliver of time").

Public regulatory systems and other governmental measures can certainly provide better protection and support to children than they currently do. That will not happen, however, unless we, as citizens, demand that it does, which is why, I believe, being a good parent today requires more than just making good choices as a parent. It requires as well that we work to change the conditions in which we make those choices; that we demand governments take action to protect children from harm at the hands of corporations and other economic actors. Being a good parent, in other words, means becoming engaged as a *citizen* in the collective practice of remaking society—in that thing called democracy.

For democracy to thrive, or even survive, however, it is not only parents, but youths as well, who must take on the tasks of citizenship.

"Summon[ing] forth the potential intelligence of the younger generation . . . [is the] one effort which can keep a democratic country healthy," according to Erik Erikson. Throughout history "intelligent youth, proud in its independence and burning with initiative," as Erikson describes it, challenged the misuses of power and comfortable acquiescence of older generations, and refuted the jaded cynicism that so often engendered corruption and injustice. Youth-driven social movements helped end apartheid in South Africa. They fought for democracy in Tiananmen Square, and more recently in Egypt and other parts of the Middle East. Around the world today youth promote peace, protest nuclear proliferation, energize a large and growing environmental movement, fight against social injustice and corporate abuse, and drive the agendas and actions of hundreds of activist organizations.[13] Free the Children, one such organization, created by two young activists, brothers Craig and Marc Kielburger, builds schools in the developing world, opposes child labor, promotes the rights of women and girls, and mounts huge "We Day" rallies each year bringing together thousands of teenagers to "celebrate the power of young people to create positive change in the world."[14] The organization is greatly aided in its work by web-based social networks, media that have quickly become powerful drivers and defining features of all youth activism. The recent overthrow of Egypt's autocratic regime—dubbed the "Facebook Revolution"—showed just how effective these media can be when it comes to organizing and mobilizing for change.

Yet there are trends in our society that threaten to repress, rather than to summon forth, the potential intelligence of the younger generation. I discussed two of these already in earlier chapters: the increasingly narrow and regimented education system that threatens to deprive young people of the critical and questioning perspectives they need to become effective democratic citizens; and the hyperconsumerist and individualistic youth culture that works against the cultivation of civic-mindedness. Within these contexts, even social networks, powerful as they are for organizing and mobilizing youth activism, might turn out to have significant downsides in terms of their overall and long-term impacts on democracy. Experience with other media suggests democratic potential depends largely upon who controls a medium and for what purposes it is used. In the 1950s and 1960s, for example, many believed television would serve to deepen democracy by helping create openness and transparency in government and a well-informed citizenry. As it turned out, the medium's democratic potential was largely squandered by commercial networks and broadcasters whose sole concern was delivering content that would attract advertisers.[15]

Currently, social networks are, like television, aimed primarily at generating profit for corporations. They do this (as I discussed in earlier chapters) by targeting youth with marketing, immersing them in consumerism and brands, eliciting compulsive engagement, and trolling users' pages for useful information. It is crucial to consider how these *core functions* of social networks, not only the inspiring examples of activist uses, might contribute to their overall democratic impact. It seems reasonable to wonder, for example, whether, in light of these functions, youths' increasing reliance on social networks could sap or at least flatten political consciousness and energy. A recent survey of college students on how they engage with "news" on social networks is worrying in this regard:

> [M]ost students report that they rarely go prospecting for "hard" news at mainstream or legacy news sites [such as The New York Times, the BBC, or Al Jazeera]. Instead they inhale, almost unconsciously, the news that is served up on the sidebar of their email account, that is on friends' Facebook walls, that comes through on Twitter. . . . The nonstop deluge of information coming via mobile phones and online means that most students across the world have neither the time nor the interest to follow up on even quite important news stories—unless they are personally engaged. For daily news, students have become headline readers via their social networks. In most cases they only learn more about a story when the details or updates are also served up via text or tweet or post.

In these ways, social networks could end up contributing to the dilution of *informed* political thought and action, and thus offsetting whatever other democratic potentials they might have.

A larger and more ominous threat is big business's ongoing campaign to co-opt the idealism of youth for its own self-interested purposes. Companies have understood for some time now that corporate social responsibility helps sell products and ward off regulators.[16] More recently they have realized that this strategy is most effective, and indeed essential, when targeting youth. As a result, corporations have begun creating, sponsoring, and infiltrating youth-driven environmental and

173

social justice campaigns as central parts of their marketing strategies. At the "We Day" events described above, for example, corporations are a large and unavoidable presence, handing out promotional goods, filling arena screens with advertisements for, among other things, Coca-Cola, Disney, and Molson Coors products, and boasting about all the good works they do around the world. "Now let's watch this video about how Telus believes in the power of young people to change the world," trumpeted a popular youth-oriented television show host, Ben Mulroney, as he introduced a slick ad featuring the company's good deeds at a recent We Day event in Vancouver.

Major corporations are involved in youth-driven social and environmental initiatives in numerous different ways. Bayer, for example, recently sponsored a United Nations Environmental Program meeting of Young Environmental Leaders; Unilever launched an advertising campaign for its Dove brand that was critical of the fashion industry's obsession with unhealthy body images; Pepsi and Domino's Pizza ran web-based contests to generate recycling ideas for their product containers; McDonald's partnered with Conservation International to create a special Happy Meal designed "to engage kids in a fun and informative way about protecting the environment" and to provide "information about eight species of endangered animals and how they are being threatened by climate change" (the meal came with plush animal toys and a code to unlock various virtual adventures at a special website).[17] These are just a few examples. There are legions more.

Many believe such initiatives provide needed resources and leadership to social and environmental causes. The deployment by companies of their substantial resources to try to do some good in the world can only help those causes, they say, a claim supported by the old adage "Do not look a gift horse in the mouth." Yet, when that gift horse may be a Trojan horse, it surely makes sense to consider what may lurk inside. Corporate "gifts" to social and environmental causes are, and indeed must be, by law, calculated strategies to advance companies' pecuniary interests, despite the usually genuine intentions of most employees. As such these initiatives are designed to position corporations as forces for good, especially when their core activities are likely to suggest otherwise. Bayer, for example, supported young environmentalists while it manufactured pesticides, Bisphenol A, phosgene, and other toxic chemicals; Unilever protested the fashion industry's encouragement of unhealthy body images while it promoted diet aids and other products associated with unhealthy body images; Pepsi and Domino's Pizza touted recycling while producing containers that are major sources of land fill waste; McDonald's publicized endangered species while being attacked for destroying wildlife habitats by clearing forests for grazing lands.

The larger and cumulative message of such campaigns is that big business is part of the solution, not part of the problem, in relation to the world's ills. The 18,000 youth in attendance at Vancouver's We Day, all "burning with initiative" to change the world, could not have helped but come away with the message that big business was, and would continue to be, their main partner in doing so. That message is profoundly misleading, however. Corporations, as large, powerful, and dominating institutions, deliberately programmed to exploit and neglect others in pursuit of wealth for themselves, are central players in causing environmental and social harms and fomenting injustice across the globe. Their attempts to convince young people otherwise are little more than calculated strategies to sell products and protect their interests, a point many young activists fully understand.

Like dominant institutions have done throughout history, big business is trying to harness youths' energy to its purposes, and ensure that energy does not work against its interests. What history has taught time and time again, however, is that the idealism and energy of youth cannot be diverted, diluted, or kept down for long. Inevitably, it rises up as a force to change the world for the better.

That is why I am optimistic about the future.

Notes

INTRODUCTION

1. As Gordon Neufeld and Gabor Mate state in *Hold Onto Your Kids: Helping the Most Important People in a Child's Life Make a Positive and Lasting Difference* (Toronto: Alfred A. Knopf Canada, 2004), 15: "Our children want to belong to us, even if they don't know or feel that and even if their words or actions seem to signal the opposite."

2. Erik Erikson, *Childhood and Society* (New York: W.W. Norton, 1963), 408 (the book was first published in 1950). An example of how industry tactics can make it difficult to "fear accurately," as I discuss in the next paragraph, can be found in relation to cell phones and children.

    Recently, my wife, Rebecca, and I struggled with the question of whether to get cell phones for our then thirteen- and fourteen-year-old kids. There is no downside to kids having cell phones, even at very young ages, according to the industry. Indeed, what parents should worry about is their kids *not* having cell phones. The teddy-bear-shaped Teddyphone, for example, billed by its maker as "the first ever safety phone for your children and grandchildren," has child tracking features and a special SOS button (www.teddyfone.com/). Firefly mobile, another phone designed specifically for kids, "gives you peace

READERS NOTE: All websites in this section were last accessed May 1, 2011.

of mind [and] keep[s] you connected and in control" (www.fireflymobile. com) according to its maker. Cingular Wireless warns parents of the dangers of child predators by hosting "Safe Kid Days" at retail outlets and distributing free fingerprint ID kits (in case their kids go missing), along with a fear fomenting book, *A Stranger in the Park*. Cell phones "help parents keep up with important details about where their kids are, who they are with and when they'll be home," according to Cingular VP Jim Thorpe, and are thus "key to helping us keep our kids safe" (see www.thefreelibrary.com/Cingular+Wireles s+Makes+Safety+Top+Priority+As+Kentucky's+Kids...-a0106467603).

That parents should fear *cell phones*, as opposed to the alleged dangers of their kids not having them, is, of course, never mentioned. Yet there are real concerns. With phones now functioning as minicomputers and texting devices, they give kids 24/7 access to online enticements, such as social networks, gaming, virtual worlds, the web, and put them at risk of constant distraction from other areas of their lives (school and family, for example), and also of becoming involved in age-inappropriate activities, such as accessing pornography, "sexting," and online gambling. There is also the issue of radiation. The industry invests heavily in research, public relations strategies, and lobbying designed to cast doubt upon possible links between cell phones and tumors. Its official position, that "no adverse health effects have been established for mobile phone use," as stated by The Wireless Association (see, www.ctia.org/consumer_info/safety/index.cfm/AID/10371), an advocacy group representing major cell phone companies, obscures the fact that there is also no proof of safety, and some suggestive, if not definitive, evidence of possible harm, especially to the young. Some countries and jurisdictions (most recently California) have taken or are considering regulatory action.

In the end, we bought our kids cell phones when they entered high school, not happily and with the queasy feeling that future research might prove correct concerns about radiation risks. But we felt we had no choice, convinced by our kids' pleas that all their friends had phones (true) and that their ability to have a social life depended on their having phones (also true). The phones we got them, however, lack internet capacity (much to their chagrin), and we prohibited them from taking their phones to school and having them in their bedrooms, thus eliminating at least some exposure and risk.

Beyond cell phones chapters 4 to 7 of this book deal with the ways business interests within the pharmaceutical and chemical industries respectively use their influence to shape public opinion and policy through lobbying governments and agencies, co-opting professionals and organizations, creating front groups, disarming critics, sponsoring science, and running marketing campaigns. One excellent and important account of how this happens in the food industry can be found in Marion Nestle, *Food Politics: How the Food Industry Influences Nutrition and Health* (Berkeley, CA: University of California Press, 2003).

3. For an excellent example of how racism, sexism, and poverty intersect to harm children, see Marlee Kline, "Complicating the Ideology of Motherhood: Child Welfare Law and First Nations Women," *Queen's Law Journal* 18(2): 306–42 (1993).

CHAPTER ONE: THE CENTURY OF THE CHILD

1. Philippe Aries, *Centuries of Childhood: A Social History of Family Life* (New York: Vintage Books, 1963), 103, as cited in Neil Postman, *The Disappearance of Childhood* (New York: Vintage Books, 1994), 17.

2. Ibid., 33.

3. From William Blake's short poem "And did those feet in ancient time," which is part of the preface to *Milton a Poem*, 1804 (set to music in 1916 by Sir Hubert Parry and known as the hymn "Jerusalem").

4. E.P. Thompson, *The Making of the English Working Class* (New York: Vintage Books, 1966), 307.

5. Quoted in Marvin Levine, *Children for Hire: The Perils of Child Labor in the United States* (Westport, CT: Prager Publishers, 2003), 1. See also, Stephen B. Wood, *Constitutional Politics in the Progressive Era: Child Labor and the Law* (Chicago: University of Chicago Press, 1968).

6. For discussions of the rise of child protection during the nineteenth and twentieth centuries, see Wood, *Constitutional Politics,* and also John E.B. Myers,

Notes

"A Short History of Child Protection in America," *Family Law Quarterly* 42 (2008); John F. Fogarty, "Some Aspects of the Early History of Child Protection in Australia," *Family Matters* 78 (2008): 52–59; Adam M. Tomison, "A History of Child Protection," *Family Matters* 60 (2001): 46; Gertrude J. Rubin Williams, "Child Protection A Journey into History," *Journal of Clinical Child Psychology* 12 (1983): 236–243; Didier Reynaert, Maria Bouverne-De Bie, and Stijn Vandevelde, "A Review of Children's Rights Literature Since the Adoption of the United Nations Convention on the Rights of the Child," *Childhood* 16 (2009): 518–534; Hugh Cunningham, *Children and Childhood in Western Society Since 1500* (New York: Longman, 1995); Colin Heywood, *A History of Childhood* (Cambridge, UK: Polity, 2006); Viviana A. Zelizer, *Pricing the Priceless Child: The Changing Social Value of Children* (New York: Basic Books, 1985).

7. The book, by Ellen Key, was published in Germany in 1900 as *Barnetsårhundrade* (Century of the Child). It was later published in English as: Ellen Key, *The Century of the Child* (New York: G.P. Putnam's Sons, 1909). It is cited in Cunningham, *Children and Childhood*, 163, in a chapter also entitled "The Century of the Child."

8. David Harvey, *A Brief History of Neoliberalism* (New York: Oxford University Press, 2005).

9. Stated by Margaret Thatcher in an interview in *Women's Own* magazine, October 31 1987. Interesting commentary on possible connections between neoliberalism and childhood can be found in Timimi Sami, "The McDonaldization of Childhood: Children's Mental Health in Neo-liberal Market Cultures," *Transcultural Psychiatry* 47 (2010): 686–706; M.K. Haly, "Neoliberalism and Child Protection: A Deadly Mix," *Labour History* 98 (2010): 121–141.

10. Polayni is quoted by Harvey, *Brief History Neoliberalism*, 36. For a broader discussion of the nature of neoliberalism's conception and practice of freedom, see Harvey, ibid., 5–38.

11. For further discussion of this point, see Joel Bakan, *The Corporation: The Pathological Pursuit of Profit and Power* (New York: Free Press, 2004), 5–59.

12. For an excellent analysis of the 2008 financial crisis that highlights the role of

inadequate regulation see John Bellamy Foster and Fred Magdoff, *The Great Financial Crisis: Causes and Consequences* (New York: Monthly Review Press, 2009).

13. A recent report to President Obama on the Gulf crisis concludes that inadequate regulation was a root cause: "The explosive loss of the Macondo well could have been prevented; The immediate causes of the Macondo well blowout can be traced to a series of identifiable mistakes made by BP, Halliburton, and Transocean that reveal such systematic failures in risk management that they place in doubt the safety culture of the entire industry; Deepwater energy exploration and production, particularly at the frontiers of experience, involve risks for which neither industry nor government has been adequately prepared, but for which they can and must be prepared in the future; To assure human safety and environmental protection, regulatory oversight of leasing, energy exploration, and production require reforms even beyond those significant reforms already initiated since the *Deepwater Horizon* disaster. Fundamental reform will be needed in both the structure of those in charge of regulatory oversight and their internal decision-making process to ensure their political autonomy, technical expertise, and their full consideration of environmental protection concerns." Report to the President, *Deep Water: The Gulf Oil Disaster and the Future of Offshore Drilling* (Washington DC: National Commission on the BP Deepwater Horizon Oil Spill and Offshore Drilling, January, 2011). Available online at: https://s3.amazonaws.com/pdf_final/1_OSC_Intro.pdf.

Many commentators have noted the connection between inadequate regulation and both the 2008 financial meltdown and the BP explosion, as well as other disasters and fiascos. See, for example, Steven Pearlstein, "Time for Industry to End Its War on Regulation," *Washington Post*, May 26, 2010, A13, which states: "The biggest oil spill ever. The biggest financial crisis since the Great Depression. The deadliest mine disaster in 25 years. One recall after another of toys from China, of vehicles from Toyota, of hamburgers from roach-infested processing plants. The whole Vioxx fiasco. And let's not forget the biggest climate threat since the Ice Age. Even if you're not into conspiracy theories, it's hard to ignore the common thread running through these recent crises: the glaring failure of government regulators to protect the public. Regulators who were cowed by industry or intimidated by politicians. Regulators who were compromised by favors or prospects of industry employment. Regulators who were better at calculating the costs of oversight than the benefits. And regulators who were blinded by their ideological bias against government interference and their faith that industries could police themselves." See also Leonard Pitts, "Free-Market Religion Lost in Gulf Oil Spill," *Chicago Tribune*, March 24, 2009; Paul Krugman, "Disaster and Denial," *Int'l Herald Tribune*, December 16, 2009; Al Meyerhoff, "Roadkill on the Deregulation Highway," *Los Angeles Times*, January 14, 2008. For a sweeping analysis, history, and critique of neoliberalism, and a documentation of how neoliberal policies have fed upon and fomented disasters and crises over the last three decades, see Naomi Klein, *The Shock Doctrine: The Rise of Disaster Capitalism* (New York: Henry Holt, 2008).

14. Bakan, *The Corporation*.
15. John Stuart Mill, *On Liberty* (New York: Penguin Classic, 2006), first published in 1859.

CHAPTER TWO: WHACK YOUR SOUL MATE AND BONELESS GIRL

1. A few examples of sites where Whack Your Soul Mate can be played: www. y8.com/games/Whack_Your_Soul_Mate; www.y3.com/games/7492/Whack_ Your_Soul_Mate.
2. At the same sites as in note 1, and also at Addictinggames.com.
3. These games, like the others discussed, are found at numerous sites across the internet, and at Addictinggames.com.
4. Quote found in the user review section of Commonsensemedia.org (www. commonsensemedia.org/website-reviews/addictinggames/user-reviews ?page=2&filter=kid). The 10 million unique user figure comes from www.addictinggames.com/aboutus/about_ag.php. Buried in Addictinggames.com's privacy policy is the requirement that individuals be at least thirteen years old and live in the United States in order to play. Based on an unscientific

survey of my son's friends, all of whom visit the site regularly, and were under thirteen years old at the time and did not live in the United States (we live in Canada), there is little knowledge of these requirements among users, and no concern to comply with them if they are made aware of them. The site has no registration requirement, nor are players asked to indicate their age before playing. By one estimate, 13 percent of visitors to the site are between the ages of three and twelve; 44 percent between the ages of thirteen and seventeen; and 53 percent are female. Just over half of households where the game is played include children between the ages of three and twelve; 43 percent of such households include children between the ages of thirteen and seventeen: www.quantcast.com/addictinggames.com/demographics?country=US.

5. Erikson, *Childhood and Society*, at 307.

6. Quote found at Commonsensemedia.org/website-reviews/user-reviews? page=2&filter=kid.

7. The quote comes from a speech by then Senator Obama at a Kaiser Foundation event on November 9, 2005, in Washington DC. The text of the speech can be found at www.kff.org/entmedia/upload/entmedia110905oth2.pdf. Obama's speech, in turn, quotes from and was clearly inspired by a famous speech by Newton Minow, Chair of the Federal Communications Commission under President John Kennedy in the early 1960s. Minow was addressing the National Association of Broadcasters, meeting in Washington D.C. on May 9, 1961. His speech pulled no punches in indicting television and the broadcasters who delivered it, and it was particularly concerned with the medium's negative impact on children. "When television is bad, nothing is worse," stated Minow to the assembled broadcasters.

> I invite each of you to sit down in front of your television set when your station goes on the air and stay there, for a day, without a book, without a magazine, without a newspaper, without a profit and loss sheet or a rating book to distract you. Keep your eyes glued to that set until the station signs off. I can assure you that what you will observe is a vast wasteland. You will see a procession of game shows, formula comedies about totally unbeliev- able families, blood and thunder, mayhem, violence, sadism, murder, west-

ern bad men, western good men, private eyes, gangsters, more violence, and cartoons. And endlessly, commercials, many screaming, cajoling, and offending. And most of all, boredom.

As noted, Minow was particularly concerned about television's impact on children:

Most young children today, believe it or not, spend as much time watching television as they do in the schoolroom. If parents, teachers, and ministers conducted their responsibilities by following the ratings, children would have a steady diet of ice cream, school holidays, and no Sunday school. What about your responsibilities? Is there no room on television to teach, to inform, to uplift, to stretch, to enlarge the capacities of our children? There are some fine children's shows, but they are drowned out in the massive doses of cartoons, violence, and more violence. Must these be your trademarks? Search your consciences and see if you cannot offer more to your young beneficiaries whose futures you guide so many hours each and every day.

A full transcript of Minow's speech can be found in Newton N. Minow and Craig L. LaMay, *Abandoned in the Wasteland: Children, Television, and the First Amendment* (New York: Hill and Wang, 1995), at 185–96.

When in a recent interview with Newton Minow I described *Whack Your Soul Mate* to him and asked him what he thought about it, this is what he said: "I think that there's room here for public shaming of the people who are doing that. I would have them up on television with their names and addresses and phone numbers so that people can let them know what they think."

8. Casual gaming sites, such as Addictinggames.com, have become advertising goldmines, with unique visits to such sites jumping 22 percent between 2008 and 2009 (from 72 to 87 million), a rate ten times the 2 percent growth of the internet as a whole (from 191 to 194 million). See www.comscore.com/ Press_Events/Press_Releases/2009/7/Online_Gaming_Continues_Strong_

Growth_in_U.S._as_Consumers_Increasingly_Opt_for_Free_Entertainment_Alternatives.

The $15 billion figure quoted here is likely conservative as it is an estimate from 2003. Still, that figure is more than double the number from 1992. See Susan Linn, *Consuming Kids: The Hostile Takeover of Childhood* (New York: The New Press, 2004), 1. A 2007 estimate of the overall amount spent marketing to kids in the U.S. is $17 billion, compared to just $100 million in 1983. See www.cbsnews.com/stories/2007/05/14/fyi/main2798401.shtml.

As noted below, children's direct buying power combined with their influence over parents' purchasing tops $1 trillion per year, an exponential rise over the last several decades. See "Trillion-dollar Kids," *The Economist*, November 30, 2008 (www.economist.com/node/8355035?story_id=8355035).

There is a plethora of different ways marketers reach children, especially now with the wide use of digital and mobile devices by youth. An excellent resource, rich with examples, for monitoring the various techniques and media that marketers use to target children is: http://digitalads.org/, a site run by the Center for Digital Democracy and the Berkeley Media Studies Group.

9. Unfortunately, I was unable to get an answer to this question from anyone at Addictinggames.com as my interview requests were rebuffed.

10. This discussion of Martin Lindstrom and his work is based on an extensive interview with him, done in two sessions, and also on his book (with Patricia B Seybold), *Brandchild: Remarkable Insights Into the Minds of Today's Global Kids and Their Relationships with Brands* (London: Kogan Page, 2005).

11. A quote from BBC World on the endorsement page of Lindstrom, *Brandchild*.

12. Lindstrom, *Brandchild*, 35.

13. See Lindstrom's detailed explanations of all of these emotional factors, ibid., 33–43.

14. The YouTube video can be found at: www.youtube.com/watch?v=n7b9SbFzIp0. The original trailer that circulated around the web is entitled *Ladies of Liberty City*. It was initially posted by IGN Entertainment, a popular internet forum for games, among other things (the site is owned by News Corporation). *Ladies of Liberty City* can now be found at: www.gametrailers.com/user-movie/

gtaiv-ladies-of-liberty/209411. Not surprisingly, considerable controversy was raised around the possibility of killing prostitutes in *GTA IV*. Sex workers' organizations called for a ban of the game, for example (see www.gamespot. com/news/6144286.html). In order to comply with Australian classification laws, *GTA IV*'s maker, Rockstar Video, edited out the possibility of killing prostitutes in the Australian version of the game (www.gamespot.com/news/6234900.html?tag=result%Btitle%3B1). Defenders of the game point out that players do not *have* to kill prostitutes in the game—they simple can. For a statement of the latter point, see Chris Baker, "It's Not Just about Killing Hookers Anymore: The Surprising Narrative Richness of Grand Theft Auto IV," *Slate*, April 29, 2008 (the article can be found at www.slate.com/id/2190207/, accessed January 13, 2011). While there may be literal truth to the argument—players do not have to visit the strip club, kill prostitutes, and so on—the tween and teenage boys who play the game are, as is their wont, likely to seek out the edgiest content as they play. Especially when such edgy content is widely circulated on the web, in trailers such as *The Ladies of Liberty City*, the possibility is high that young players will find it.

15.   D. A. Gentile, "Pathological Video Game Use Among Youth 8 to 18: A National Study," *Psychological Science*, 20 (2009): 594–602. For similar statistics, see Lawrence Kutner and Cheryl Olson, *Grand Theft Childhood: The Surprising Truth About Violent Video Games* (New York: Simon and Schuster, 2008, 90–94). A recent Kaiser Family Foundation report, *Generation M2*, January 2010 (at www.kff.org/entmedia/upload/8010.pdf), found that: "Over half (56 percent) of all 8- to 18-year-olds say they have played *GTA*, including 25 percent of 8- to 10-year-olds, 60 percent of 11- to 14-year-olds, and 72 percent of 15- to 18-year-olds. *GTA* is especially popular among boys, with 70 percent of all 8- to 18-year-old boys saying they've played it, including 38 percent of 8- to 10-year-old boys, 74 percent of 11- to 14-year-old boys, and 85 percent of 15- to 18-year-old boys" (at 26).

It is fairly easy for underage players to get their hands on mature-rated games. WikiHow even provides a convenient how-to guide, "How to Buy M Rated Games," which can be found at www.wikihow.com/Buy-M-Rated-Games. A recent study shows that retailers are becoming better at not selling industry-rated mature games to underage shoppers, though some retailers continue to do a poor job. See, AJ Glasser, "Study: K-Mart, Sears Fail to Enforce ESRB Ratings," *Gamepro.com*, October 26, 2010 (www.gamepro.com/article/news/217066/study-k-mart-sears-fail-to-enforce-esrb-ratings/).

16. Quoted in Matt Richtel, "Thou Shalt Not Kill, Except in a Popular Video Game at Church," *The New York Times*, October 7, 2007 (www.nytimes.com/2007/10/07/us/07halo.html).

17. A large number of the most popular video games over the last couple of decades have been violent ones, such as *Halo, Counter Strike, Street Fighter, God of War, Grand Theft Auto*, and *Resident Evil*. See www.buzzle.com/articles/most-popular-video-games.html. The same holds true on a year-by-year basis. In 2010, for example, violent games were among the most popular according to MobyGames.com's list of best games of 2010: www.mobygames.com/stats/top_games/k,by_year/listType,1/p,-1/ssid,2010/.

18. The information in this paragraph is based upon David Kushner, "The Neopets Addiction," *Wired Magazine*, December 2005, 13 (www.wired.com/wired/archive/13.12/neopets.html). According to Viacom's website, Neopets currently has around 50 million members and over 5 billion page views per month; over 200 million virtual pets have been created over the life of the site, and it is now delivered in eleven languages. See www.viacom.com/ourbrands/medianetworks/mtvnetworks/Pages/neopets.aspx; see, for further analysis of Neopets, http://biz.yahoo.com/ic/114/114314.html. For more information on Neopets, see "Neopets Case Analysis," at www.criticallythought.com/tag/industry-valuation/.

19. For in-depth analysis of the manipulative casino-style tactics used at virtual pet sites, such as Club Penguin and Webkinz, and also at kids' websites more generally, see Warren Buckleitner, *Like Taking Candy from a Baby: How Young Children Interact with Online Environments* (Yonkers, NY: Consumer Reports WebWatch, 2008) (found at www.consumerwebwatch.org/pdfs/kidsonline.pdf). For discussions of Club Penguin and Webkinz in particular, see pages 21–25, 39–40, and 55–56 of the report. Overall, in relation to pet sites, the report states that: "Web sites frequently tantalize children, presenting enticing options and even threats that their online creations will become inaccessible

unless a purchase is made. Some sites show attractive options that invite a click, but lead to a registration form instead. Some sell a child's prior experience—a room they've built for a virtual pet, for instance—back to them, using statement such as, 'If you cancel your membership, then your belongings will go into storage and will be automatically retrieved when you re-subscribe'" (at 14).

20. Ibid. and www.clubpenguin.com.

21. Ibid. and www.neopets.com.

22. Complaint from "faizaan" on August 8, 2008 at 12:20 p.m. at the online forum, http://mybiggestcomplaint.com/webkinz-and-the-issues-we-face/878/.

23. Kushner, "The Neopets Addiction."

24. Interview with Kristian Segerstrale.

25. Warren Dunlop, "Grand Theft Auto IV Review: It's Like the Video Game Version of Heroin," Gamingexcellence.com, May 2, 2008 (www.gamingexcellence.com/ps3/games/857/review.shtml).

26. Arik Hesseldahl, "Apple: Soon to be a Mobile Gaming Force," *Bloomberg Businessweek*, November 4, 2008 (www.businessweek.com/technology/content/nov2008/tc2008113_963033.htm).

27. Steve Tilley, " 'Civilization V' Highly Addictive," *Toronto Sun*, October 5, 2010 (www.torontosun.com/entertainment/videogames/2010/10/01/15546896.html).

28. The statement was made by Ken Kavanagh, president of Clicktoy, about the company's new game, *The Meadow*. It is quoted in Marke Andrews, "Video Game Entrepreneurs Aim for Young, Online Eyeballs," *Vancouver Sun*, November 13, 2009.

29. Jamie Cannon, "Addiction—Design Success or Failure?" December 16, 2007 (posted at http://jmecannon.wordpress.com/2007/12/16/addition-design-success-or-failure/). For lists of "most addictive video games," see: Lee Andrew Henderson, "Ten Most Addictive Video Games of All-Time," *Associatedcontent.com* (Yahoo), October 12, 2007 (www.associatedcontent.com/article/408004/ten_most_addictive_video_games_of_alltime.html?cat=19); Shubhankar Parijat, "10 Most Addictive Games This Generation," *Gamingbolt.com*, November 10, 2010 (http://gamingbolt.com/10-most-addictive-games-this-generation).

30. These statements can be found at Viacom's website. The full text is as follows: "AddictingGames is a wild, unpredictable space for simple-game junkies to gorge themselves on games, and find great fodder to share with friends. Users drive the experiences, having a big influence over programming and even creating games themselves. With a huge collection of addictive, simple, impulsive, popular games, players always have a game to check out. And because new selections are added to AddictingGames.com every weekday, our audience has access to the latest games to fuel their addiction" (www.viacom.com/ourbrands/medianetworks/mtvnetworks/pages/addictinggames.aspx).

31. Interview with Douglas Gentile.

32. See John Hopson, "Behavioral Game Design," April 27, 2001 (www.gamasutra.com/view/feature/3085/behavioral_game_design.php). Another game designer, Jonathon Blow, criticizes the Hopson-inspired behaviorist strategies used by most game designers as unethical: See an account of Blow's views in Jason Hill, "Ethical Dilemmas," *Sydney Morning Herald*, September 20, 2007 (www.smh.com.au/news/articles/ethical-dilemmas/2007/09/19/1189881577195.html). For another interesting take on the subject of gaming addiction, with some interesting examples, see David Wong, "5 creepy ways video games are trying to get you addicted," March 8, 2010 (www.cracked.com/article_18461_5-creepy-ways-video-games-are-trying-to-get-you-addicted.html).

33. Hopson, "Behavioral Game Design."

34. Ibid.

35. Ibid.

36. Ibid.

37. Ibid.

38. The addictive pull of gaming has only been strengthened by improvements in games' graphic and audio quality and realism, speedier downloads, and all-the-time-everywhere availability through mobile devices. Indeed, availability is a key factor in all forms of addiction, according to Douglas Gentile. "If there isn't a gambling casino anywhere near you, you're not going to get addicted to it," he stated in an interview. With games "more available and ubiquitous on every screen that we have around us," he says, compulsive playing is likely to continue to grow. Indeed, transforming gaming into a ubiquitous pres-

ence, an obsession and "addiction" for everyone, and especially for kids, has been the gaming industry's stated goal for the last decade. The idea, executed with much fanfare and success, has been to expand markets beyond small reserves of hardcore gamers into the entertainment mainstream—to "sell to more people [rather than] sell more and more to less [sic] people," as Nintendo executive Cammie Dunaway is reported to have described it (see Brian Crescente, "Nintendo: Wii Gamers Are Hardcore Gamers," *Kotaku*, May 21, 2008; http://kotaku.com/#!5010227/nintendo-wii-gamers-are-hardcore-gamers?comment=5815234:5815234).

Marketers are now moving their advertising dollars from television to online sites, including gaming sites (see Yankee Group, "US Online Advertising Market to Reach $50B in 2011," www.marketingcharts.com/interactive/us-online-advertising-market-to-reach-50b-in-2011-3128/). Advertisers are attracted to gaming by the uniquely powerful opportunities it offers for placing and pitching brands and products, as well as by the rising numbers of players. In a game or virtual world, brands and products can be represented as characters, objects, themes, or places to visit and hang out, creating possibilities for players to interact with them in exciting ways and for long periods of time. Games thus "create engagement with a brand," says Segerstrale in an interview, "not just the kind of interruption advertising that's possible on TV." Or, as one commentator describes the views of Lauren Bigelow of WeeWorld.com, a virtual world for kids: "Bigelow says it's all about giving kids what they want . . . Rather than advertisers pushing ads at them, they accept the brands as part of the fun." See Laurie Sullivan, "Will Virtual Worlds Collide with Real Life in 2009," *MediaPost News*, January 6, 2009 (www.mediapost.com/publications/?fa=Articles.showArticle&art_aid=97746).

39. Interview with Kristian Segerstrale.
40. Ibid.
41. Ibid.
42. http://www.zynga.com/games/mafia-wars.php.
43. See warning at www.facebook.com/MafiaWarsFans?sk=info. As well, buried in Zynga's "terms of service" is a prohibition on children under the age of

thirteen playing *Mafia Wars* and other Zynga games. See www.zynga.com/about/terms-of-service.php.

44. See www.facebook.com/group.php?gid=354359800714.

45. As quoted in Ryan Kim, "Selling to Denizens of the Virtual Worlds," *San Francisco Chronicle*, November 2, 2009, DC-1 (www.sfgate.com/cgi-bin/article.cgi?f=/c/a/2009/11/02/BUKC1ACTTHE.DTL).

   Pet Society currently sells 90 million virtual goods a day, which adds up to 32.85 billion a year, according to Playfish co-founder Sebastian de Galleux, who is now a vice president at EA Interactive (see Ben Parr, " 'Pet Society' Sells 90 Million Virtual Goods Per Day," December 8, 2010 (http://mashable.com/2010/12/08/pet-society-sells-90-million-virtual-goods-per-day/#). According to one recent analysis, social gaming is the wave of the not-too-distant-future in gaming, and virtual goods sales will become a major source of revenue (as is already the case in Asia). See Lolapps, "Social Gaming and the Next Five Years," *Marketwire.com*, March 23, 2010 (www.marketwire.com/press-release/Social-Gaming-and-the-Next-Five-Years-1198078.htm). An in-depth analysis of the "stickiness" of social games can be found at Eric von Coellen, "How Big Social Games Maintain Their Sticky Factors," November 4, 2009 (www.insidesocialgames.com/2009/11/04/how-big-social-games-maintain-their-sticky-factors/). As another analysis states, the stickiness of social games and applications lies with their connection to users' social status and their need to be recognized—two factors of acute importance for tweens and teens: "The stickiest content for consumers is that which delivers social status, enabling them to appear smarter, more connected, more successful, etc with their friends. 'Game-Based Marketing' is premised on the notion that an effective loyalty and reward system in the 21st century is based on social status: Facebook, Twitter and rewards that emphasize users' individual desires to be recognized" (see Amada Batista, "Game-based Marketing Author Shares Insights on Scoring Loyalty Points with Funware," June 3, 2010, www.retailtouchpoints.com/retail-crm/508-game-based-marketing-author-shares-insights-on-scoring-loyalty-points-with-funware.html#).

46. This statement was reported to have been made by Internet Gaming Gate (IGG) co-founder Kevin Xu at the 2009 Virtual Goods Summit in San Fran-

cisco (see Michael Arrington, "Scamville: The Social Gaming Ecosystem from Hell," October 31, 2009, http://techcrunch.com/2009/10/31/scamville-the-social-gaming-ecosystem-of-hell/#).

47. Interview with Kristian Segerstrale. For information on PlayFish sale, see Eric Schonfeld, "Not Playing Around: EA Buys Playfish for $300 Million, Plus $100 Million Earnout," November 9, 2009 (http://techcrunch.com/2009/11/09/not-playing-around-electronic-arts-buys-playfish-for-275-million/).

48. http://www.facebook.com/friendsforsale. The 1 million users per day figure is cited in Dean Takahashi, "Serious Business Looks for Life Beyond Friends For Sale!," November 30, 2009, http://venturebeat.com/2009/11/30/serious-business-looks-for-life-beyond-friends-for-sale/#. There are currently 5 million active monthly users of the site, according to Leigh Alexander, "Zynga buys Friends for Sale Creator Serious Business," February 11, 2010, www.gamasutra.com/view/news/27197/Zynga_Buys_Friends_For_Sale_Creator_Serious_Business.php. The following questions and answers from the "basic information" section at www.facebook.com/friendsforsale provide some insight into the nature of the game:

> Q: How can I make myself worth more money? A: Every time someone buys you as a pet your value increases, earning you more money in the "Value" category. The more people buy you, the higher your value!
> Q: How do I earn cash on Friends For Sale? A: When you buy a pet and then later sell that pet you make a profit. When you buy a pet their value increases. When you sell them, the sale price is their increased value. The more pets you buy and sell the more money you make. Simple! You can also earn money by clicking on Bonus Money at the top of your profile and exploring the offers and bonus shopping options.
> Q: A total stranger just bought me. What do I do? A: You should feel honored when someone buys you! When people buy you, your value goes up and when you buy people and then sell them you make money, too. The more you play, the more money you make!

49. Interview with Kristian Segerstrale.
50. www.honestybox.com.

51. See, www.facebook.com/honestybox#!/honestybox?v=info.

52. From a videotaped presentation by Peguine, which can be found at www
     .viddler.com/explore/allfacebook/videos/4/. While the overall number of
     users is 8 million, according to the site, the number of monthly active users on
     March 13, 2011, also according to the site, was 249,015. As one independent
     "how-to" web entry on *Honesty Box* explains, harassing other people is key to
     what the site is about. "Drama on the Internet is slightly less interesting than
     drama in real life. But that shouldn't stop you from harassing people! Here are
     some demonstrations. It's short, it's simple, it's offensive. Perfect! "I've got shit
     to say but I refuse to say it to your face." [Response]: "I know it's you. I know
     what you're doing and it needs to stop" (see Sam Weber, "Proper technique for
     Facebook's 'Honesty Box'," September 7, 2010, http://gadgets.gunaxin.com/
     proper-technique-for-facebooks-honesty-box/69574#.

53. See http://apps.facebook.com/honesty/feature.php. Virtual goods, such as
     HB points, and the various virtual goods at sites such as *Pet Society, Mafia
     Wars*, and *Friends for Sale*, are becoming a monetizing miracle for social net-
     works and the companies that offer them. In Asia virtual goods sales already
     top $7 billion annually. Comparable figures in Europe and North America
     are lower, but that will soon change, according to Kristen Segerstrale in an
     interview.

54. Fifty-five percent of twelve-to-seventeen-year-olds in the United States were
     on Facebook in October 2009, up from 28 percent a year earlier (see Katie
     Hafner, "To Deal with Obsession, Some Defriend Facebook," *New York
     Times*, December 20, 2009 (www.nytimes.com/2009/12/21/technology/
     internet/21facebook.html). A helpful graphic representation of Facebook
     demographics can be found here: http://cdn.mashable.com/wp-content/
     uploads/2010/07/Facebooks-500-million-infographics.jpg.

55. Television, with its distant characters and stories, unrelated to kids' lives and
     untouched by their interventions, is having trouble competing and is mov-
     ing toward integration with social media. "Television is—I don't know what
     the opposite of 'heyday' is, but it's a long way down the scale from 'hey,'"
     according to Ogilvy and Mather ad executive Janet Kestin. "This [2009] is
     the tipping point year where you will really see a great deal of creativity going

elsewhere. Everything's changing so fast" (quoted in "Digital Media Creativity Dominates Cannes," *Globe and Mail*, July 3, 2009). And it keeps changing. Kids are moving from television to social media, and marketers are moving with them. The following account is from a 2008 Securities and Exchange Commission filing by the internet company GoFish (at 56): "We believe that the 6–17 year old demographic is relatively underserved by the current Internet content and website market. The 6–17 year old demographic market tends to be on the cusp of the most recent online trends, including gaming, virtual worlds and social networking. . . . There are 31.5 million 6- to 17-year-old Internet users per month in the United States. We believe that advertisers must reach this demographic online as this is where they spend most of their time compared to other media" (www.sec.gov/Archives/edgar/data/1349274/000114420408056383/v128090_s-la.htm).

56. Though some prisons adopted certain of its features, such as the Illinois State Penitentiary in Stateville, Illinois, built in 1925.

57. Michel Foucault, *Discipline and Punish: The Birth of the Prison* (New York: Pantheon Books, 1977).

58. Facebook press release, November 6, 2007 (www.facebook.com/press/releases.php?p=9176).

59. Bob Garfield, "Widgets Are Made for Marketing, So Why Aren't More Advertisers Using Them?" *Advertising Age*, December 01, 2008 (http://adage.com/article?article_id=132778).

60. Other examples of viral marketing can be found in the following sources: Dan Zerella, "Examples of Viral Marketing Campaigns," October 12, 2007 (http://danzarella.com/examples-of-viral-marketing-campaigns.html#); Curtis Silver, "Organized Chaos: Viral Marketing, Meet Social Media," *Wired*, October 29, 2009 (www.wired.com/epicenter/2009/10/organized-chaos-2/#); James Grainger, "47 Outrageous Viral Marketing Examples over the Last Decade," June 28, 2009 (www.ignitesocialmedia.com/social-media-examples/viral-marketing-examples/#). Many companies create their own branded virtual worlds, games, and social networks where every experience for users revolves around the brand and its allies. Examples of such sites aimed at children and teens can be found in Buckleitner, *Like Taking Candy from a Baby*.

61. The central idea of the Panopticon metaphor—that marketing is most powerful when least visible—is not limited to social media, but extends to other media as well. Marketers and marketing disappear for example, in guerilla and buzz marketing campaigns where actors pretending to be just regular folks rather than marketing operatives use and talk about products (see discussion in Bakan, *The Corporation*, 132–34); or in movies and television shows that feature products, and build story lines, vignettes, and dialogue around them; or when ads and images of products appear in games and become part of the game play. Through these (and other) techniques the boundaries between marketing and content and life are blurred, or disappear altogether, and marketers and their campaigns effectively become both invisible and omnipresent.

62. David Rowan, "Six Tech Trends to Expect in 2011," *Wired*, January 11, 2011 (www.wired.co.uk/news/archive/2011-01/11/david-rowan-predictions-2011); William M. Bulkeley, "Social TV: Relying on Relationships to Rebuild TV Audiences," *Technology Review*, MIT publishers, May/June 2010 (www.technologyreview.com/communications/25084/?a=f). Typical of recent trends is the alliance formed between CNN and Facebook, which grants the CNN access to users' Facebook data. In a similar vein, MySpace, Intel, and Yahoo recently formed a partnership to turn TV sets into platforms for accessing social networks.

63. Others have connected the idea of the Panopticon to surveillance in social networking and on the internet more generally. See, for example, Tom Brignall III, "The New Panopticon: The Internet Viewed as a Structure of Social Control," *Theory and Science* 3 (2002) (http://theoryandscience.icaap.org/content/vol003.001/brignall.html).

64. Advertising Research Foundation press release, "ARF Using Social Media to Transform Research," January 7, 2009 (www.thearf.org/assets/pr-2009-01-07).

65. A useful discussion of "social graphs" can be found at Jeff Korhan, "What Your Business Needs to Know about Social Graphs," January 7, 2011 (www.socialmediaexaminer.com/what-your-business-needs-to-know-about-social-graphs/#).

66. JPMorgan, "Nothing But Net: 2008 Internet Investment Guide," January 2, 2008, 27 (https://mm.jpmorgan.com/stp/t/c.do?i=2082C248&u=a_p*d_170762.pdf*h_-3ohpnmv).

67. The full list of Mindset's personality traits can be found at www.mindset-media.com/agencies/. For the original announcement of the new psychographic service, see www.mindsetmedia.com/about/press/releases/pdf/Mindset%20Media%20and%2024.7_042808.pdf.

68. See Scobleizer, "Zuckerberg: Facebook's 'Intense' Year," January 29, 2009 (http://scobleizer.com/2009/01/29/zuckerberg-facebooks-intense-year/).

69. "Buzzlogic Whitepaper: Tales from the Trenches—4 Tips for Driving Social Media," November 2007 (www.scribd.com/doc/36241186/BUZZLOGIC-4-Tips-for-Driving-Social-Media).

CHAPTER THREE: THE NEW CURRICULUM OF CHILDHOOD

1. Recall that "making fun of adults," as Lindstrom described it, is at the heart of tween and teen humor; and "mastery," which includes the desire to be independent and hence to rebel against parents, is a core teen emotion (see chapter 2). Importantly, it is not only natural but also healthy and essential to maturation for teens to rebel and seek autonomy. The problem lies not with these tendencies, but with the calculated manipulation and exploitation of the tendencies by marketers, as I explore more fully below. Neufeld and Mate, *Hold Onto Your Kids*, speak of "healthy rebellion" as "the genuine quest for autonomy: the maturing, individuating child [who] resists coercion whatever the source may be." That is distinct from "counterwill," which involves seeking "freedom from one person [parents], only to succumb to the influence and will of another" (98). My concern here is that the rebelliousness stoked by marketers is more about counterwill than healthy rebellion. It is, as I shall argue, aimed at severing ties to parents and family in order to create bonds to brands, products, endorsed celebrities and athletes, websites, TV shows and networks, mascots, characters, bands and musicians, and anything else that will help marketers and corporations generate profit. The "another," in other words, in terms of Neufeld and Mate's phrase "the will of another," is the coterie of marketers who target children. A limitation of Neufeld and Mates' is that they confine that "another" strictly to peers

and thus do not adequately account for the way marketers cultivate attachments to their creations, and also redefine peer attachments in ways that are mediated through those creations. With that correction, I believe Neufeld and Mate's analysis is powerful. I agree, for example, with their observation that mistaking "counterwill" for "healthy rebellion" is common in parenting today. "Many parents idealize teenage rebellion," they say, when counterwill is what is really happening. Viewing the latter as "healthy teenage self-assertion, they may prematurely back away from the parenting role." This is not a good idea, they say. "While it's wise to give adolescents the space to be themselves, to allow them to learn from their own mistakes, many parents just throw in the towel. Out of sheer exasperation or frustration, usually unannounced and without ceremony, they retire nonetheless. To back off prematurely, however, is unwittingly to abandon a child who still needs us dearly but doesn't know that she does" (98).

2. The article appeared in the *Journal of Retailing*, Summer 1969, 15–22. McNeal recounts the background to his writing it in James U. McNeal, *Kids as Customers: A Handbook of Marketing to Children* (New York: Lexington Books, 1992), 4–5.

3. See Newton N. Minow and Craig L. LaMay, *Abandoned in the Wasteland: Children, Television and the First Amendment* (New York: Hill and Wang, 1995), 95–102.

4. Ibid., 102–104.

5. Ibid. Modest reregulation occurred in 1990 when the Children's Television Act was passed by Congress. The act limited commercials in children's programming to ten minutes an hour on weekends and 12.5 minutes an hour on weekdays. It also required broadcasters to provide educational programming. In 1996, three hours per week was set as a minimum amount of educational and informational content that broadcasters had to provide to children. These measures have served poorly to achieve their objectives (for critiques, see Children Now, "Emotionally/Insufficient?: An Analysis of the Availability and Educational Quality of Children's Programming," 2008, available at www.childrennow.org/; and Lisa de Moraes, "PBS President Paula Kerger says Commercial Networks Neglect Young Viewers," *Washington Post*, January 14,

2010). As children move from television to digital media, the impact of the act will be further diminished.

6. Quoted at Online Encyclopedia, "Laybourne, Geraldine—Overview, Personal Life, Career Details, Social and Economic Impact," available at http://encyclopedia.jrank.org/articles/pages/6299/Laybourne-Geraldine.html.

7. The almost cultish parent-excluding devotion solicited from kids by the network was well captured by a popular company slogan in the 1990s—"I believe in Nick, 'cause it believes in me."

8. For a more detailed description of these initiatives, and the rise of Nickelodeon more generally, see Kathryn C. Montgomery, *Generation Digital: Politics, Commerce, and Childhood in the Age of the Internet* (Cambridge, MA: MIT Press, 2007), 16–17.

9. Nickelodeon currently dominates the kid-web and recently made a comeback in television as well after being challenged for kid's TV supremacy by Disney through the mid-2000s. "We're winning in a way we haven't been in a very long time," stated company president Cyma Zarghami in October, 2010, speaking of the escalating numbers of viewers among its target demographics. Viacom CEO, Phillipe Dauman, recently stated of Nickelodeon that it is "perhaps our most important asset." See Brooks Barnes, "Making Sure Nickelodeon Hangs with Cool Kids," *New York Times*, October 30, 2010 (www.nytimes.com/2010/10/31/business/media/31nick.html).

10. Neufeld and Mate, *Hold On to Your Kids*, 10.

11. Ibid., 11.

12. This account of Brandon Crisp's story is compiled from the following sources: Colin Campbell and Jonathon Gatehouse, "What Happened to Brandon?" *Macleans*, October 30, 2008 (www.macleans.ca/culture/lifestyle/article.jsp?content=20081030_22084_22084&page=1); CTV News, "Witness Spoke with Teen the Day He Went Missing," March 16, 2011 (www.ctv.ca/CTVNews/TopStories/20081021/barrie_teen_081022/); CBC News, "Not Just a Video Game: The Obsessive World of Gaming and Its Young Stars," March 6, 2009 (www.cbc.ca/news/canada/story/2009/03/03/f-video-gaming.html).

13. Andy Patrizio, "Did Game Play a Role in Suicide?" *Wired*, April 3, 2002 (www.wired.com/gaming/gamingreviews/news/2002/04/51490).

14. See, for accounts of these stories: Terri Wells, "Online Gaming Addiction—Myth or Reality?" January 11, 2006 (www.devhardware.com/c/a/Opinions/Online-Gaming-Addiction-Myth-or-Reality/). See also Christopher S. Stewart, "Obsessed with the Internet: A Tale from China," *Wired Magazine*, January 13, 2010 (www.wired.com/magazine/2010/01/ff_internetaddiction/); and Choe Sang-Hun, "South Korea Expands Aid for Internet Addiction," *New York Times*, May 28, 2010 (www.nytimes.com/2010/05/29/world/asia/29game.html).

15. Quoted in Patrick Wintour, "Facebook and Bebo Risk 'Infantilising' the Human Mind," Guardian online, February 24, 2009 (www.guardian.co.uk/uk/2009/feb/24/social-networking-site-changing-childrens-brains).

16. C.H. Ko et al., "Brain Activities Associated with Gaming Urge of Online Gaming Addiction," *Journal of Psychiatric Research* 43 (2009): 739–47.

17. The American Psychiatric Association recently stated that it will continue to monitor the accumulating evidence on "internet addiction," though it currently has no plans to include it as an official disorder in its *Diagnostic and Statistical Manual*. See www.dsm5.org/ProposedRevisions/Pages/Substance-RelatedDisorders.aspx. Similarly the American Medical Association does not view "internet addiction" as a medical disorder. See American Medical Association, "Report of the Council on Science and Public Health: Emotional and Behavioral Effects, Including Addictive Potential, of Videogames," January 2007 (www.ama-assn.org/ama1/pub/upload/mm/467/csaph12a07.doc).

    A fascinating and far-reaching analysis of addiction in modern society, and one which I believe has considerable purchase with respect to internet and gaming "addiction," can be found in Bruce Alexander, *The Globalization of Addiction: A Study in the Poverty of Spirit* (New York: Oxford University Press, 2010). Alexander argues that individualism, competition, and the focus on products and consumption in free market societies combine to sever the bonds among people that sustain social and spiritual life, thus compelling them toward substitutes (whether in the form of substances or practices) to fill the void. Addiction is the result. The power of Alexander's analysis lies in his notion that addiction is a product of social and political forces, rather than simply being a matter of individual pathology.

Game designer and head of the corporate-supported Institute for the Future, Jane McGonigal, argues in her *Reality Is Broken: Why Games Make Us Better and How They Can Change the World* (New York: Penguin Press, 2011) that gaming—especially in its social forms—promotes cooperation among individuals and thus can provide a means for solving world problems. While in theory it may be true that games can be designed to promote such positive effects (much as social networks can be used to promote political organizing around issues and hence democratic movement—see conclusion for further discussion of this point), that is unlikely to happen when the design, marketing, and distribution of games is in the hands of for-profit corporations. Television was once heralded as a powerful democratizing force. No doubt the technology has that potential. But it was (and is) naïve to expect private for-profit broadcasters to use television in aid of democratic ends (see Minow and LaMay, *Abandoned in the Wasteland*, who discuss both television's democratic promise and its abject failure to realize that promise). Online gaming is similar to television in this way. In theory it may be possible to design games that serve positive social ends (McGonigal claims she has done this). In practice, however, the delivery of gaming is governed by the imperative to create profit—and that imperative inevitably leads to the kinds of manipulative strategies, violent and sexual contents, and addictive ambitions that, as I document in the previous chapter, define gaming today.

18. Interview with Douglas Gentile.

19. Ibid.

20. Greenfield is similarly concerned that the "constant reassurance—that you are listened to, recognized, and important" provided by social networks may erode our abilities to engage in "far more perilous" real life interaction which "require a sensitivity to voice tone, body language and perhaps even pheromones." Quoted in Wintour, "Facebook and Bebo." Even more ominously, Sheryl Turkle reports, as "we move from technologies that tether us to people [such as e-mail and phones] to those that . . . tether us to the web sites and avatars that represent people [such as Facebook and *Pet Society*]" we (and our kids) become "more closely coupled" to the machines and gadgets themselves,

and risk dehumanizing our relationships to others. See Turkle, "Always-on/Always-on-you: The Tethered Self," *Handbook of Mobile Communication Studies*, James E. Katz, ed. (Cambridge, MA: MIT Press, 2008) (http://web.mit.edu/sturkle/www/pdfsforstwebpage/ST_Always%20On.pdf).

21. Dr. Phil Speaking on *Larry King Live* on April 16, 2007: See http://transcripts.cnn.com/TRANSCRIPTS/0704/16/lkl.01.html.

22. As quoted in Matt Richtel, "Though Shalt Not Kill, Except in a Popular Video Game at Church," *New York Times*, October 7, 2007 (www.nytimes.com/2007/10/07/us/07halo.html).

23. The overall message of the scientific literature, according to Dr. Gentile, is that children's exposure to media violence can, depending on how much violence, what kind, and individual differences among children, "increase the likelihood of aggressive and violent behavior in both immediate and long-term contexts." The conclusions of the American Medical Association are similar. According to a recent review of the literature by that organization: "Results from multiple small studies suggest an association between exposure to or playing violent games and negative actions such as aggressive thoughts and aggressive behaviors. In their 2001 metaanalysis, Anderson and Bushman quantified the effects of exposure to violent video games on five variables (aggressive behavior, aggressive cognition, prosocial behavior [ie, cooperation], aggressive affect, and physiological arousal) and found that short-term exposure to video game violence was significantly associated with temporary increases in aggression among all subjects. In 2004, using an improved methodology, Anderson again concluded that a positive association exists between exposure to video game violence and aggression. In a literature review, Gentile and Stone confirm an association between violent video games and aggressive behaviors, while noting that given the limitations of current studies, it is difficult to definitively conclude a causal effect on long-term aggressive behaviors. Additional studies by other researchers have found that exposure to video game violence may promote increased aggressive behaviors and decreased prosocial behaviors in social interactions. Not surprisingly, the video game industry's own research has concluded that there is no causal relationship between video game violence and aggression. Additionally, researchers such as VanEenwyk and Bensley and

Griffith found that the most compelling evidence for a positive association between video game violence and aggressive behavior in youth occurs in children younger than age ten, but when older children were evaluated, the evidence was not as strong. Research by Huesman and Taylor supports short-term increases in aggression but cannot document a demonstrable long-term effect. In spite of the research on the relationship of video game exposure and aggressive behavior, there is little evidence of a substantial link between exposure to violent interactive video games and serious violence or crime. *However, the preponderance of research from both sides of the debate does support, without controversy, the conclusion that exposure to violent media increases aggressive cognition, affect, and behavior, and decreases prosocial behavior in the short term.* There also appears to be agreement that definitive long-term studies are lacking" (emphasis added). American Medical Association, "Report of the Council on Science and Public Health."

For further discussion of media violence and childhood, among other things, see Nancy Carlsson-Paige, *Taking Back Childhood: Helping Your Kids Thrive in a Fast-Paced, Media-Saturated, Violence-Filled World* (New York: Hudson Street Press, 2008).

24. Interview with Douglas Gentile. As is true in other areas (pharmaceuticals and environmental toxins, for example, as we shall see in subsequent chapters) industry is very adept at producing its own science and putting forward its own scientific "experts" to counter claims of independent researchers that are adverse to industry interests.

25. Carlsson-Paige, *Taking Back Childhood*, 1. Another important work that deals with media violence and many of the other themes looked at in this and the previous chapter is Susan Linn, *Consuming Kids: The Hostile Takeover of Childhood* (New York: The New Press, 2004).

26. Shirley R. Steinberg and Joe. L. Kincheloe, "Introduction," in Shirley R. Steinberg and Joe. L. Kincheloe, eds., *Kinderculture: The Corporate Construction of Childhood* (Cambridge, MA: Westview, 2004), 1, at 11.

27. American Psychological Association, *Report of the APA Task Force on the Sexualization of Girls* (Washington DC: American Psychological Association, 2007), or at http://www.apa.org/pi/women/programs/girls/report-summary.pdf.

28. Ibid.

29. American Psychological Association, *Report*.

30. Diane E. Levin, "So Sexy, So Soon: The Sexualization of Childhood," in *Childhood Lost: How American Culture Is Failing Our Kids*, S. Olfman, ed. (Westport, CT: Praeger Press, 2005).

31. Tim Kasser, *The High Price of Materialism* (Cambridge, MA: MIT Press, 2002).

32. See interview with Tim Kasser at http://transitionculture.org/2010/02/25/tim-kasser-on-consumerism-psychology-transition-and-resilience-part-one/.

    See also Benjamin Barber, *Consumed: How Markets Corrupt Children, Infantilize Children, and Swallow Citizens Whole* (New York: W.W. Norton, 2007), 128–144. Barber speaks of "civic schizophrenia" as the product of consumerist culture. "We are encouraged to withdraw from our public selves into the sanctuary of 'I want'," he says (130). He provides examples of "how this civic schizophrenia . . . can defeat the commonweal" (136): our consumer desire for big cars trumps our citizen concerns about the environment and oil dependence; our consumer desire for good health care for our family trumps our citizen desire for access to quality health care for everyone. One of Barber's examples of a hypothetical conflicted citizen is particularly germane. "As a career marketing executive for, say, Nickelodeon, I work to open kids up to the influencers I can buy and control—celebrities, athletes, or friends and peers I can pay to be 'buzz' leaders—and avoid the gatekeepers I can't buy (moms and teachers, for example). But as a citizen I want to live in a country that protects kids from exploitation and marketing, and I want the influencers to be tough gatekeepers like pastors and teachers and imams and moms—the very people I am trying to freeze out of the influence circle in my work as a marketer" (136–37). See also, Bakan, *The Corporation* 50–56 for discussion of such conflict among business excutives.

33. Federal Trade Commission, "Perspectives on Marketing, Self-Regulation and Childhood Obesity: A Report of the Federal Trade Commission and the Department of Health and Human Services," (Washington DC.: Federal Trade Commission, 2006), 1 (www.ftc.gov/os/2006/05/PerspectivesOnMarketing-Self-Regulation&Chil dhoodObesityFTCandHHSReportonJointWorkshop.

pdf). It is important to recognize that obesity and related diseases are not the only kinds of ill effects linked to consumption of "junk food." Behavioral, emotional, and cognitive problems also appear to be linked: See Carol Simontacchi, *The Crazy Makers: How the Food Industry is Destroying Our Brains and Harming Our Children* (New York: The Penguin Group, 2007).

34. Food and Drug Administration, "News Release: Candy and Fruit Flavored Cigarettes Now Illegal in United States; Step Is First Under New Tobacco Law," September 22, 2009 (www.fda.gov/NewsEvents/Newsroom/PressAnnouncements/2009/ucm183211.htm).

35. *Marketing alcoholic beverages to youth*: One widely used technique is to produce flavored drinks likely to appeal to children: see Derrick Z. Jackson, "Targeting Youth to Start Drinking," *Boston Globe*, Nov 20, 2010 (www .boston.com/bostonglobe/editorial_opinion/oped/articles/2010/11/20/ targeting_youth_to_start_drinking/); Wency Leung, "The Latest Boozy Gimmick: Alcoholic Whipped Cream," *Globe and Mail*, November 30, 2010 (www.theglobeandmail.com/life/the-hot-button/the-latest-boozy-gimmick-alcoholic-whipped-cream/article1819042/); Susan Linn, *Consuming Kids*, 157–174.

   Marketing caffeine drinks to youth: Purveyors of coffee and caffeinated energy drinks target youth despite the growing body of research linking caffeine consumption to serious health consequences in children and teens: see Noni MacDonald, MD MSc; Matthew Stanbrook, MD, PhD; and Paul C. Hébert, MD, MHSc, " 'Caffeinating' Children and Youth," *Canadian Medical Association Journal*, October 19, 2010, 182 (www.cmaj.ca/cgi/content/full/182 /15/1597?maxtoshow=&hits=10&RESULTFORMAT=&fulltext=caffeine+ drinks&searchid=1&FIRSTINDEX=0&sortspec=date&resourcetype=HW CIT); Jane E. Brody, "Scientists See Dangers in Energy Drinks, *New York Times*, January 31, 2011 (www.nytimes.com/2011/02/01/health/01brody .html); Reuters, "Energy Drinks Putting Kids, Young Adults at Risk?" *Toronto Sun*, February 14, 2011 (www.torontosun.com/life/healthandfitness/ 2011/02/14/17270566.html).

   Marketing gambling to youth: Children and adolescents are routinely exposed to advertising for online gambling sites, a likely factor in the rise of gambling among youth: see Sally Monaghan, Jeffrey Derevensky, and Alyssa Sklar, "Impact of Gambling Advertisements and Marketing on Children and Adolescents: Policy Recommendations to Minimise Harm," *Journal of Gambling Issues* 22 (2008): 252–75 (available at http://pdfcast.org/pdf/impact-of-gambling-advertisements-and-marketing-on-children-and-adolescents-policy-recommendations-t).

36. For a thorough and up-to-date analysis of marketing and commercialism in schools, with numerous examples and illustrations, see Alex Molnar, Faith Boninger, Gary Wilkinson, Joseph Fogarty, and Sean Geary, *Effectively Embedded: Schools and the Machinery of Modern Marketing—The Thirteenth Annual Report on Schoolhouse Commercializing Trends: 2009–2010* (Boulder, CO: National Education Policy Center, 2010; http://nepc.colorado.edu/files/CommTrends2010.pdf).

37. There are no precise numbers describing marketing's growing presence in schools, but one indicator, according to the authors of a recent report, is the amount of media attention devoted to the topic of marketing in schools. Between 1990 and 2006, the number of media stories increased 656 percent, from 991 in 1990 to 6,506 in 2006: Alex Molnar, William Koski and Faith Boninger, *Legislation Policy Brief: Policy and Statutory Responses to Advertising and Marketing in Schools* (Arizona State University: Commercialism in Education Research Unit, 2010; www.eric.ed.gov/PDFS/ED509764.pdf).

38. Ibid., 7–9.

39. Ibid., 5. Adding insult to injury, schools derive little overall benefit from their willingness to serve as platforms for advertising and marketing campaigns. The large majority of schools that participate with food companies in advertising activities make no money at all from such participation, and the rest make very little. School beverage contracts, for example, raise, on average, a paltry $18 per student per year. For programs such as Channel One that demand student time and attention be devoted to some commercial presentation, the cost of lost instructional time generally exceeds the benefits provided by commercial partners. Ibid., at 6.

40. This paragraph is based on a discussion of *Ginsberg v. New York* in Minow and LaMay, *Abandoned in the Wasteland*, 124.

41. *Irwin Toy v. Quebec (Attorney General)*, [1989] 1 S.C.R. 927.

42. As quoted in Minow and LaMay, *Abandoned*, 136.

43. James U. McNeal, *On Becoming a Consumer: Development of Consumer Behavior Patterns in Childhood* (New York: Elsevier, 2007), 378–89.

44. Interview with James McNeal.

45. McNeal, *On Becoming a Consumer*, 382.

46. Ibid., 389.

47. Interview with James McNeal.

48. See Susan Krashinsky, "Advertising Whiz Bogusky Takes His Leave," *Globe and Mail*, July 2, 2010 (www.theglobeandmail.com/report-on-business/industry-news/marketing/advertising-whiz-bogusky-takes-his-leave/article1626783/).

49. Bogusky suggests, partly in jest, that the best way to make this happen is to create an award for *not* advertising to children: "So my hope for the 2011 Cannes Crystal award is some brilliant agency works with their client to pull all the advertising to children and takes home the Cannes Crystal Gran Prix Lion in the inaugural year. And that would be the end of that. Because as soon as you can win an award for it, we ad folk are all over [it]." From Bogusky's blog, "The First Cannes Lion for Not Advertising At All." (http://alexbogusky. posterous.com/the-first-cannes-lion-for-not-advertising-at).

50. Interview with Martin Lindstrom.

51. Lindstrom, *Brandchild*, 196.

52. Federal Communications Commission, "Notice of Inquiry: Empowering Parents and Protecting Children in an Evolving Media Landscape," MB Docket No. 09-194, October 23, 2009 (http://raunfoss.fcc.gov/edocs_public/attach-match/FCC-09-94A1.pdf).

53. As quoted in White House Task Force on Childhood Obesity, "Report to the President: Solving the Problem of Childhood Obesity Within a Generation," May 2010, 18 (available at www.letsmove.gov/sites/letsmove.gov/files/TaskForce_on_Childhood_Obesity_May2010_FullReport.pdf). The Report recommends that these guidelines be made more available to parents, and that they should be the basis of standards in early childhood settings. For older children, the report states, media exposure should be treated as "a special occasion activity rather than a daily event."

54.   Victoria J. Rideout, Ulla G. Foehr, and Donald F. Roberts, *Generation M2: Media in the lives of 8- to 18-year-olds* (Menlo Park, CA: Kaiser Family Foundation, 2010).

55.   Here are the exact figures from the *Generation M2* report, ibid.: Tweens and teens (those between the ages of eight and eighteen years old) spend an average of 7 hours and 38 minutes a day using entertainment media (compared to 6:21 in 2004), and because they often are using more than one medium at a time, they actually consume 10 hours and 45 minutes worth of media content during that time (compared to 8:33 in 2004). Another 1 hour and 35 minutes a day is spent sending and receiving texts on cell phones, and 33 minutes talking on cell phones. Over the last five years, time spent watching traditional TV declined by 25 minutes a day, though total television watching—including watching on the internet, cell phones, and iPods—increased 38 minutes from 3:51 to 4:29. Time spent with all other media (except print and movies) increased as well—by 47 minutes a day for music/audio, 27 minutes for computers, 24 minutes for video games. Mobile technologies, such as cell phones and iPods, are driving these increases. In 2004, 39 percent of tweens and teens owned cell phones; today that number is 66 percent. Ownership of iPods and other MP3 players increased from 18 percent to 76 percent. On average today, tweens and teens spend 49 minutes each day watching TV, playing games, and listening to music on their cell phones.

56.   The Federal Communications Commission has taken various measures to help parents control their children's media use. It has, since 2000, for example, required television manufacturers to include "V-chips"—built-in devices that allow parents to block programming in accordance with broadcast industry ratings—on TV sets thirteen inches and larger. In its aptly titled inquiry, "Empowering Parents and Protecting Children in an Evolving Media Landscape," launched in the fall of 2009 (see note 52), the agency undertook to examine, among other things, ways to make such blocking technologies more effective and widely used, not only for television but for the internet and mobile devices as well. More generally, it undertook to examine how to make media literacy and education programs for parents, teachers, and children "a key way to enable children to enjoy the benefits of electronic media while

avoiding the potential harms." The FCC is interested in means to encourage parents to use existing resources (such as the Center for Media Literacy's MediaLit Kit and the FTC's Admongo.org), and also in the questions of what types of new resources should be created, and what roles schools do and might play in teaching media literacy.

Currently, the actual operation of parental controls is limited and ineffective. Awareness among parents of the V-chip, for example, is estimated at somewhere between 49 and 69 percent of parents. The FCC is examining whether a single rating system across all content and media would make parental controls more effective, and whether it is feasible (the commission was mandated to carry out this investigation by the Child Safe Viewing Act of 2008).

57. Nancy Carlsson-Paige, *Taking Back Childhood.*

58. The ban applies to meals with more than 600 calories, 640 milligrams of sodium, and 35 percent of calories derived from fat—which includes most such meals.

59. CTV Calgary, "McDonald's Slams San Francisco Happy Meal Ban," November 4, 2010 (http://calgary.ctv.ca/servlet/an/local/CTVNews/20101104/happy-meals-101103/20101104/?hub=CalgaryHome).

60. Rachel Gordon, "Mayor Gavin Newsom Vetoes Fast-Food Toy Ban," *San Francisco Chronicle*, November 13, 2010 (http://articles.sfgate.com/2010-11-13/bay-area/24830064_1_toy-ban-toys-in-kids-meals-vetoes).

61. CTV Calgary, "McDonald's Slams."

62. Jennifer L. Harris et al., *Fast Food F.A.C.T.S: Evaluating Fast Food Nutrition and Marketing to Youth* (New Haven, CT: Rudd Center for Food Policy and Obesity, 2010).

63. It is therefore no surprise that in a typical week nearly half of the seven out of ten parents who take a child to McDonald's report their child has asked to go (Harris et al., ibid). This is an example of what has come to be known as the "nag factor"—children's nagging of their parents to get them to buy things, or take them to fast food restaurants, or amusement parks, and so on—which marketers strategically manipulate. I explore the nature and origins of the nag factor in Bakan, *The Corporation*, 118–22.

64. Currently, there are few regulations aimed at protecting children in the contexts of media and marketing. In terms of federal law, there is little beyond

the Children's Television Act of 1990 (see note 5), and a federal prohibition on indecent broadcasts between 6 a.m. and 10 p.m.

65. John Eggerton, "Rockefeller Will Push for Government Oversight of Violent Media Content," July 22, 2009 (www.broadcastingcable.com/article/316151-Rockefeller_Will_Push_For_Government_Oversight_Of_Violent_Media_Content.php).

66. FCC, "Empowering Parents and Protecting Children in an Evolving Media Landscape," 10.

67. Ibid., 2.

68. Federal Trade Commission, "Comments of the Federal Trade Commission: Empowering Parents and Protecting Children in an Evolving Media Landscape," MB Docket No. 09-194, 5 (www.ftc.gov/os/2010/04/V100006empowerparents.pdf). Even the hard-hitting Rudd Center report on food and beverage marketing (Harris et al., *Fast Food F.A.C.T.S.*) failed to raise regulation as a possible solution to the problems it revealed. Instead, it proposed, companies should, on their own initiative, "take some responsibility for the influence of marketing on the products that young people and their parents choose to purchase" and "take action to ensure that young people visit fast food restaurants less often and, when they do visit, that they consume less of the primarily calorie-dense nutrient-poor foods typically purchased" (136–7). It is ironic that the First Amendment (or at least people's understanding of it) effectively forecloses any serious discussion of regulation. As Newton Minow, attorney and former FCC chief, and his co-author LaMay remark in *Abandoned in the Wasteland*, "it would surely come as a surprise to those who wrote the First Amendment to see that Americans now cite it not to begin discussion of the public interest, but as a reason to *close* it."

69. As quoted in Andrew Martin, "Critics Say Watchdog Group Too Soft on Advertising Industry," *Chicago Tribune*, October 31, 2005.

70. Campaign for a Commercial Free Childhood, "Transformers Marketing: Still Not Transformed," Press Release, June 25, 2009 (www.commercialfreechildhood.org/pressreleases/pg1309.html).

71. Better Business Bureau, "Children's Food and Beverage Advertising Initiative" (available at www.bbb.org/us/children-food-beverage-advertising-initiative/).

72. The CFBAI's "core principles statement" can be found at www.bbb.org/us/
storage/0/Shared%20Documents/Enhanced%20Core%20Principles%20
Third%20Edition%20-%20Letterhead.pdf.

73. Dale Kunkel et al., *The Impact of Industry Self-Regulation on the Nutritional
Quality of Foods Advertised on Television to Children* (Oakland, CA: Children
Now, 2009), 35 (www.childrennow.org/uploads/documents/adstudy_2009.
pdf).

74. The department recommends such food only be consumed on "special occasions, such as your birthday." Quoted in ibid.

75. The department recommends such food only to be consumed "sometimes, at
most several times a week." Quoted in ibid. The number of ads for healthy
foods (representing 1 percent of all food ads) has not increased since the self-
regulation initiative began, according to the Children Now report, ibid., 73.
Over the same period, however, the proportion of ads using licensed characters from popular television shows and movies nearly doubled (from 8.8 percent to 15.2 percent). Using licensed characters has proved to be a particularly
effective technique for stoking desire among young children.

76. As well, in just one year, 2008 to 2009, the company increased its total spending on media by 12.5 percent (from $800 million to $900 million). Harris et
al., *Fast Food F.A.C.T.S*, ix-x and 131–132.

77. Ibid.

78. As quoted in Kunkel et al., *Industry Self-Regulation*.

79. Ibid., 35.

80. White House Task Force on Childhood Obesity, *Report to the President*, 32–
33.

81. Douglas Gentile, Muniba Saleem and Craig Anderson, "Public Policy and
the Effects of Media Violence on Children," *Social Issues and Policy Review*
1 (2007): 15–61, 51; Hans-Bredow-Institut for Media Research, "Final Report: Study on Co-Regulation Measures in the Media Sector," University of
Hamburg, 2006 (http://ec.europa.eu/avpolicy/docs/library/studies/coregul/
final_rep_en.pdf).

82. Minow and LaMay, *Abandoned in the Wasteland*, 131.

83. As quoted and discussed, ibid.

84. Gentile et al., "Public Policy," 45–46.

85. Ibid.

86. Ibid.

87. Tor Thorsen, "Schwarzenegger Signs Game-Restriction Bill," October 7, 2005 (www.gamespot.com/news/6135332.html).

88. The case *Schwarzenegger v. EMA* was, at the time of writing, still pending a decision by the United States Supreme Court. The official title of California's law is: 2005 California Civil Code Sections 1746–1746.5 Title 1.2a. Violent Video Games (can be found at www.justia.com/codes/california/2005/civ/1746-1746.5.htm).

CHAPTER FOUR: PRESCRIPTIONS FOR PROFIT

1. The account of Kyle Warren's story is based on Duff Wilson, "Child's Ordeal Shows Risks of Psychosis Drugs for Young," *New York Times*, September 1, 2010 (http://www.nytimes.com/2010/09/02/business/02kids.html?_r=2&pagewanted=print). Statistics on ADHD are from Rick Mayes, Catherine Bagwell, and Jennifer Erkulwater, *Medicating Children: ADHD and Pediatric Mental Health* (Cambridge, MA: Harvard University Press, 2009), 1. In the last decade alone, psychotropic drug use among two- to five-year-olds doubled: M. Olfson, et al., "Trends in antipsychotic drug use by very young, privately insured children," *Journal of the American Academy of Child and Adolescent Psychiatry* (49) 2010: 3–6 (http://www.ncbi.nlm.nih.gov/pubmed/20215922). See also a report by the Food and Drug Administration's Center for Drug Evaluation and Research, 2009, on children's use of anti-psychotic drugs (www.fda.gov/downloads/AdvisoryCommittees/Committees MeetingMaterials/PediatricAdvisoryCommittee/UCM191615.pdf). For more discussion of increased psychotropic drug use among youth, see Elizabeth Roberts, *Should You Medicate Your Child's Mind? A Child Psychiatrist Makes Sense of Whether to Give Kids Psychiatric Medication* (New York: Marlowe and Company, 2006). Poor children, such as Kyle Warren, tend to be medicated for mental problems significantly more frequently than their middle-class counterparts, and gen-

erally for less severe conditions. See Duff Wilson, "Poor Children Likelier to Get Antipsychotics," *New York Times*, December 12, 2009 (www.nytimes.com/2009/12/12/health/12medicaid.html). Children in foster care are also more heavily medicated than those who are not. See Laurel K. Leslie, et al., *Multi-State Study in Psychotropic Drug Medication Oversight in Foster Care* (Boston, MA: Tufts Clinical and Translational Science Institute, 2010), 1.

One reason for increasing use of psychotropic drugs, in addition to those discussed below, is the fact drug therapies are cheaper for health care insurers and management organizations, both public and private, than other forms of therapy—such as talk therapy—which can be time consuming and therefore expensive. See Mayes et al., *Medicating Children*; and also Gardiner Harris, "Talk Doesn't Pay, So Psychiatry Turns Instead to Drug Therapy," *New York Times*, March 5, 2011 (www.nytimes.com/2011/03/06/health/policy/06doctors.html?ref=americanpsychiatricassn).

2. Patricia Wen, "Father Guilty in Girl's Fatal Drugging," *Boston Globe*, March 27, 2010 (www.boston.com/yourtown/framingham/articles/2010/03/27/father__guilty_in__girls_fatal_drugging/).

3. The account of Rebecca Riley's tragedy is compiled from the following sources: WCVB-TV, "Parents Charged in Death of Daughter, 4" February 6, 2007 (http://www.thebostonchannel.com/news/10943835/detail.html); WCVB-TV, "Parents Charged in Daughters Overdose Death," February 6, 2007 (www.thebostonchannel.com/news/10940941/detail.html); Benedict Carey, "Debate over Children and Psychiatric Drugs," *New York Times*, February 15, 2007 (www.nytimes.com/2007/02/15/us/15bipolar.html); CBS News *60 Minutes*, "What Killed Rebecca Riley," September 30, 2007 (http://www.cbsnews.com/stories/2007/09/28/60minutes/main3308525.shtml).

4. Interview with Lawrence Diller. See also Diller, "But Don't Call It Science," in Sharma Olfman (ed.), *Bipolar Children* (Westport, CT: Prager Publishers, 2007), 28; and Diller, "Misguided Standards of Care," *Boston Globe*, June 19, 2007 (www.boston.com/yourlife/health/other/articles/2007/06/19/misguided_standards_of_care/). I personally heard Diller state his allegations about Biederman at a conference at Point Park University, Pittsburgh, PA on June 8 and 9, 2007. See also Scott Allen, "Backlash on Bipolar Diagnoses

in Children: MGH Psychiatrist's Work Stirs Debate," *Boston Globe*, June 17, 2007 (www.boston.com/yourlife/health/diseases/articles/2007/06/17/back-lash_on_bipolar_diagnoses_in_children/).

5. Interview with Lawrence Diller.

6. Benedict Carey, "Bipolar Illness Soars as a Diagnosis for the Young," *New York Times*, September 4, 2007 (www.nytimes.com/2007/09/04/health/04psych.html?_r=2&oref=slogin&ref=health&pagewanted=print).

7. See, for example, Mary Ann McDonnell, *Is Your Child Bipolar: The Definitive Resource on How to Identify, Treat, and Thrive with a Bipolar Child* (New York: Bantam Dell, 2008), 17.

8. The critique is increasingly prominent. See, for some examples, Diller, "Misguided Standards"; Roberts, *Should You Medicate*; Mayes et al., *Medicating Children*; Carey, "Debate"; Gardiner Harris, "Use of Antipsychotics in Children Is Criticized," *New York Times*, November 19, 2008 (www.nytimes.com/2008/11/19/health/policy/19fda.html). With respect to nutrition, as just one factor that can contribute to mental problems among children, see: Carol Simontacchi, *The Crazy Makers: How the Food Industry Is Destroying Our Brains and Harming Our Children* (New York: The Penguin Group, 2007).

9. Dr. Bessel van der Kolk, professor of psychiatry at Boston University, quoted in Carey, "Debate." Dietary issues have been linked to various behavioral and emotional problems. See, for example, Rita Bakan et al. "Dietary Zinc Intake of Vegetarian and Nonvegetarian Patients with Anorexia Nervosa," *Int'l J of Eating Disorders*, 13(2): 229–33 (1993).

10. See sources cited above, note 4.

11. Letter from Joseph Biederman to Clark Hoyt, Reader Representative, *New York Times*, December 1, 2008. This letter was circulated, along with letters to the editor of the *New York Times*, to members of the psychiatric community by Biederman's assistant. It listed, among other things, a litany of complaints with Gardner Harris's stories in that paper. It is on file with the author.

12. Jocelyn Kaiser, "Private Money, Public Disclosure," *Science* 325 (July 3, 2009) 30; Gardiner Harris and Benedict Carey, "Researchers Fail to Reveal Full Drug Pay," *New York Times*, June 8, 2008 (www.nytimes.com/2008/06/08/us/08conflict.html).

13. As quoted in Gardiner Harris, "Drug Marker Told Studies Would Aid It," *New York Times*, March 19, 2009 (www.nytimes.com/2009/03/20/us/20psych. html?ref=gardinerharris). See also Gardiner Harris, "3 Researchers at Harvard Are Named in Subpoena," *New York Times*, March 27, 2009 (www.nytimes. com/2009/03/28/health/policy/28subpoena.html?ref=gardinerharris).

14. Except where indicated, the following account of Robert Spitzer is based upon Alix Spiegel, "The Dictionary of Disorder: How One Man Revolutionized Psychiatry," *New Yorker*, January 3, 2005 (www.newyorker.com/ archive/2005/01/03/050103fa_fact).

15. Mayes et al., *Medicating Children*, 74.

16. He would later say of his own experiences with psychoanalytic therapy, which he used as a young psychiatrist to treat patients in the early 1960s: "I was always unsure that I was being helpful, and I was uncomfortable with not knowing what to do with [patients'] messiness. I don't think I was uncomfortable listening and empathizing—I just didn't know what the hell to do." Quoted in Spiegel, "Dictionary of Disorder."

17. Mayes et al., *Medicating Children*, 73–74.

18. In addition to Spiegel, "Dictionary of Disorder," see Mayes et al.'s discussion of Spitzer in *Medicating Children*, 74–75.

19. Mayes et al., *Medicating Children*, 79–84 and 87–95.

20. Ibid., 77–78.

21. The official name of the Bayh-Dole Act is: Bayh-Dole University and Small Business Patent Procedure Act of 1980, 35 U.S.C. s. 200 (2006). It can be found at www.law.cornell.edu/uscode/35/usc_sup_01_35_10_II_20_18.html.

22. Ibid.

23. Thomas J. Siepmann, "The Global Exportation of the U.S. Bayh-Dole Act," *University of Dayton Law Review* 30 (2004): 209 at 214 (www.ipeg.eu/blog/ wp-content/uploads/Thomas-Siepmann-THE-GLOBAL-EXPORTATION-OF-THE-U.S.-BAYHDOLE-Act.pdf).

24. For accounts of this culture, and the Bayh-Dole Act's role in creating it, see Kaiser, "Private Money," note 12, at 29; Clifton Leaf, "The Law of Unintended Consequences," *Fortune*, September 19, 2005 (http://money.cnn.com/maga-zines/fortune/fortune_archive/2005/09/19/8272884/index.htm); Annette

Lin et al., "The Bayh-Dole Act and Promoting the Transfer of Technology of Publicly Funded-Research," Universities Allied for Essential Medicines, 2008 (http://essentialmedicine.org/sites/default/files/archive/uaem-white-paper-on-indian-bd-act.pdf); Shannon Brownlee, "Doctors Without Borders: Why You Can't Trust Medical Journals Anymore," *Washington Monthly*, April 2004 (www.washingtonmonthly.com/features/2004/0404.brownlee.html).

25. Epidemiologist and current Occupational Safety and Health Administration head David Michaels is concerned that science, as a whole, is too closely connected to commerce. His following comment has particular relevance for medical and pharmaceutical science. "The separation between academic science and the business world is disappearing," he says. "As a result, the model of the disinterested scientist searching for truth with no financial interest in the outcome . . . is no longer held up as an ideal, not even by scientists. This concept is no longer operative. Laughable is more like it. Instead, the most valued scientist is the one whose work contributes most to the bottom line." See David Michaels, *Doubt Is Their Product: How Industry's Assault on Science Threatens Your Health* (New York: Oxford University Press, 2008), 244.

26. This account of Caitlin McIntosh's story is drawn from the testimony of her father, Glen McIntosh, before the FDA panel. Transcripts of that testimony can be found at: www.ablechild.org/fda_hearing_testimonies%202-2-04.htm and also at www.ritalindeath.com/FDA-Hearing-Testimonies.htm.

27. Jim Rosack, "FDA Warns of Suicide Risk with Paroxetime," *Psychiatric News* 38 (2003): 1 (http://pn.psychiatryonline.org/content/38/14/1.2.full). For a recent study confirming the link between SSRIs and suicidality in youth, see: Corrado Barbui et al., "Selective Serotonin Reuptake Inhibitors and Risk of Suicide: A Systematic Review of Observational Studies," *Canadian Medical Association Journal* 180 (2009): 291.

28. Lawrence Diller, "Keeping Doctors in the Dark," *The Washington Post*, March 24, 2004, p. A21.

29. Rosack, "FDA Warns"; Diller, "Keeping Doctors."

30. Erick Turner et al., "Selective Publication of Antidepressant Trials and Its Influence on Apparent Efficacy," *New England Journal of Medicine* 358 (2008): 252–60.

31. Beezy Marsh and Tim Utton, "Shamed Glaxo's U-Turn on 'Suicide' Drug," *Daily Mail Online*, June 15, 2004 (http://www.dailymail.co.uk/health/article -306667/Shamed-Glaxos-u-turn-suicide-drug.html).

32. Interview with David Healy.

33. Ibid.

34. This account of events at the meeting is based upon: David Healy, "Academic Stalking and Brand Fascism" (unpublished article on file with author). Relevant correspondence between Healy and various officials and faculty at the University of Toronto can be found at www.healyprozac.com/AcademicFree dom/default.htm; see also, Sarah Boseley, "Bitter Pill," *The Guardian*, May 7, 2001 (www.guardian.co.uk/education/2001/may/07/medicalscience.higher education); and Boseley, "Bitter Pill (2)," *The Guardian*, May 21, 2002 (www. guardian.co.uk/education/2002/may/21/internationaleducationnews.men-talhealth/print).

   For more on Healy's tangles with pharmaceutical companies, see David Healy, "Contra Pfizer," *Ethical Human Psychology and Psychiatry*, 7 (2005) (www.healyprozac.com/AcademicStalking/Post%204%20-%20Contra%20 Pfizer.pdf).

35. Brownlee, "Doctors Without Borders."

36. Gardiner Harris, "Top Psychiatrist Didn't Report Drug Makers' Pay," *New York Times* October 3, 2008 (www.nytimes.com/2008/10/04/health/ policy/04drug.html). Healy implies Nemeroff may have played a role in University of Toronto's retraction of his offer. See Healy, "Academic Stalking."

37. Interview with David Healy

38. Ibid.

39. Ibid.

40. David Healy and Dinah Cattell, "Interface Between Authorship, Industry and Science in the Domain of Therapeutics," *The British Journal of Psychiatry* 183 (2003): 22–27.

41. Ghostwriting is a "systematic manipulation and abuse of scholarly publishing [that should] make you very concerned and angry if you depend on your doctor or health care provider getting unbiased information from medical journals," according to an editorial in one journal, *PLoS Medicine*. The latter

journal, along with just about every other major medical journal, has, according to a recent survey, unknowingly published scores of ghostwritten articles. The survey is reported in The PLoS Medicine Editors, "Ghostwriting: The Dirty Little Secret of Medical Publishing That Just Got Bigger," 2009: 6, 1. See also Natasha Singer, "Medical Papers by Ghostwriters Pushed Therapy," *New York Times*, August 4, 2009 (www.nytimes.com/2009/08/05/health/research/05ghost.html); Duff Wilson and Natasha Singer, "Ghostwriting Is Called Rife in Medical Journals," *New York Times*, September 11, 2009 (www.nytimes.com/2009/09/11/business/11ghost.html).

An entire ghost journal, the *Australasian Journal of Bone and Joint Medicine*, published by a leading medical publisher, Elsevier, went undetected by the medical community for years. The journal looked genuine, but the six issues published between 2000 and 2005 were little more than advertisements for Merck products, "a series of sponsored article compilation publications, on behalf of pharmaceutical clients [Merck], that were made to look like journals and lacked proper disclosures," as one Elsevier official described the issues in an apology for his company's wrongdoings (after the fake journals had been revealed in a lawsuit, filed on another matter, against Merck). See "Statement from Michael Hansen, CEO of Elsevier's Health Sciences Division, Regarding Australia Based Sponsored Journal Practices Between 2000 And 2005," Philadelphia, PA, May 2009, at www.elsevier.com/wps/find/authored_newsitem.cws_home/companynews05_01203. See also Stuart Laidlaw, "Drug 'Reports' Found to Be Faked," *Toronto Star*, June 22, 2009 (www.thestar.com/living/article/654423).

42.   Shirley S. Wang, "Eli Lilly's Payments to Doctors Revealed," *Wall Street Journal Health Blog*, July 31, 2009 (http://blogs.wsj.com/health/2009/07/31/eli-lillys-payments-to-doctors-revealed/). For a discussion of the kinds of venues drug companies use to host "education" events, see Ray Moynihan, *Sex, Lies, and Pharmaceuticals: How Drug Companies Plan to Profit from Female Sexual Dysfunction* (Vancouver, B.C.: Greystone Books, 2010), chapter 4 (entitled "Educating Doctors with Ski Trips and Strip Clubs").

43.   Dr. Eric Campbell quoted in Bob LaMendola and Fernando Quintero, "Eli Lilly Paid Area Doctors to Discuss Drugs," *Orlando Sentinel*, September 23, 2009

(http://articles.orlandosentinel.com/2009-09-23/news/0909220159_1_lilly-payments-to-doctors-companies-pay-doctors).

44. As quoted in Brownlee, "Doctors Without Borders."

45. Ibid.

46. Richard Smith, "Medical Journals Are an Extension of the Marketing Arm of Pharmaceutical Companies," *PLoS Med* 2005: 2, e138 (www.plosmedicine. org/article/info:doi/10.1371/journal.pmed.0020138).

47. G. Schott et al., "The Financing of Drug Trials by Pharmaceutical Companies and Its Consequences," *Deutsches Ärzteblatt International* 107 (2010): 279–85 (www.aerzteblatt.de/int/article.asp?id=74342).

48. This quote and the following account of Clinical Research Organizations are based upon Danielle Egan, "Ghost in the Machine," *BC Business*, August 2009, 35–39 (www.bcbusinessonline.ca/bcb/topstories/2009/08/05/ghost-machine).

49. Ibid.

50. Lisa Cosgrove et al., "Financial Ties Between DSM-IV Panel Members and the Pharmaceutical Industry," *Psychotherapy and Psychosomatics* 75 (2006): 154–160.

51. Allen Frances and Robert Spitzer, "Letter to the APA Board of Trustees," July 6, 2009 (http://www.scribd.com/doc/17172432/Letter-to-APA-Board-of-Trustees-July-7-2009-From-Allen-Frances-and-Robert-Spitzer).

52. Ibid.

53. Allen Frances, "A Warning Sign on the Road to DSM-V: Beware of Its Unintended Consequences," *Psychiatric Times* 26 (2009); see also Gary Greenberg, "Inside the Battle to Define Mental Illness," *Wired Magazine*, December 27, 2010 (http://www.wired.com/magazine/2010/12/ff_dsmv/all/1).

54. Brownlee, "Doctors Without Borders."

CHAPTER FIVE: POM-POMS FOR PILLS

1. Quoted in Stephanie Saul, "Gimme an Rx! Cheerleaders Pep up Drug Sales," *New York Times*, November 28, 2005 (www.nytimes.com/2005/11/28/business/28cheer.html). For a list of professional sports team cheerleaders

who allegedly also work as drug reps, see "Introducing . . . the All-Pharma Cheerleading Squad," January 11, 2007 (www.edrugsearch.com/edsblog/introducing-the-all-pharma-cheerleading-squad/).

2. "Career Opportunities" (http://spiritedsales.com/default.asp?page=careers).

3. "Employers" (http://spiritedsales.com/default.asp?page=placement).

4. Jamie Reidy, *Hard Sell: The Evolution of a Viagra Salesman* (New York: Andrews McMeel Publishing, 2005); Jim Edwards, "Pfizer Sales Reps Discuss Having Sex with Doctors," July 24, 2009 (www.bnet.com/blog/drug-business/pfizer-sales-reps-discuss-having-sex-with-doctors/2256). Having sex with drug sales reps is a key story line in two recent Hollywood movies, *The Little Fockers* and *Love and Other Drugs*.

5. Quoted in Chris Ayers, "The Rise of the Rah-Rah Reps: Cheerleaders Are Being Used to Sell Pharmaceuticals in the US," *The Sunday Times*, January 9, 2006 (www.timesonline.co.uk/tol/life_and_style/health/features/article785873.ece).

6. The following account is based on an interview with Sharim Ahari.

7. Since then he has been seeking something akin to absolution by revealing and criticizing drug company marketing tactics. "The things I did, I realize they were mistakes," he says. "I learned lessons and now try to share my experiences with other people. I don't expect to change the world, but I sure as hell am going to try."

8. McKinnell quote is from Bakan, *The Corporation*, 30.

9. Press Release, "Justice Department Announces Largest Health Care Fraud Settlement in its History," Washington DC: U.S. Department of Justice, September 2, 2009 (www.hhs.gov/news/press/2009pres/09/20090902a.html).

10. The Food and Drug Administration's approval of Zyprexa was limited to the treatment of adult schizophrenia and bipolar disorder.

11. Press Release, "Eli Lilly and Company Agrees to Pay 1.415 Billion to Resolve Allegations of Off-label Promotion of Zyprexa," Washington DC: U.S. Department of Justice, January 15, 2009 (www.justice.gov/opa/pr/2009/January/09-civ-038.html).

12. Eli Lilly and Company, "Lilly Reports Strong Second-Quarter 2010 Results," July 22, 2010 (www.pharmpro.com/News/Feeds/2010/07/pharmaceutical-companies-eli-lilly-lilly-reports-strong-second-quarter-2010-results/).

13. The $50 billion figure is an estimate based upon the fact Zyprexa has been on the market since the mid-1990s, and earned around $4 billion a year over the last few years. Earnings were even higher prior to controversies, beginning in the mid-2000s, about the drug's adverse side effects. The latter point is made by Alex Berenson, "U.S. Wonders if Zyprexa Drug Data Was Accurate," *New York Times*, April 25, 2007 (www.nytimes.com/2007/04/25/business/worldbusiness/25iht-25drug.5431663.html).

14. I discuss in detail the difficulties associated with successfully prosecuting corporations for unlawful activity in Bakan, *The Corporation*, 79–84.

15. Press Release, "Pharmaceutical Manufacturer to Pay $280 million to Settle False Claims Act Case," Washington DC: U.S. Department of Justice, December 20, 2010 (www.scribd.com/doc/45771225/12-20-10-DOJ-Press-Release-Dey-280-Million-Settlement).

16. Associated Press, "New Jersey Firm to Pay Nearly $25 million in Kickbacks Case," *Business Insider*, September 14, 2009 (www.businessinsider.com/nj-drug-firm-to-pay-nearly-25m-in-kickbacks-case-2009-9).

17. Carrie Johnson, "Merck to Pay $650 Million in Medicaid Settlement," *Washington Post*, February 8, 2008 (www.washingtonpost.com/wp-dyn/content/article/2008/02/07/AR2008020701336.html).

18. Linda Loyd, "Cephalon Settles Charges for $425 Million," *Philadelphia Inquirer*, September 30, 2008 (http://articles.philly.com/2008-09-30/business/24991664_1_cephalon-provigil-gabitril).

19. Press Release, "Pfizer Subsidiary Agrees to Plead Guilty to Offering Kickback; Agrees to Pay $19.68 Million Criminal Fine," FBI's Year in Review: Top News Stories of 2007, Federal Bureau of Investigation, 2007, 04/06/07 (www.fbi.gov/news/pressrel/press-releases/fbi2019s-year-in-review-top-news-stories-of-2007).

20. Press Release, "Bristol-Myers Squibb to Pay More Than $515 Million to Resolve Allegations of Illegal Drug Marketing and Pricing," Washington DC: U.S. Department of Justice, September 28, 2007 (www.justice.gov/opa/pr/2007/September/07_civ_782.html).

21. *U.S. v. Purdue Frederick*, U.S.D.C. (Western District of Virginia), Case. No. 1:07CR00029, July 23, 2007.

22. Press Release, "Aventis Pays More Than $190 Million to Settle Drug Pricing Fraud Matters," Washington DC: U.S. Department of Justice, September 10, 2007 (www.justice.gov/opa/pr/2007/September/07_civ_694.html).

23. Karen Gullo and Margaret Cronin Fisk, "InterMune Will Pay $37 Million to Resolve U.S. Probe," October 26, 2006 (www.bloomberg.com/apps/news?pid=newsarchive&sid=aKY6b4_KAB9k&refer=healthcare).

24. Press Release, "Serono to Pay $704 Million for the Illegal Marketing of AIDS Drug," Washington DC: U.S. Department of Justice, October 17, 2005 (www.justice.gov/opa/pr/2005/October/05_civ_545.html).

25. Press Release, "Eli Lilly and Company to Pay U.S. $36 Million Relating to Off-Label Promotion," Washington DC: U.S. Department of Justice, December 21, 2005 (www.justice.gov/opa/pr/2005/December/05_civ_685.html).

26. Press Release, "Pharmaceutical Company, Dey, Inc. to Pay U.S. and Texas $18.5 Million to Settle Allegations of Medicaid Fraud," Washington DC: U.S. Department of Justice, June 11, 2003 (www.justice.gov/opa/pr/2003/June/03_civ_350.htm).

27. Noted in Press Release, "Justice Dept. Civil Fraud Recoveries Total $2.1 Billion for FY 2003; False Claims Act Recoveries Exceed $12 Billion Since 1986," Washington DC: U.S. Department of Justice, November 10, 2003 (http://www.justice.gov/opa/pr/2003/November/03_civ_613.htm).

28. Press Release, "Astrazeneca Pharmaceuticals LP Pleads Guilty to Healthcare Crime; Company Agrees to Pay $355 Million to Settle Charges," Washington DC: U.S. Department of Justice, June 20, 2003 (www.justice.gov/opa/pr/2003/June/03_civ_371.htm).

29. Noted in The Department of Health and Human Services and The Department of Justice Health Care Fraud and Abuse Control Program, *Annual Report For FY 2003*, December, 2004 (http://oig.hhs.gov/publications/docs/hcfac/hcfacreport2003A.htm).

30. "Pfizer to Pay $49 Million in Fraud Case," *New York Times*, October 29, 2002 (www.nytimes.com/2002/10/29/business/pfizer-to-pay-49-million-in-fraud-case.html).

31. Press Release, "Tap Pharmaceuticals Products Inc. and Seven Others Charged

with Health Care Crimes; Company Agrees to Pay $875 Million to Settle Charges," Washington DC: U.S. Department of Justice, October 3, 2001 (www.justice.gov/opa/pr/2001/October/513civ.htm).

32. Michelle Meadows, "Company Gets a Guilty Reading in Glucose Monitor Case," *FDA Consumer*, March 21, 2001 (http://findarticles.com/p/articles/mi_m1370/is_2_35/ai_73064355/).

33. Press Release, "F. Hoffman-La Roche and BASF Agree to Pay Record Criminal Fines for Participating in International Vitamin Cartel," Washington DC: U.S. Department of Justice, May 20, 1999 (www.justice.gov/atr/public/press_releases/1999/2450.htm).

34. Mary Ann Tawasha, "Hoeschst to Pay $36 Million Fine for Price-Fixing," May 5, 1999 (www.icis.com/Articles/1999/05/05/79381/hoechst-to-pay-36m-fine-for-price-fixing.html).

35. "Genentech Agrees to Pay $50 Million to End Probe," *Baltimore Sun*, April 19, 1999 (http://articles.baltimoresun.com/1999-04-19/business/9904170059 _1_genentech-biotechnology-dwarfism).

36. Press Release, "U.S. Pharmaceutical Giant Agrees to Pay Criminal Fines for Participating in Two International Food Additive Conspiracies," Washington DC: U.S. Department of Justice, July 19, 2009 (www.justice.gov/opa/pr/1999/July/311at.htm).

37. U.S. Department of Justice, *Health Care Fraud Report*, 1997 (www.justice.gov/archive/dag/pubdoc/health97.htm).

38. Reuters, "Bayer Unit to Plead Guilty to Price-Fixing," *The Los Angeles Times*, January 30, 1997 (http://articles.latimes.com/1997-01-30/business/fi-23491_1_prices-fix-guilty).

39. National Drug Intelligence Center, "Oxycontin Diversion and Abuse," Washington DC: U.S. Department of Justice, January, 2001 (www.justice.gov/ndic/pubs/651/).

40. John M. Annese, "On Staten Island, Prescription Drug Abuse A Teen Epidemic," *Staten Island Real-Time News*," March 08, 2009, www.silive.com/news/index.ssf/2009/03/on_staten_island_rx_drug_abuse.html.

41. Ibid.

42. Press Release, "McDonnell, Brownlee Announce Maker of OxyContin Pleads

Guilty to Felony Misbranding," Richmond Virginia, Office of the Attorney General, Virginia, May 10, 2007 (www.oag.state.va.us/press_releases/newsarchive/051007_oxycontin.html).

43. *U.S. v. Purdue Frederick.*

44. Elizabeth Roberts, *Should You Medicate Your Child's Mind?: A Child Psychiatrist Makes Sense of Whether or Not to Give Kids Meds* (Cambridge, MA: Da Capo Press, 2005).

45. FDA Amendments Act of 2007, Public Law 110-85, Title VIII. Fines of up to $10,000 a day can be levied for breach of the registration requirements (the act can be found at http://frwebgate.access.gpo.gov/cgi-bin/getdoc.cgi?dbname=110_cong_public_laws&docid=f:pub1085.110).

46. Roger Collier, "Clinical Trial Registries Becoming a Reality, But Long-Term Effects Remain Uncertain," *Canadian Medical Association Journal* 180(2009): 1007–1008 (www.cmaj.ca/cgi/reprint/180/10/1007.pdf).

47. Thomas O. McGarity and Wendy E. Wagner, *Bending Science: How Special Interests Corrupt Public Health Research* (Cambridge, MA: Harvard University Press 2008), 249–50.

48. There is no evidence of proactive, or indeed any, enforcement of the 2007 law; and no information or analysis on how many and what types of trials are *not* being registered and thus still hidden from public view. Though the law appears to have had some effect in increasing the raw numbers of trials being registered—between 2007 and 2009, for example, the number of weekly clinical trial registrations jumped from 250 to as many as 350—it is unclear to what extent, if any, suppression of negative results has been limited, and whether decision making in the daily practices of physicians has been affected. See Collier, "Clinical Trial Registries."

49. McGarity and Wagner, *Bending Science*, 233–39.

50. These are all proposed reforms in ibid., 236–38.

51. David Michaels, *Doubt Is Their Product: How Industry's Assault on Science Threatens Your Health* (New York: Oxford University Press, 2008), 256.

52. Ibid., 246–47. Michaels points out that similar recommendations have been made by Senator Gaylord Nelson in 1971, and Sheldon Krimsky in his book *Science in the Private Interest.*

53. Cal Woodward, "New US Law Applies 'Sunshine' to Physician Payments and Gifts from Drug, Device Industries," *Canadian Medical Association Journal* 182(2010): E467–E468 (www.cmaj.ca/cgi/reprint/182/10/E467.pdf).

54. As quoted in Colleen O'Connor, "Drug Firms' Payments to Doctors Raise Ethical Concerns for Many," *The Denver Post*, October 31, 2010 (www.denverpost.com/news/ci_16480972).

55. Obama's new health bill requires a system be in place by 2013. See Kevin B. O'Reilly, "Health Reform Mandates Disclosure of Industry Gifts," April 5, 2010 (www.ama-assn.org/amednews/2010/04/05/prsa0405.htm). Major drug companies already disclose some of this information, which can be found at the investigative news website ProPublica.org at a page called "Dollars for Docs." At this page, users can obtain information about drug company payments to particular doctors. See http://projects.propublica.org/docdollars/#.

CHAPTER SIX: A DANGEROUS AND UNNATURAL EXPERIMENT

1. Maude Barlow and Elizabeth May, *Frederick Street: Life and Death on Canada's Love Canal* (Toronto: Harper Collins Canada, 2000); see also, Timothy W. Lambert and Stephanie Lane, "Lead, Arsenic, and Polycyclic Aromatic Hydrocarbons in Soil and House Dust in the Communities Surrounding the Sydney, Nova Scotia, Tar Ponds," *Environmental Health Perspectives* 112(2004): 35–41.

2. The chronicler was French traveler M. Arthur de Gobineau. The quote is from Barlow and May, *Frederick Street*, 5.

3. Ibid., 119

4. Ibid.

5. Ibid. See also Pierre Band et al., *Mortality Rates Within Sydney, Nova Scotia, by Exposure Areas to Airborne Coke Ovens and Steel Mill Emissions: 1961–1988* (Ottawa, ON: Health Canada, 1999); Daniel Rainham, "Risk Communication and Public Response to Industrial Chemical Contamination in Sydney, Nova Scotia: A Case Study" *Journal of Environmental Health* 65(2002): 25

(available at http://emaychair.dal.ca/documents/Rainham_2002.pdf); Lambert and Lane, "Lead, Arsenic."

6. Barlowe and May, *Frederick Street*, 98.

7. Ibid. 132–35.

8. The 99.8 percent figure is calculated as follows: there are approximately 86,000 industrial chemicals in commercial use; only 200 of these (0.2 percent) have been tested by the U.S. Environmental Protection Agency (EPA) for adverse health and environmental effects. That leaves 99.8 percent of them untested.

9. The current asthma rate among children and youth (0–17 years old) in the United States is 9.6 percent (though higher for certain populations, particularly Black, Puerto Rican, and poor children): See Lara J. Akinbami et al., "Asthma Prevalence, Health Care Use, and Mortality: United States, 2005–2009," *National Health Statistics Report* (2011): 32 (www.cdc.gov/nchs/data/nhsr/nhsr032.pdf). In 1980 the asthma rate for five- to fourteen-year-olds was 4.3 percent and for 0 to 4-year-olds 2.2 percent: See National Institutes of Health, "Data Fact Sheet: Asthma Statistics, U.S. Department of Health and Human Services," January 1999 (www.nhlbi.nih.gov/health/prof/lung/asthma/asthstat.pdf).

10. According to the National Cancer Institute, rates increased from 3.3 to 4.6 cases per 100,000 children (an increase of 42 percent) between 1975 and 1985 and have leveled off since then; rates for all invasive cancers in children jumped from 11.5 cases per 100,000 to 14.8 between 1975 and 2004, representing a 29 percent increase: See National Cancer Institute, "Fact Sheet: Childhood Cancers" (www.cancer.gov/cancertopics/factsheet/Sites-Types/childhood).

11. That is since the mid-1990s. See Safer Chemicals, Healthy Families Coalition, "The Health Case for Reforming the Toxic Substances Control Act," January 2010, 8 (http://healthreport.saferchemicals.org/PDFs/The_Health_Case_for_Reforming_the_Toxic_Substances_Control_Act.pdf). Around 30 percent of this increase is due to diagnostic changes and inclusion of milder cases, according to estimates (ibid). In California 3,000 new cases of autism were reported in 2006, compared to 205 in 1990. The authors of the study

attribute the dramatic increase to environmental factors though acknowledge that part of it may be due to other factors, including broader diagnostic categories. See Marla Cone, "Autism: It's the Environment, Not Just Doctors Diagnosing More Disease," *SFGate.com*, July 16, 2009 (http://articles.sfgate.com/2009-07-16/living/17118511_1_autism-autistic-children-household-products).

12. This increase is since the mid-1990s. See Safer Chemicals, Healthy Families Coalition, "The Health Case," 12.

13. Ibid. The most common such abnormality is hypospadias, a birth defect involving the opening of the penis being displaced to somewhere on the shaft.

14. Ibid., 8.

15. Trasande is quoted in Jordana Miller, "Tests Reveal High Chemical Levels in Kids' Bodies," *CNNTech*, October 22, 2007 (http://articles.cnn.com/2007-10-22/tech/body.burden_1_flame-retardants-chemicals-bodies?_s=PM:TECH). Over the last three decades the quantity of industrial chemicals produced or imported by U.S. companies has increased from 200 billion to 15 trillion pounds, a seventy-five-fold jump. And chemicals commonly used in household and consumer goods (such as bisphenol A, phthalates, PBDEs, and PFCs, all recently deemed by the EPA to be "chemicals of concern" because they interfere with hormonal processes) have led the pack. Production of bisphenol A jumped almost 150-fold—from 7,260 tons to over 1 million tons—for example; and phthalates, which did not even exist in commerce until the 1970s, are now produced at a rate of 8 billion kilograms a year. See Philip Shabecoff and Alice Shabecoff, *Poisoned Profits: The Toxic Assault on Our Children* (New York: Random House, 2008), 44. See also the following of the U.S. EPA's "Existing Chemical Action Plans": "Bisphenol A Action Plan," March 29, 2010; "Phthalates Action Plan," December 30, 2009; "Long-Chain Perfluorinated Chemicals (PFCs) Action Plan," December 30, 2009); "Polybrominated Diphenyl Ethers (PBDEs) Action Plan," December 30, 2009. For summaries and links to the EPA's action plans, see: www.epa.gov/opptintr/existingchemicals/pubs/ecactionpln.html.

Recent biomonitoring data collected as part of wide-ranging government-sponsored study in Canada suggest that our—and our children's—bodies are polluted with numerous industrial chemicals. See Health Canada, "Report on Human Biomonitoring of Environmental Chemicals in Canada: Results of the Canadian Health Measures Survey Cycle 1 (2007–2009)," Ottawa, Canada, 2010 (www.hc-sc.gc.ca/ewh-semt/pubs/contaminants/chms-ecms/index-eng.php).

16. Douglas Fischer, "Bill to Monitor Body Toxins Advances in the Assembly," *The Oakland Tribune*, June 29, 2005 (www.insidebayarea.com/oaklandtribune/localnews/ci_2830506); and Miller, "Tests Reveal Chemical Levels."

17. Interview with Leo Transande. Over the last thirty years or so scientists came to realize that prenatal exposure to chemicals and pollutants, along with prenatal traumas and low birth weight, could have profound impacts on the health of individuals later in life. That idea, only recently considered controversial, is now broadly accepted among scientists. For early awareness of the idea, see Paul Bakan, "NonRight-Handedness and the Continuum of Reproductive Casualty," in Stanley Coren (ed.), *Left-Handedness: Behavioral Implications and Anomalies* (New York: North-Holland, 1990) 33–74. For further pioneering work in the area, see D.J.P.Barker, *Mothers, Babies, and Disease in Later Life* (London: BMJ Publishing Group, 1994). An informative and engaging account of Barker's work can be found in Stephen S. Hall, "Small and Thin: The Controversy Over the Fetal Origins of Adult Health," *New Yorker,* November 19, 2007, 52–57. That article quotes early development expert Richard Schultz as saying: "A few years ago, it [the link between prenatal events and later health] was considered controversial. But it's my sense that it's no longer controversial, and people have moved on. The discussion now is about what are the underlying cellular and molecular mechanisms" (at 57).

18. See Shabecoff and Shabecoff, *Poisoned Profits.*

19. The site for the "fact sheet" is: U.S. Department of Health and Human Services, "Bisphenol A (BPA) Information for Parents" (www.hhs.gov/safety/bpa/).

20. See, for overviews of and examples from the low-dose literature: U.S. EPA, "Bisphenol A Action Plan"; U.S. Food and Drug Administration, "Update on Bisphenol A for Use in Food Contact Applications," U.S. Department of Health and Human Services, 2010 (www.fda.gov/newsevents/publichealthfocus/ucm197739.htm); Theo Colborn, Dianne Dumanoski, and John Peterson

Myers, "Scientific Findings of the Impacts of Endocrine Disrupters at Low Doses" (www.ourstolenfuture.org/newscience/lowdose/lowdoseresults.htm).

21. Colborn et al., ibid.

22. Quoted in Rick Smith and Bruce Lourie, *Slow Death by Rubber Duck: How the Toxic Chemistry of Everyday Life Affects our Health* (Toronto: Alfred A. Knopf Canada, 2009), 237.

23. As explained to me in an interview with children's environmental health expert, Dr. Bruce Lanphear.

24. Ibid.

25. As recounted by Lanphear, ibid., and also in Shabecoff and Shabecoff, *Poisoned Profits*, 97.

26. From a study (Guilliand et al. 2004) cited in Bruce Lanphear, "Origins and Evolution of Children's Environmental Health," in T.J. Goehl, *Essays on the Future of Environmental Health Research: A Tribute to Dr. Kenneth Olden* (Research Triangle Park, NC: Environmental Health Perspectives/National Institute of Environmental Health Sciences, 2005) 28.

27. For a description of this condition which, as earlier noted, has doubled in frequency since phthalates were first introduced into the environment, see note 13, above.

28. Shanna H. Swan, "Environmental Phthalate Exposure in Relation to Reproductive and Other Health Endpoints in Humans," *Environmental Research* 108(2008): 177–84 (http://shswan.com/wp-content/uploads/2010/03/Swan-2008-Environmental-phthalate-exposure-in-relation-to-reproductive-outcomes-and-other-health-endpoints-in-humans.pdf).

29. S. H. Swan et al., "Prenatal Phthalate Exposure and Reduced Masculine Play in Boys," *International Journal of Andrology* 32 (2009): 1–9 (http://shswan.com/wp-content/uploads/2010/02/Swan-2009-Prenatal-phthalate-exposure-and-reduced-masculine-play-in-boys.pdf).

30. Test Results, " 'Green Baby' Recycling Shirt," (www.healthystuff.org/departments/toys/product.details.php?getrecno=15360).

31. Test Results, "Dora the Explorer Activity Tote" (www.healthystuff.org/departments/toys/product.details.php?getrecno=15307).

32. Report, "Chemicals Up Close: Plastic Shoes from All Over The World"

(Stockholm: Swedish Society for Nature Conservation, 2010; www.natur-skyddsforeningen.se/upload/Foreningsdokument/Rapporter/engelska/chem-icals_in_plastic_shoes.pdf).

33. In most jurisdictions the law requires that only *intended* ingredients be listed on labels for personal care products. That means chemicals considered to be by-products rather than intended ingredients—such as formaldehyde and 1,4 dioxane, both known carcinogens—are not listed. As well, laws do not require a breakdown of proprietary concoctions, such as fragrances (the rationale is the need to protect trade secrets), which means chemical ingredients, such as phthalates, which are common in scented products, are not listed. With respect to scents, for example, labels will simply list "parfum," an almost certain indicator that a product contains phthalates.

   Formaldehyde and 1,4 dioxane, though not listed on labels, have been found in numerous children's and baby personal care products, including Johnson's Baby Shampoo, Sesame Street Bubble Bath, Grins and Giggles Milk and Honey Baby Wash, and Huggies Naturally Refreshing Cucumber and Green Tea Baby Wash. See report, *No More Toxic Tub* (San Francisco: The Campaign for Safe Cosmetics, 2009; www.safecosmetics.org/downloads/No-MoreToxicTub_Mar09Report.pdf).

34. U.S. EPA, "Long-Chain Perfluorinated Chemicals (PFCs) Action Plan."

35. Environmental Working Group, "New Study from CDC and Boston University Shows Babies Getting Unsafe Dose of Perchlorate," March 2007 (www.ewg.org/report/new-study-cdc-and-boston-university-shows-babies-getting-unsafe-dose-perchlorate).

36. These are the government lists I used: U.S. Department of Health and Human Services, "Household Products Database" (http://householdproducts.nlm.nih.gov/); National Toxicology Program, "11th Report on Carcinogens," U.S. Department of Health and Human Services, 2005 (http://ntp.niehs.nih.gov/?objectid=035E5806-F735-FE81-FF769DFE5509AF0A); Environmental Protection Agency (State of California), "Chemicals Known to the State to Cause Cancer or Reproductive Toxicity," January 7, 2011 (http://oehha.ca.gov/prop65/prop65_list/files/P65single010711.pdf).

37. Ibid.

38. Household dust, which collects on floors and carpets, especially in the nooks and crannies where children like to play—under beds, behind furniture, and so on—is laden with toxic chemicals, as are the carpets and floors themselves, along with the soil outside that children play on (which is then tracked inside to become household dust, the reason household dust contains chemicals such as lead, arsenic, and pesticides when those chemicals are in the soil outside. See Lambert and Lane, "Lead, Arsenic," 40).

39. Environmental Working Group, *Body Burden—The Pollution in Newborns* (Washington DC, July 14, 2005) (www.ewg.org/reports/bodyburden2/exec-summ.php).

40. U.S. EPA, "Long-Chain Perfluorinated Chemicals (PFCs) Action Plan."

41. Though banned chemicals, such as PCBs, stop accumulating, they continue to persist in the environment, which is why, despite bans on PCBs, the chemical is still detected in humans, including recently born babies.

42. As quoted in Miller, "Tests Reveal Chemical Levels."

43. U.S. Centers for Disease Control and Prevention, "National Report on Human Exposure to Environmental Chemicals: Executive Summary," Washington DC, 2005 (www.cdc.gov/exposurereport/executive_summary.html).

44. Interview with Bruce Lanphear.

CHAPTER SEVEN: PRECAUTIONARY TALES

1. See Susanne Rust and Meg Kissinger, "BPA Industry Seeks to Polish Image," *Milwaukee Journal Sentinel Online*, May 29, 2009 (www.jsonline.com/watchdog/watchdogreports/46510647.html). See also Meg Kissinger, "What Goes on Behind Closed Doors," *Milwaukee Journal Sentinel Online*, June 1, 2009 (this item contains the actual minutes from the meeting: www.jsonline.com/blogs/news/46630742.html); Lyndsey Layton, "Strategy Is Being Devised to Protect Use of BPA," *Washington Post*, May 31, 2009 (www.washingtonpost.com/wp-dyn/content/article/2009/05/30/AR2009053002121.html).

2. Kissinger, "What Goes on Behind Closed Doors."

3. Ibid.

4. For more on industry websites, see Rust and Kissinger, "BPA Industry Fights Back," *Milwaukee Journal Sentinel Online*, August 22, 2009 (www.jsonline.com/watchdog/watchdogreports/54195297.html).

5. This statement was no longer available at the website on May 1, 2011. A print copy is on file with author.

6. Rust and Kissinger, "Donation Raises Questions for Head of FDA's Bisphenol A Panel," *Milwaukee Journal Sentinel Online*, October 12, 2008 (www.json-line.com/news/32431234.html).

7. As quoted in ibid. Gelman believes regulation of a chemical is not justified in the absence of definitive proof it causes ill effects. He backs numerous organizations opposed to "junk science" and to environmental regulation more generally (his own company was known for breaching environmental law while he was at the helm), according to the article.

8. Press Release, "Gift Positions U-M as National Leader in Studying Risks to Public Health," University of Michigan News Service, July 1, 2008 (http://ns.umich.edu/htdocs/releases/story.php?id=6630).

9. As quoted in Rust and Kissinger, "Donation Raises Questions."

10. Philbert's salary was paid by the university, not the center, it reasoned, and that ensured money from Gelman's gift would not end up in Philbert's pockets.

11. Rust and Kissinger, "Donation Raises Questions."

12. Steven Hentges, for example, was on a first-name basis with them, according to Rust and Kissinger, "FDA Relied Heavily on BPA Lobby," *Milwaukee Journal Sentinel*, May 16, 2009 (www.jsonline.com/watchdog/watchdogreports/45228647.html). "Laura and Mitch," wrote Hentges in one email to two FDA officials, according to Rust and Kissinger, "I send you this note to give you a head's up on something we understand is coming next week [an NGO's report highlighting safety concerns about BPA] . . . It might be appropriate for FDA to consider issuing a statement to reassure consumers about the safety of the food supply." When a Japanese study revealed that exposure to BPA could cause miscarriages, Rust and Kissinger further point out, FDA officials turned to Hentges for help in "determin[ing] if there are problems with that data." On at least two further occasions, according to Rust and Kissinger—first, when the

CDC released a study showing that 93 percent of the population had BPA in its urine, and next when independent researchers discovered that BPA leaches from heated bottles—it was Steven Hentges to whom the FDA turned for opinions.

13. Ibid.

14. Rust and Kissinger, "Plastics Industry Behind FDA Research on Bisphenol A, Study Finds," *Milwaukee Journal Sentinel*, October 22, 2008 (www3.json-line.com/story/index.aspx?id=809282). The report was widely condemned: Rust and Kissinger, "Scientists Slam FDA Report on Bisphenol A Chemical," *Milwaukee Journal Sentinel*, October 24, 2008 (www.jsonline.com/watchdog/watchdogreports/33200554.html).

15. The reasons for these charges are as follows: Two of the studies used a strain of rat, Sprague-Dawley, which is known to be uniquely insensitive to bisphenol A, thus increasing the chances of results supporting the chemical's safety. In some studies, including the most recent of the four (on which Steven Hentges is a coauthor) positive control animals (ones exposed to a non-BPA estrogenic chemical known to cause effects at low doses) did not show effects from exposure, meaning some flaw in the researchers' methods and analyses rendered the experiment insensitive to estrogenic chemicals' effects. In other studies, negative control animals (ones not exposed to estrogenic chemicals) *did* show effects meaning either that the animals had already been contaminated with an estrogenic substance, or that post-exposure dissection methods were flawed. Either way, any effects from exposure to BPA would be masked. See F. Vom Saal and W. Welshons, "Large Effects From Small Exposures II: The Importance of Positive Controls in Low-Dose Research on Bisphenol A," *Environmental Research* 100(2006): 50–76; John Peterson Myers and Frederick vom Saal et al., "Why Public Agencies Cannot Depend on Good Laboratory Practices as a Criterion for Selecting Data: The Case of Bisphenol A," *Environmental Health Perspectives* 117(2009): 309–315.

16. Myers and vom Saal et al., "Why Public Agencies." In addition, vom Saal and Welshon, "Large Effects," note that a National Toxicology Program reanalysis of the data from one of the industry studies found the authors' conclusion that there were no adverse effects from BPA to be "flawed," "illogical," and "misleading."

17. Vom Saal and Welshons, "Large Effects."

18. In an interview, Bruce Lanphear offered the example of a young researcher, up for tenure in a few years. Her chairman has told her she needs to get funding. Along comes a research scientist from a plastics corporation. He wines and dines her, flatters her about her work, and asks her to become involved in a study. "You feel good about it, they think you're important," says Lanphear. "You fall into this. And before you know it, you're on the plastic company's advisory committee, your research lab is dependent upon them, and you think they're really nice guys anyway." The problem, says Lanphear, is that while the researcher may feel confident in her ability to remain independent—"it doesn't seem like there's any harm to [the collaboration]; you're a scientist, you're going to set up studies in such a way that the data are objective"—researchers too easily become complicit in serving the goals of their collaborators rather than those of science. We have a "natural tendency intentional or otherwise," says Lanphear, to want to please those we work for, facilitate their processes, and presume they are well-intentioned. And that tendency can put at risk the independence of otherwise independent scientists when they collaborate with and are supported by industry.

19. Interview with Bruce Lanphear. Though Dr. Lanphear notes there have been some improvements in this area under the Obama administration.

20. Lennart Hardell et al., "Secret Ties to Industry and Conflicting Interests in Cancer Research," *American Journal of Industrial Medicine* 2006, Jan 5, at 5. (www.avaate.org/IMG/pdf/article.SecretTies.pdf).

21. Smith and Lourie, *Slow Death by Rubber Duck*, 207.

22. Quoted in David Michaels, *Doubt Is Their Product* (New York: Oxford University Press, 2008), at x.

23. Pierre Band et al., "Mortality Rates Within Sydney, Nova Scotia, by Exposure Areas to Airborne Coke Ovens and Steel Mill Emissions: 1961–1988," (Ottawa, ON: Health Canada, 1999); Daniel Rainham, "Risk Communication and Public Response to Industrial Chemical Contamination in Sydney, Nova Scotia: A Case Study," *Journal of Environmental Health*, 65(2002):25 (http://emaychair.dal.ca/documents/Rainham_2002.pdf); Timothy W. Lambert and Stephanie Lane, "Lead, Arsenic, and Polycyclic Aromatic Hydrocarbons in Soil

and House Dust in the Communities Surrounding the Sydney, Nova Scotia, Tar Ponds," *Environmental Health Perspectives* (2004):112, 35–41.

24. See Michaels, *Doubt Is Their Product*, for an in-depth description and discussion of the "doubt" industry.

25. Cantox.com, "History," at www.cantox.com/history.aspx.

26. See Barlow and May, *Frederick Street: Life and Death on Canada's Love Canal* (Toronto: Harper Collins Canada, 2000), 132–35, which includes the quote from the Cantox report.

27. Michaels, *Doubt Is Their Product*, at 38–39.

28. Lead was linked to the health and purity of clean white paint in public relations campaigns by the National Lead Company as a proactive measure against mounting evidence of ill health effects. See ibid., 39.

29. Indeed, by the mid-1940s, paint manufacturers had begun to reduce the amounts of lead in their paints partly in response to public concerns, but also because zinc and titanium pigments were found to make better and more easily used paints. Lead was declared a potential health hazard by the U.S. surgeon general in the early 1970s, and in 1971, President Nixon signed the Lead-Based Paint Poisoning Prevention Act, which restricted the use of lead in paint. See ibid., 38–39.

30. This account of the leaded gasoline story is based upon: Frank Ackerman, *Poisoned for Pennies: The Economics of Toxics and Precaution* (Washington DC: Island Press, 2008), 34–39.

31. Gastric juices likely dissolved the other metals leaving mainly lead. Testing on other pendants revealed that some had very little lead in them, while others—like the one Jarnell swallowed—were composed predominantly of lead. See Caroline E. Mayer, "Reebok Recalls Trinkets Linked to Death," *Seattle Times*, March 24, 2006 (http://seattletimes.nwsource.com/html/health/2002885628_recall24.html).

32. Sara Lemagie, "Reebok's Deadly Lead Charm Draw $1 Million Federal Fine," *Minneapolis-St. Paul Star Tribune*, March 18, 2008 (www.startribune.com/local/west/16769521.html).

33. See Healthystuff.org for a large collection of assessments of the chemical composition of toys and other items. For Green Baby suit, see Test Re-

sults, " 'Green Baby' Recycling Shirt," *Healthystuff.org* (www.healthystuff.
org/departments/toys/product.details.php?getrecno=15360); for Dora the
Explorer activity tote, see Test Results, "Dora the Explorer Activity Tote,"
Healthystuff.org (www.healthystuff.org/departments/toys/product.details.php?
getrecno=15307).

See also U.S. Consumer Product Safety Commission, "Toy Hazard Recalls" (www.cpsc.gov/CPSCPUB/PREREL/CATEGORY/toy.html). For
new U.S. federal rules concerning lead content in toys and other items, see
Consumer Product Safety Improvement Act of 2008, s. 101 (www.cpsc.gov/
ABOUT/Cpsia/sect101.html).

34. Bruce P. Lanphear, "The Conquest of Lead Poisoning: A Pyrrhic Victory,"
Environmental Health Perspectives 115(2007):484–85. Companies continue
to resist regulation of leaded gasoline in the developing world. As recently as
2010, the United Kingdom's Serious Fraud Office announced that Innospec,
a British company that manufacturers lead additives, admitted to bribing
Indonesian officials to delay banning leaded gasoline. See Philippe Grand-
jean, "Even Low-Dose Lead Exposure Is Hazardous," *The Lancet* 376(2010):
855–856.

35. Michaels, *Doubt Is Their Product*, 60.

36. Ibid.

37. Austin Bradford Hill, "The Environment and Disease: Association or Causation?" *Proceedings of the Royal Society of Medicine* 58(1965): 295–300.

38. Interview with Michael Transande.

39. Bradford Hill, "The Environment and Disease."

40. As Lanphear told me in an interview, "maybe after the twentieth or thirtieth
or three-hundredth study we do something; or if there's a crisis maybe we'll do
it sooner; it takes somebody to jump on a grenade before anything is done."
As a result, he said, millions of children are becoming unnecessarily ill, some
of them dying.

41. Interview with Bruce Lanphear.

42. Ibid.

43. A number of government and nongovernment organizations' websites provide useful information on what chemicals are used in various products, and

whether or not they are dangerous. See, for example, http://householdprod-ucts.nlm.nih.gov/; www.ewg.org/; www.healthystuff.org.

44. Interview with Lanphear. As noted in chapter 3 cosmetic and personal care product companies target girls with marketing campaigns designed to exploit their tendencies to focus on personal appearance. It is now not uncommon for girls as young as eight to be heavy and regular users of cosmetics. A recent study of girls between the ages of fourteen and nine-teen showed that, on average, they used seventeen different personal care products each day compared to twelve for adult women. Testing of these same girls' blood and urine revealed thirteen hormone-disrupting chemicals from several chemical families, including phthalates, triclosan, and para-bens. See Rebecca Sutton, "Adolescent Exposures to Cosmetic Chemicals of Concern," Environmental Working Group, September 2008 (www.ewg. org/reports/teens).

45. Interview with Bruce Lanphear. A typical argument made against more robust regulation is that the costs it creates for industry outweigh whatever benefits it might yield. Environmental economist Frank Ackerman rigorously refutes this argument in his *Poisoned for Pennies: The Economics of Toxics and Precau-tion* (Washington DC: Island Press, 2008).

46. U.S. FDA, "Update on Bisphenol A for Use in Food Contact Applications: January 2010" (www.fda.gov/newsevents/publichealthfocus/ucm197739.htm).

47. As quoted in Denise Grady, "F.D.A. Concerned About Substance in Food Packaging," *New York Times*, Jan 15, 2010 (www.nytimes.com/2010/01/16/health/16plastic.html).

48. To its credit, however, the Obama administration committed $30 million to investigate BPA's health effects.

49. Two further, albeit related factors contributing to that ineffectiveness are: (1) "dose makes the poison" thinking, as discussed earlier; and (2) the system's tendency to analyze chemicals' health effects one chemical at a time. With respect to the latter, a recent report states that "with over 80,000 chemicals in commerce, it is clear that a chemical-by-chemical regulatory approach cannot solve the problem." See Monica Becker, Sally Edwards and Rachel Massey, "Toxic Chemicals in Toys and Children's Products: Limitations of Current

Responses and Recommendations for Government and Industry," *Environmental Science and Technology* 44(2010): 7986–7991, 7989.

50. This information is from Senator Lautenberg's summary of the Safe Chemicals Act and the reasons behind it. See http://lautenberg.senate.gov/assets/SCA2010Summary.pdf.

51. Press Release, "Lautenberg Introduces 'Safe Chemicals Act' to Protect Americans from Toxic Chemicals," Senator Frank Lautenberg, April 15, 2010. The "EPA does not have the tools to deal with dangerous chemicals," Senator Lautenberg says, and "parents are afraid because hundreds of untested chemicals are found in their children's bodies." See http://lautenberg.senate.gov/newsroom/record.cfm?id=323863.

52. Robert F. Service, "A New Wave of Chemical Regulations Just Ahead?" *Science* 325(2009): 692–93 (www.chemicalspolicy.org/downloads/2009-0807Scienceonchemicalregs.pdf).

53. Ibid.

54. Senator Lautenberg press release.

55. Lautenberg, summary of Safe Chemicals Act.

56. Joseph Picard, "Americans Exposed to Thousands of Untested Chemicals," *International Business Times*, October 27, 2010 (www.ibtimes.com/articles/76477/20101027/chemicals-industry-environment.htm#).

CHAPTER EIGHT: IN OUR OWN BACKYARD

1. Both countries have ratified the United Nations International Labour Organizations Convention Concerning the Minimum Age for Admission to Employment of 1973 (known as the ILO Minimum Age Convention) which, in Article 2, sets fifteen years as the minimum age for work in nonhazardous jobs, provides a mechanism for member countries to raise that age, and also permits them to lower the age to fourteen if their "economy and educational facilities are insufficiently developed." For a list of countries that have ratified the convention, see http://webfusion.ilo.org/public/db/standards/normes/appl/applbyConvYear.

cfm?hdroff=1&Lang=en&conv=C138. For the text of the convention, see www.ilo.org/ilolex/cgi-lex/convde.pl?C138.

2.   The only limitation in the law is that children between the ages of twelve and fourteen must have the consent of one parent. Prior to the change a child under the age of fifteen could not work without special permission of the director of employment standards. Under the new law a child of twelve or over can work without such permission, while those under twelve still require such permission to work. Regulations under the new law provide that until children reach sixteen, they can only work outside of school hours, and for limited hours each day and week—in particular, no more than four hours on school days and seven hours on nonschool days; and no more than twenty hours in weeks with five school days, or thirty-five hours with fewer than five school days due to holidays, professional days, or the fact a school district has shortened the week to four days. See *Employment Standards Act*, RSBC 1996, chapter 113, s. 9(1) (as amended by the *Skills Development and Labour Statutes Amendment Act*, otherwise known as Bill 37, of 2003) and regulations (www.bclaws.ca/EPLibraries/bclaws_new/document/ID/freeside/00_96113_01); See also Fact Sheet, "General Employment of Young People," Employment Standards Branch, B.C. Ministry of Labour, December 2008 (www.labour.gov.bc.ca/esb/facshts/pdfs/youth_general.pdf).

For detailed discussion and critical commentary of B.C.'s child labor regime, see Helesia Luke and Graeme Moore, *Who's Looking Out for Our Kids: Deregulating Child Labour in British Columbia* (Vancouver: Canadian Centre for Policy Alternatives, 2004). The following passage from the report captures the gist of its critique: "Bill 37 transfers child labour oversight from government to parents. The Minister of Skills Development and Labour contends that parents are in the best position to decide about employment on behalf of their child. This position assumes that all parents have expert knowledge of employment standards and can ensure their child's employment is developmentally appropriate, not detrimental to their education, safety or physical and mental well-being, *and* can define and enforce the terms of employment. It also assumes that parents and children always share the same interest and that parents have the same authority over employers as does the Director of Employment Standards. This self-regulated system does away with workplace inspections by employment standards officers who would monitor a child at work to ensure employers are respecting any restrictions imposed by parents. The new regulations state only that children must be 'under the direct, immediate supervision of an adult in the workplace at all times.' There is no benchmark by which to judge whether that adult is trained in the supervision of children or has a thorough grasp of tasks that are appropriate to the child's development or ability. Many employers do not appreciate the physical and intellectual limits to a child's ability to perform certain tasks. For example, working with adult-sized equipment and performing repetitive tasks that require sustained strength are usually inappropriate for children" (at 8).

3. As indicated by, among other measures, the 1000 percent jump in workplace injuries to 12 to 14 year olds since 2004. See, Daphne Bramham, "Child Labour Injuries Skyrocket in B.C.," *Vancouver Sun*, October 8, 2009 (www2. canada.com/vancouversun/news/story.html?id=3cbdbcba-0b58-4baa-85b7-cf62ad2f625b&p=2).

4. A fact cemented into law in British Columbia until just this year, and still in the United States, by exemptions from minimum wage laws that allow employers to pay young workers less than minimum wage for a certain "training" period. Until very recently in British Columbia an employee with no previous paid work experience (generally a youth) could be paid $6 an hour for the first 500 hours of work as compared to the general minimum wage of $8. On March 16, 2011, however, the new premier of British Columbia announced that the "training wage" would be repealed on May 1, 2011, and that from that date forward all employees, regardless of their previous experience, would be entitled to the general minimum wage (see News Release, "Premier Announces Increase to Minimum Wage," Office of the Premier, March 16, 2011).

    In the United States, federal labor law permits employers to pay employees under the age of twenty years old 60 percent of the minimum wage for the first ninety days of their employment (currently $4.25 instead of $7.25). See U.S. Department of Labor, "Youth and Labor: Wages," at www.dol.gov/dol/topic/youthlabor/wages.htm.

5. More than half of these children—roughly 126 million of them—are en-

gaged in the worst forms of child labor (work that is harmful, unhealthy, and unsafe, including slavery, prostitution, pornography, and drug trafficking). Many of these children work in slave-like conditions (see "The End of Child Labour," *World of Work: Magazine of the ILO*, 2007:61, 4, at 5, www.ilo.org/wcmsp5/groups/public/---dgreports/---dcomm/documents/publication/wcms_090161.pdf).

Forced child labor has become a serious problem in China, for example, where children are lured to cities from poorer regions of the country with false promises of lucrative work, or kidnapped or bought from parents by shadowy employment agencies who then auction the children off to factories. The children, once sold, are effectively captives of the factory owners, and must endure long work hours, minimal pay, and slave-like working conditions (see Summary Report, "Child Labor, Forced Labor, and Forced Child Labor in China," United States Department of Labor, July 2009, www.dol.gov/ilab/media/reports/external/20091209-Report-China.pdf).

6. The ILO Minimum Age Convention of 1973, see note 1, above. As noted, the convention permits a country to drop the age to fourteen if economic exigencies make it necessary to do so. "Light work" is permitted for younger children, so long as it it does not harm their health or interfere with their schooling. Through the convention and similar measures, the ILO hopes to eradicate child labor in its worst forms by the year 2016 (though the organization acknowledges the obstacles in the way of reaching this target). See *Accelerating Action Against Child Labour* (Geneva: International Labour Office, 2010) (www.ilo.org/global/resources/WCMS_126752/lang--en/index.htm).

7. Rick Rousos and Yesenia Mojarro, "Accident Highlights Child Care and Labor Law Issues," *The Ledger*, January 12, 2007 (www.theledger.com/article/20070112/NEWS/701120392).

8. *Fields of Peril: Child Labor in U.S. Agriculture* (Washington DC: Human Rights Watch, 2010), 40–41 (www.hrw.org/node/90126); Jennie Rodriguez, "No Prison Time in Teen Farm Worker's Death," *Recordnet.com*, January 21, 2011 (www.recordnet.com/apps/pbcs.dll/article?AID=/20110121/A_NEWS/101210313).

9. *Fields of Peril*, 38.

10. Ibid. Also see National Consumers League website entries on child labor: www.nclnet.org/worker-rights/82-child-labor?start=3. Poverty is all but ensured by farmworkers' meager pay. The piece rate for tomato pickers in Florida, for example, has lagged behind inflation to the point where in 2004, when compared to 1980, nearly twice as many tomatoes had to be picked in order to make a minimum wage. See *Like Machines in the Fields: Workers Without Rights in American Agriculture* (Boston: Oxfam, 2004), 12–13. More than 80 percent of farmworkers are Hispanic (compared to 14 percent of all U.S. workers). Generally, they are driven to work in the fields by extreme poverty. Children work on farms because they must in order for them and their families to survive. Sometimes they work on their own to send money home to their families, usually in Mexico. More typically, they work, alongside parents and siblings. "Typical families we work with earn $7000 to $10,000 a year, per family," according to one social service program director in Florida. "As soon as you are old enough you have to go to work to earn for your family" (see *Fields of Peril*, at 18).

11. Mainly on small family farms that are exempt from minimum wage requirements.

12. Brian Ross et al., "ABC News Investigation: The Blueberry Children," October 30, 2009 (http://abcnews.go.com/Blotter/young-children-working-blueberry-fields-walmart-seversties/story?id=8951044).

13. *Fields of Peril*, note 8, 20.

14. That pronouncement is quoted in Ross et al., *Blueberry Children*. In similar spirit, Walmart's CEO Lee Scott recently pronounced at a conference: "A company that cheats on . . . the age of its labor . . . will ultimately cheat on the quality of its products." See Stephanie Rosenbloom, "Wal-Mart to Toughen Standards," *New York Times*, October 22, 2008 (www.nytimes.com/2008/10/22/business/22walmart.html).

15. Steven Greenhouse, "Wal-Mart Agrees to Pay Fine in Child Labor Cases," *New York Times*, February 12, 2005 (www.nytimes.com/2005/02/12/national/12wage.html); Steven Greenhouse, "In-House Audit Says Wal-Mart Violated Labor Laws," *New York Times*, January 13, 2004 (www.nytimes.com/2004/01/13/us/in-house-audit-says-wal-mart-violated-labor-laws.html).

Walmart is, of course, not the only major company recently charged with violating child labor laws in the United States. For example, a 2008 investigation of Agriprocessors, an Iowa kosher meatpacking plant, found fifty-seven underage workers, all of them illegal immigrants, and many employed in hazardous jobs. The former manager of the plant was acquitted of sixty-seven criminal charges that he *knowingly* hired underage workers, but the jury had no doubts the underage workers were employed at the plant. See Julia Preston, "Former Manager of Iowa Slaughterhouse Is Acquitted of Labor Charges," *New York Times*, June 7, 2010 (www.nytimes.com/2010/06/08/us/08immig.html).

16. Press Release, "Child Labor Advocates Call Wal-Mart Settlement Disastrous," Child Labour Coalition, National Consumers League, February 16, 2005. More generally, Walmart has been plagued by allegations, most of them confirmed and acknowledged, that its developing world suppliers and manufacturers use child labor. The issue was put front and center by the Kathy Lee Gifford scandal of the late 1990s, documented in my earlier book, and the film based upon it. See Bakan, *The Corporation*, 65–70. Walmart's Kathy Lee Gifford line of clothing was being made by children working in sweatshops in Honduras and other developing countries, in horrible conditions for meager pay. Despite its pious promises at the time, Walmart has been unable to shake the charge that its developing-world suppliers use child labor, with regular revelations in subsequent years, and to this day, of suppliers using child labor—whether in factories in Bangladesh or on cotton farms in Uzbekistan.

17. *Fields of Peril*, 76.

18. Ibid., 5.

19. Ibid., 5, 74.

20. Ibid.

21. Ibid. In 2009, however, the division hired several hundred new inspectors as part of a plan to boost the number of inspectors from 750 to 1,000. By April 2010, there were 894 (ibid., 77). The Obama administration, through Labor Secretary Hilda Solis (herself the daughter of an immigrant farmworker), recently made it a priority to enforce the rules governing child labor on farms,

and there has been movement in Congress toward bringing those rules into line with the rules governing nonfarm work. Erik Eckholm, "U.S. Cracks Down on Farmers Who Hire Children," *New York Times*, June 18, 2010 (http://www.nytimes.com/2010/06/19/us/19migrant.html). Also, see note 31, below.

22. See www.nclnet.org/worker-rights/82-child-labor?start=3.

23. As quoted in Viviana A. Zelizer, *Pricing the Priceless Child: The Changing Social Value of Children* (New York: Basic Books, 1985), 61.

24. Ibid, 64–70.

25. Ibid., 70–72; see also Stephen P. Wood, *Constitutional Politics in the Progressive Era* (Chicago: Chicago University Press, 1968), 3–80.

26. Zelizer, *Pricing the Priceless.*

27. Wood, *Constitutional Politics.*

28. International Programme on the Elimination of Child Labour, "Background Information on Child Labour and ILO," 2011 (www.ilo.org/ipec/Campaignandadvocacy/Youthinaction/C182-Youth-oriented/C182Youth_Background/lang--en/index.htm).

29. As stated at "Themes: Child Labour" (www.ilo.org/global/topics/child-labour/WCMS_CON_TEX_CHI_EN/lang--en/index.htm).

30. International Programme on the Elimination of Child Labour. Jim McKechnie and Sandy Hobbs, British psychologists, draw a useful distinction between "child labor" and "child work." The former is work that is not good for children, while the latter is work that can serve their interests as well as being beneficial for the economy. See McKechnie and Hobbs, "Changing Perceptions of Child Employment," in *Child Focused Research and Practice with Working Children*, Beatrice Hungerland et al., eds. (London: Jessica Kingsley Publishers, 2007), 225–33 at 226.

31. The $26 million figure comes from Daya Gamage, "U.S. Allows Child Labor by Law but Chastises Other Nations for Human Rights Abuses, *Asian Tribune*, July 8, 2010 (www.asiantribune.com/news/2010/07/08/US-allows-child-labor-by-law-but-chastises-other-nations-for-human-rights-abuses).

There are, however, signs the federal government is committed to addressing the issue, as noted above in note 21. During the summer of 2010, the U.S. Department of Labor cracked down on child labor on blueberry farms in North Dakota, the opening volley in Secretary Hilda Solis's new resolve to enforce child labor laws on farms. "I am totally changing the direction of this department," said Ms. Solis. In addition to adding to hiring new inspectors (see note 21), her plan includes raising fines for infractions, and a campaign to provide education to workers about their rights.

Though better enforcement of existing laws is an improvement, the lax laws themselves remain on the books. For years, a proposed law that would bring farmworker child labor standards into line with standards governing nonfarm work, the *Children's Act for Responsible Employment*, has languished in both houses, despite the efforts of the bill's sponsors, Congresswoman Louise Roybal-Allard and Senator Tom Harkin. Such a law would certainly be a welcome start to addressing the problem. The bill has been vigorously opposed, however, by the American Farm Bureau, the major farm lobby organization in the United States.

In the meantime, the fallout from providing better enforcement of child labor laws only underlines the importance of attacking the root of the problem—namely, the deep poverty that creates a *need* for children to work in the fields. Many parents and teenagers were caught by surprise when, in response to the federal initiative in North Dakota, blueberry farms and labor contractors stopped hiring teens and prohibited parents from taking their children to the fields to work. Some parents and teens complained of the lack of child care and the difficulties caused for families as a result of lost income. See Eckholm, "U.S. Cracks Down."

32. See *Accelerating Action*.

CHAPTER NINE: RACE TO NOWHERE

1. This account of events relating to Albert and Truitt is based upon the following items: Kristen Mack and Stephanie Banchero, "16-year-old Boy Beaten to Death in Roseland," September 25, 2009 (http://archive.chicagobreakingnews.com/2009/09/boy-16-found-slain-on-far-south-side.html); Azam Ahmed, "The Gantlet: Dodging Gangs, Violence and Drug Addicts, Many Chicago School Stu-

dents Find It a Daily Ordeal Just to Get to Class," *Chicago Tribune*, October 16, 2009 (http://articles.chicagotribune.com/2009-10-16/news/chi-safe-passage-intro-16-oct16_1_chicago-public-schools-school-students-gangs); Azam Ahmed et al., "Fenger Kids Tell Why They Fight," *Chicago Tribune*, October 6, 2009 (http://articles.chicagotribune.com/2009-10-06/news/chi-fenger-safe-passage-06-oct06_1_derrion-albert-youth-violence-fenger-high-school-s tudent); Mallory Simon, "Official: Suspect Admits Role in Beating Death of Chicago Teen," *CNN Justice*, September 28, 2009 (http://articles.cnn.com/2009-09-28/justice/chicago.teen.beating_1_factions-street-fight-honor-student?_s=PM:CRIME); "Teen's Beating Death Puts Pressure on Officials," September 28, 2009 (www.msnbc.msn.com/id/33057768/ns/us_news-crime_and_courts/); Kenneth Saltman, *The Gift of Education: Public Education and Venture Philanthropy* (New York: Palgrave Macmillan, 2010), 58 (I first learned of this story from this book).

2. Looking only at shootings of students (excluding deaths by other forms of violence, such as beating and stabbing, in other words), the numbers are chilling. Before 2006, ten to fifteen Chicago students died each year from being shot. In 2006–7 and 2007–8 the numbers were twenty-four and twenty-three respectively. In 2008–9 the number was 34. See "Teen's Beating Death Puts Pressure on Officials."

3. Ahmed, "The Gantlet."

4. Saltman, *Gift of Education*, 58.

5. As discussed in Henry A. Giroux and Kenneth Saltman, "Obama's Betrayal of Public Education?" *Truthout*, December 17, 2008 (http://216.78.200.159/documents/RandD/Duncan%20Arne/Duncan%20and%20the%20Corpora%20model%20of%20Schooling%20-%20Giroux%20Saltman.pdf).

6. Duncan is quoted in ibid.; see also Kenneth Saltman, *Capitalizing on Disaster: Taking and Breaking Public Schools* (Boulder, CO: Paradigm Publishers, 2007), chapter 3.

7. As quoted in Giroux and Saltman, "Obama's Betrayal."

8. As a result, Renaissance 2010 promised, there would be "greater choice and competition, and all families [would be provided] with high-quality education options." See www.rsfchicago.org/About.html.

9. Some schools, rather than being closed, were subject to "turnaround" pro-

grams, often delivered by for-profit companies, and sometimes resulting in the firing and replacement of entire teaching staffs (which is what happened at Fenger in 2009, where the entire staff was fired and replaced after the Gates Foundation pulled money from attempts, all failed, to turn the school around: See Saltman, *Gift of Education*, at 58).

10. Stephanie Banchero, "Daley School Plan Fails to Make Grade," *Chicago Tribune*, January 17, 2010 (http://articles.chicagotribune.com/2010-01-17/news/1001160276_1_charter-schools-chicago-reform-urban-education). Studies commissioned by the Renaissance Schools Fund itself reveal that the program's new schools are either no better than, or by some measures worse than, traditional schools in the system: See Viki M. Young et al., *Renaissance Schools Fund-Supported Schools: Early Outcomes, Challenges and Opportunities* (Menlo Park, CA: SRI International, 2009) (http://policyweb.sri.com/cep/publications/RSF_FINAL_April_15v2.pdf).

11. The National Commission on Excellence in Education, *A Nation at Risk: The Imperative for Educational Reform* (Washington DC: Department of Education, 1983) (www2.ed.gov/pubs/NatAtRisk/index.html).

12. Scattered references to the importance of democracy and citizenship can be found in the report, but there is no sense at all that part of education's mandate is to cultivate critical thinking about political and economic arrangements. For example, the report limits the purpose of teaching about social issues to ensuring students "understand the fundamentals of how our economic system works and how our political system functions; and grasp the difference between free and repressive societies."

13. U.S. Department of Education, "Race to the Top Program: Executive Summary," Washington DC, November 2009 (www2.ed.gov/programs/racetothetop/executive-summary.pdf). The program offers the possibility of federal funds at a time when, as the American Association of School Administrators describes it, "the scope and number of challenges presented by recent developments [the 2008 economic crisis] . . . threaten to overwhelm even the resilient public school system." See Noelle Ellerson, Federal Education Legislative Update, American Association of School Administrators, January 13, 2010, at slide 37 (www.ssaonline.org/documents/AL0110Ellerson.ppt).

14. Diane Ravitch, *The Death and Life of the Great American School System: How Testing and Choice Are Undermining Education* (New York: Basic Books, 2010, Kindle version), location 271.

15. As Giroux and Saltman state in "Obama's Betrayal": "The greatest threat to our children does not come from lowered standards, the absence of privatized choice schemes or the lack of rigid testing measures that offer the aura of accountability. On the contrary, it comes from a society that refuses to view children as a social investment, consigns 13 million children to live in poverty, reduces critical learning to massive testing programs, promotes policies that eliminate most crucial health and public services and defines rugged individualism through the degrading celebration of gun culture, extreme sports and the spectacles of violence that permeate corporate controlled media industries."

16. Interview with Aunt Ally.

17. Ibid.

18. Ibid.

19. Ibid.

20. Ibid.

21. The schools that were closed at Erasmus were the High School for Business and Technology, The High School for Math and Science, and the High School for Humanities. The schools reopened in their place were the Academy of Hospitality and Tourism, Academy for Youth and Community Development, High School for Service and Learning, the Science, Technology & Research Early College High School, and the Academy for College Preparation and Career Exploration. Erasmus is part of a larger experiment, a joint project of the Bloomberg administration and the Bill and Melinda Gates Foundation (which has contributed more than $100 million to New York City schools), that involves breaking up large schools into smaller units that each have a particular thematic, and often vocational, focus.

    The Bloomberg administration, like Mayor Daly's in Chicago, has been strongly business-oriented in its approach to the city's school system. Both former school chancellor Joel Klein and his replacement recently resigned chancellor Cathie Black had backgrounds in business, not education. Joel Klein had been chairman and CEO of media giant Bertlesmann prior to becoming chancellor. After leaving his position as chancellor, he became chief executive of News Corp's new education unit. Resigned chancellor Cathie Black was formerly chairwoman of Hearst Magazines and publisher of New York magazine and USA Today. The new chancellor, Dennis Walcott, has a background in education.

It is no coincidence that both Klein and Black previously held high positions in large media companies (and Klein does currently). Media concerns have a substantial interest in education and school reform as areas in which they can develop markets for their "edutainment" products—websites, curriculum packages, games, and so on—and also as places to target children with advertising.

22. Which it does by providing funding and also by helping schools forge partnerships with companies that represent the industries for which they train students. See http://naf.org/.

23. The Gates foundation has been a major backer of market-led reform initiatives. One reason business interests and their supporters tend to advocate that schools become more involved in training students for particular jobs, according to Kenneth Saltman, is to ensure "that schools teach what is useful for corporations, thereby saving companies worker training costs." See Kenneth Saltman's *The Edison Schools: Corporate Schooling and the Assault on Education* (New York: Routledge, 2005) and *The Gift of Education*.

24. Clara Hemphill and Kim Nauer, *The New Marketplace: How Small-School Reforms and School Choice Have Reshaped New York City's High Schools* (New York: The New School Center for New York City Affairs, 2009) (www.newschool.edu/milano/nycaffairs/documents/TheNewMarketplace_Report.pdf).

25. Unless otherwise stated, the following account is from Jonathon Kozol, *The Shame of The Nation: The Restoration of Apartheid Schooling in America* (New York: Three Rivers Press, 2005).

26. See "Health Opportunities High School," High School Directory, New York City Department of Education (http://schools.nyc.gov/ChoicesEnrollment/High/Directory/school/?sid=1376).

27. Kozol, *Shame*, 94.

28. Career academies, according to Kozol, "take from [children's] education far too many of the opportunities for cultural and critical reflectiveness without

which citizens become receptacles for other people's ideologies and ways of looking at the world but lack the independent spirits to create their own" (ibid., 98). "Beginning in the early 1980s and continuing with little deviation right up to the present time," Kozol says, "the notion of producing 'products' who will then produce more wealth for society has come to be embraced by many politicians and, increasingly, by principals of inner-city schools that have developed close affiliations with the representatives of private business corporations. . . . Children, in this frame of reference, are regarded as investments, assets, or productive units—or else, failing that, as pint-sized human deficits who threaten our competitive capacities. . . . These ways of viewing children, which were common at the start of the last century, have re-emerged over the past two decades in the words of business leaders, influential educators and political officials" (95–96).

29. Ravitch, *Death and Life*, locations 347–48.

30. Many of the criteria of "Race to the Top" and the overall spirit of the program bear close resemblance to the prescriptions of "Tough Choices or Tough Times: The Report of the New Commission on the Skills of the American Workforce," 2007 (for the Executive Summary of the report, see www. skillscommission.org/wp-content/uploads/2010/05/ToughChoices_EXEC-SUM.pdf). Business organizations, along with some unions and states, are calling for even closer alignment between the report and federal education policy (see " 'Tough Choices' Education Initiative Grows with the Addition of Three States and a Newly Announced NEA-Business Coalition," April 13, 2010: www.skillscommission.org/?p=16).

The panel that created "Tough Choices or Tough Times" was heavily weighted with individuals who work—or had worked—for companies and business organizations with stakes in education. Prominent members with such backgrounds were former New York City schools chancellor, and current CEO of News Corp's education unit, Joel Klein; Viacom's Michael Dolan; Susan Sclafani and Michael Page from Chartwell Education Group; William Wiggenhorn from Educational Development Associates; John Engler, president of the National Association of Manufacturers; Judy Codding from America's Choice Inc.; Paul Elsner from Paul Elsner Associates; Henry

S. Schacht, former chairman and CEO of Lucent Technologies (see Executive Summary of "Tough Choices or Tough Times," 22–23).

The report, echoing "A Nation at Risk," states that its proposed education reforms are necessary for the United States to regain its prominence in "producing the most important new products and services" and for it to maintain "the worldwide technological lead, year in and year out." According to it, we are now competing with countries such as India and China, where workers, especially in science and technology sectors, are better trained and willing to work for less. We need to reform our education system to produce workers who can compete in the new globalized economy and, the report implies, who are willing to work for less. "Today, Indian engineers make $7,500 a year against $45,000 for an American engineer with the same qualifications," the reports states. "If we succeed in matching the very high levels of mastery of mathematics and science of these Indian engineers—an enormous challenge for this country—why would the world's employers pay us more than they have to pay the Indians to do their work." See Executive Summary of "Tough Choices or Tough Times."

"Race to the Top" similarly seeks "improved results for students, long-term gains in school and school system capacity, *and increased productivity and effectiveness*," and follows recommendations of both "Tough Choices or Tough Times" and "A Nation at Risk" in proposing "a longer school day, week, or year schedule to significantly increase the total number of school hours," and prescribing that children should have more rigorous preparatory schooling before entering kindergarten. Measures aimed at bolstering proficiencies in technology is another area of similar prescription as "Race to the Top," like its predecessors, encourages states to boost the study of mathematics, science, technology, and engineering. See U.S. Dept. of Education, "Race to the Top."

CHAPTER TEN: NARROWING MINDS

1. Editorial, "Top of The Heap: N.Y. Must Put $700 Million in Federal Education Funds to Work for Kids," *New York Daily News*, August 28, 2010 (www.nydailynews.com/opinions/2010/08/25/2010-08-25_top_of_the_heap.html).

2. U.S. Department of Education, "Race to the Top Program: Executive Summary," Washington DC, November 2009 (www2.ed.gov/programs/racetothetop/executive-summary.pdf).

3. Recent reforms in New York State require that 40 percent of teachers' performance evaluations be based upon standardized test scores. See Jennifer Medina, "Agreement Will Alter Teaching Evaluations," *New York Times*, May 10, 2010 (www.nytimes.com/2010/05/11/nyregion/11teacher.html).

4. Some districts, such as Chicago's and New York's were already doing this, as noted earlier, well before Race to the Top was in place. In New Orleans, a natural disaster, Hurricane Katrina, led to the closing of many schools. Rebuilding the system post-Katrina has been governed by market-driven philosophies and initiatives. For accounts of post-Katrina privatization in New Orleans' schools see Kenneth Saltman, *Capitalizing on Disaster: Taking and Breaking Public Schools* (Boulder, CO: Paradigm Publishers, 2007), chapter 1; Henry A. Giroux, *Stormy Weather: Katrina and the Politics of Disposability* (Boulder, CO: Paradigm Publishers, 2006); Naomi Klein, T*he Shock Doctrine: The Rise of Disaster Capitalism* (New York: Henry Holt, 2008).

5. These problems are only deepened by school funding systems (typical of those in the United States) that rely heavily on local property taxes. On average, property taxes account for around half of the revenue available for schools in most systems with the rest coming from state and federal coffers. The result is that poorer communities, where property tax revenue is low and conditions are most challenging for schools, tend to get fewer funds for their schools than richer ones, a dynamic further exacerbated by "No Child Left Behind," which grants or withdraws funds on the basis of whether a school is above or below state performance averages.

6. Funding schools equitably across a state, for example, rather than relying on local property tax revenues would allow for significant improvements in inner-city schools. In most Canadian cities, in contrast to those in the United States, schools are funded out of general tax revenues rather than through property taxes. Disparities among schools are less pronounced as a result. Hawaii is the one state in the United States that currently funds schools out of state coffers and does not rely on property taxes.

7. "Never has the nation's education system been so reliant on standardized tests and the companies that make them," according to Michael Winerip, "Standardized Tests Face a Crisis Over Standards," *New York Times*, March 22, 2006 (www.nytimes.com/2006/03/22/education/22education.html). Winerip made this observation *before* two developments that have further increased reliance on standardized testing—the 2007 extension of the mandatory testing requirements of "No Child Left Behind" to science; and the 2009 "Race to the Top" initiative.

8. "Race to the Top" requires these standards to be internationally benchmarked and aimed at preparing students for college and the workforce. While states are permitted to add (but not subtract) from these standards, additional standards can constitute only 15 percent or less of the overall number of standards in a given area. "Race to the Top" encourages states to sign on to new national standards (created in 2010 by the National Governors Association and the Council of Chief State School Officers, and backed by Gates Foundation money) by allocating extra points in the competition to those who sign on. A majority of states have now committed to these standards. In the not too distant future, the United States is likely to have a national curriculum from coast to coast, with standardized testing to complement it. Tamar Lewin, "Many States Adopt National Standards for Their Schools," *New York Times*, July 21, 2010 (www.nytimes.com/2010/07/21/education/21standards.html).

    Here again, "Race to the Top" bears resemblance to "Tough Choices or Tough Times." The latter, in similar sprit to the former, calls for performance measures based on standardized test results that would be publicly available and serve as a basis for parents and students to choose schools, and also as a basis for rewarding, penalizing, and firing teachers. These measures would also form the basis for districts contracting with schools that are privately owned and run (which ideally, according to the report, would be most of them).

    At the same time, "Tough Choices or Tough Times" goes further in its privatization prescriptions than "Race to the Top." The former envisions teachers forming limited-liability companies through which they would offer their services to districts and the public, much like the firms formed by lawyers, doctors, and architects. The role of local districts would be limited to selecting which firms to contract with, and to determining whether or not to renew contracts on the basis of performance. As "Tough Choices or Tough Times" states (at 16): "Schools would no longer be owned by local school districts. Instead, schools would be operated by independent contractors, many of them limited-liability corporations owned and run by teachers. The primary role of school district central offices would be to write performance contracts with the operators of these schools, monitor their operations, cancel or decide not to renew the contracts of those providers that did not perform well, and find others that could do better." See *"Tough Choices or Tough Times"* (www.skillscommission.org/wp-content/uploads/2010/05/ToughChoices_EXECSUM.pdf). "Race to the Top" does not call for such deep privatization. Nor, however, does it discourage or bar it.

9. Testing companies operate in secrecy and with virtually no regulatory oversight, prompting one expert, Robert Shaeffer of the National Center for Fair and Open Testing, to observe that there is "absolutely no accountability for the corporations that make those tests." As a result, he says, "companies over-promise and under-deliver and states, particularly in the last several years because of the fiscal crisis, take the lowest bidder who promises to do the job whether that company's track record demonstrates that they can do it [or not]" (as quoted in "FCAT Scores Delayed Due to Grading Problem," June 6, 2010: www.winknews.com/Local-Florida/2010-06-06/Report-FCAT-scores-delayed-due-to-grading-problem). Over the last decade, there have been numerous incidents of flawed marking, late delivery, and poor performance by the companies states rely upon to create and mark tests. As early as 2001, there were problems, according to Diana B. Henriques and Jacques Steinberg, "Right Answer, Wrong Score: Test Flaws Take Toll," *New York Times*, May 20, 2001 (www.nytimes.com/2001/05/20/business/20EXAM.html?pagewanted=all). Since then, those problems have only grown, especially as standardized testing has become more widespread: See Todd Farley, *Making the Grades: My Misadventures in the Standardized Testing Industry* (San Francisco: Polipoint Press, 2009). The Florida Department of Education, for example, recently paid NCS Pearson $254 million to design and grade the state's Comprehensive Assessment Tests, despite being so burdened with debt that it was cutting teaching jobs

and extracurricular activities. NCS Pearson had managed to secure the lucrative contract by bidding lower than its competitor, CTB-McGraw-Hill, which had previously held the contract. But NCS Pearson failed to deliver results on time and jeopardized the validity of many results by failing to employ sufficient numbers of staff to mark the test's essay questions (see "FCAT Scores Delayed Due to Grading Problem").

10. As quoted in Pedro Noguera, "A New Vision of School Reform," *The Nation*, May 27, 2010 (www.thenation.com/article/new-vision-school-reform).

11. "Tough Choices or Tough Times" similarly takes aim at multiple-choice testing. "A major overhaul of the American testing industry" is necessary, according to the report, to "move from America's tests to the kinds of examinations and assessments that will capture [creativity, innovation, work management skills] and other qualities at the level of accomplishment required." See "Tough Choices or Tough Times," 14–15.

12. There has been a litany of scandals, legal battles, and unfulfilled contracts as a result of marking foul-ups at major testing companies. See Noguera, "A New Vision."

13. As stated by Todd Fairley at the *Washington Post* blog of Valerie Strauss, "Author: 'My Misadventures in the Standardized Testing Industry,'" December 18, 2009 (http://voices.washingtonpost.com/answer-sheet/standardized-tests/-gerald-martineaupost-today-my.html). See also Fairley, *Making the Grades*.

14. Ibid.

15. Ibid.

16. Todd Fairley, "Standardized Tests Are Not the Answer. I Know, I Graded Them," *Christian Science Monitor*, October 28, 2009 (www.csmonitor.com/Commentary/Opinion/2009/1028/p09s01-coop.html). Further problems arise when education authorities, desperate to show improvements in test scores when federal and grant money hangs in the balance, manipulate test-score numbers. In New York dramatic jumps in the proportion of students reaching proficiency between 2006 and 2009 in math and English were not a result of increased proficiency, but rather of the fact the proficiency standard had been dropped from 60 to 44 percent. In Chicago, similar results between 2004 and 2008 were due to similar reasons. In respect to the latter, a study

commissioned by the Commercial Club of Chicago found that the "huge increases [in performance measures in the city's schools] reflect changes in the tests and testing procedures—not real student improvement." As quoted and discussed in Diane Ravitch, *The Death and Life of the Great American School System: How Testing and Choice Are Undermining Education* (New York: Basic Books, 2010) (Kindle version).

17. Ibid., location 3068.

18. See, for elaboration on this point, Henry A. Giroux and Kenneth Saltman, "Obama's Betrayal of Public Education?" *Truthout*, December 17, 2008 (see also above, chapter 9, note 5). Even by their own limited measures of success, there is considerable doubt about whether standardized tests work. According to Ravitch, *Death and Life*, location 2919: "School districts have invested hundreds of millions of dollars in programs and training materials that teach students the specific types of questions that will appear on the state tests. For weeks or even months before the state test, children are drilled daily in test-taking skills on questions mirroring those that are likely to appear on the state test. The consequence of all that practice is that students may be able to pass the state test, yet unable to pass a test of precisely the same subject for which they did not practice. They master test-taking methods, but not the subject itself. In the new word of accountability, students' acquisition of the skills and knowledge they need for further education and for the workplace is secondary. What matters most is for the school, the district, and the state to be able to say that more students have reached 'proficiency.' This sort of fraud ignores the students' interests while promoting the interests of adults who take credit for nonexistent improvements." Ravitch goes on to discuss the work of Daniel Koretz, a psychometrician at Harvard who argues that test-taking preparation undermines the validity of testing. According to Ravitch, Koretz demonstrates that "changes induced by accountability pressures corrupt the very purpose of schooling by causing practitioners to focus on the measure rather than on the goals of education" (location 2958).

19. As quoted in Bakan, *The Corporation*, 115.

20. Ibid.

21. Major players in the testing industry are CTB/McGraw-Hill, Houghton Mif-

flin, and NCS Pearson (which recently swallowed up a fourth giant, Harcourt Assessment).

22. See PBS Nightly Business Report transcript, "The New Business of Education—Standardized Testing," February 18, 2008 (www.pbs.org/nbr/site/onair/transcripts/080218a/).

23. Substantial revenue is also generated by "wraparounds"—teaching manuals, practice tests, and textbooks that schools and students use for test preparation. Kaplan, for example, a $70 million test-prep company in 1991, had $2 billion in sales in 2008 as a result of the growth in K–12 testing and is now the largest source of revenue for its parent company, The Washington Post Company. PBS transcript, "The New Business of Education."

24. United States Government Accounting Office, "Highlights of GAO-04-62: A Report to the Chairman, Committee on Education and the Workforce, House of Representatives," Washington DC, October 2003 (the full report can be found at www.gao.gov/cgi-bin/getrpt?GAO-04-62).

25. Ibid.

26. Alex Molnar et al., *Profiles of For-Profit Education Management Organizations: Twelfth Annual Report—2009–2010* (Boulder, CO: National Education Policy Center, December 2010), (http://nepc.colorado.edu/files/EMO-FP-09-10.pdf). The report notes that EMOs operate in thirty-one states, and teach more than 300,000 students (a 25 percent increase over the previous year). Between 2003 and 2009 the number of EMOs operating in the United States increased from fourteen to ninety-five; the number of schools they run increased from 131 to 733; and the number of states in which EMOs operate jumped from sixteen to thirty-one. The vast majority of students in schools run by EMOs are in schools run by the largest EMOs. Among the latter are Imagine Schools, Inc., with the largest number of schools (76), and Edison Learning, with the largest number of students (37,574). In terms of different states, Michigan has the largest number of schools run by for-profit EMOS (191), followed by Florida (136), Arizona (103), Ohio (95), and Pennsylvania (39).

27. While encouraging privatization, in the form of charter schools, "Race to the Top" places no limitations on how far such privatization can go. A state proposal could, in theory, score high points on all the program's criteria with

a plan that, as the "Tough Choices or Tough Times" report recommends (at 16), privatizes the management and operation of all schools in a state.

28. An up-to-date collection of news articles about various scandals at EMO schools can be found at http://charterschoolscandals.blogspot.com/.

29. Kenneth Saltman, *The Edison Schools: Corporate Schooling and the Assault on Public Education* (New York: Routledge, 2005), 88.

30. As Erik Erikson states in his *Childhood and Society* (New York: W.W. Norton, 1963), the "one effort which can keep a democratic country healthy [is] the effort to 'summon forth the potential intelligence of the younger generation.'" The greatest threat to doing so, he argues, is the training of youth to be "machinelike and clocklike . . . standardized" (323) and to be subservient to the authority of "bosses." Such training, he says, fails to cultivate the natural idealism and scepticism of power that is necessary for the health and survival of both individuals and democracy. "Political ideals are part and parcel of an evolution in conscience structure which, if ignored, must lead to illness," he says. "Political conscience cannot regress without catastrophic consequences." Societies that opt for mechanical rather than humanistic ethos are, accordingly, in trouble. "If man permits his ethics to depend on the machineries he can set in motion," Erikson warned, "he may find himself helplessly harnessed to the designs of total destruction along with those of total production" (325).

CONCLUSION

1. As quoted above in chapter 1.

2. This is not to say that regulators never act to protect children's interests. Rather, my argument is that existing regulatory regimes are often inadequate and poorly enforced, and that these effects are, at least in part, the results of ideologically fueled presumptions against regulation. The regulatory regimes that do exist tend to be in areas where harms have been definitively proven (as opposed to reasonably supported by evidence, as the precautionary principle would demand), or where there is near unanimous public support for a regime, or slight or nonexistent industry opposition. The various regimes I

look at in earlier chapters—those restricting, for example, leaded paint and gasoline, offensive and obscene children's television content, marketing of pharmaceutical drugs for off-label pediatric uses, and nefarious forms of child labor—meet some or all of these criteria, as do regulations around various childhood safety issues such as car seats, bike helmets, and toy choking hazards. It is also important to take note of the numerous organizations, some of which have already been mentioned, devoted to lobbying, among other things, for more robust protection of children. Here are just a few of these, all excellent resources for concerned parents and citizens in relation to the various topics covered in this book: Campaign for a Commercial-Free Childhood (www.commercialfreechildhood.org/); Centre for Child Honouring (http://childhonouring.org/); Children's Environmental Health Network (www.cehn.org/); The Child Labor Coalition (http://clc.designannexe.com/); Children Now (www.childrennow.org/index.php/); Commercialism in Education Research Unit (http://nepc.colorado.edu/ceru-home); The Kaiser Family Foundation (www.kff.org/entmedia/index.cfm); Rudd Center for Food Policy and Obesity (http://www.yaleruddcenter.org/).

3. This account is based upon Lenore Skenazy, "Why I Let My 9-Year-Old Ride the Subway Alone," *New York Sun*, April 1, 2008 (http://www.nysun.com/editorials/why-i-let-my-9-year-old-ride-subway-alone).

4. Lenore Skenazy, "America's Worst Mom?" *New York Sun*, April 8, 2008 (www.nysun.com/opinion/americas-worst-mom/74347/).

5. As a parent, I try not to be overprotective. My wife, Rebecca, and I have encouraged our kids to play ice hockey (at least until our son's fourth concussion), train and compete in martial arts, ski, snowboard, sail, and mountain bike. We try to be firm but realistic about adolescent rituals—the partying and late nights among other things—and we have let our kids roam the city freely and take public transit since they were eleven years old. We set and enforce firm but realistic limits around TV watching, video gaming, computer screen time and content, cell phones, and diet. The latter are not always easy to enforce—for all the reasons discussed in chapters 2 and 3—but we, like most parents, do the best we can.

6. Erikson, *Childhood and Society*, 408.

7. As quoted in Paul Krugman, "Gordon the Unlucky," *New York Times*, June 7, 2009 (www.nytimes.com/2009/06/08/opinion/08krugman.html?_r=1).

8. For a fuller elaboration on this point, see Bakan, *The Corporation: The Pathological Pursuit of Profit and Power* (New York: The Free Press, 2004).

9. As quoted in: Andrew Clark and Jill Treanor, "Greenspan—I Was Wrong About the Economy, Sort Of," *The Guardian*, October 24, 2008 (www. guardian.co.uk/business/2008/oct/24/economics-creditcrunch-federal-reserve-greenspan). See also Edmund L. Andrews, "Greenspan Concedes Error on Regulation," *New York Times*, October 23, 2008 (www.nytimes. com/2008/10/24/business/economy/24panel.html).

10. Willem Buiter, "Self Regulation Means No Regulation," *Williambuiters's mavercon*, April 10, 2008 (http://blogs.ft.com/maverecon/2008/04/self-regulation-means-no-regulation/).

11. Co-regulation models warrant consideration in some areas, as I suggested in chapter 3, for example, as do "new regulation" models, which seek to create cultures of compliance within firms rather than just punishing firms for failing to comply with regulatory norms. For discussion of "new regulation," see Cristie Ford, "New Governance in the Teeth of Human Frailty: Lessons From Financial Regulation," 2010 Wisconsin Law Review 101 (2010).

    My prescription here for more regulation is, needless to say, at odds with the views and premises of free market advocates and neoliberals and consistent with those who see public regulation as a legitimate and necessary means for addressing social and environmental ills (such as myself, in *The Corporation* and here again, and also those who have called for more robust regulation in the wake of the 2008 economic crisis and the BP Gulf of Mexico disaster: see chapter 1, note 13). For an excellent critique of free market economics, see Paul Krugman, "How Did Economists Get It So Wrong?" *New York Times Magazine*, September 6, 2009 (www.nytimes.com/2009/09/06/magazine/06Economic-t.html).

12. See Bakan, *The Corporation*, chapters 4 and 6.

13. For numerous inspiring stories about youth activism in the environmental movement, as well as practical advice about how youth can become involved, see Sharon J. Smith, *The Young Activists Guide to Building a Green Movement and Changing the World* (Berkeley, CA: Ten Speed Press, 2011). For Erik Er-

ikson quotes, see his *Childhood and Society* (New York: W.W. Norton, 1963), 323, 325.

14. See http://weday.freethechildren.com/about/.

15. See Newton H. Minow, *Abandoned in the Wasteland: Children, Television, and the First Amendment* (New York: Hill and Wang, 1995), at 95. Newton Minow spoke eloquently in an interview with me about early hopes that television would play a key role in bolstering democracy. He was himself instrumental in the creation of televised presidential candidate debates, beginning with the famous Nixon-Kennedy debate. See Newton N. Minow and Craig L. Lamay, *Inside the Presidential Debates: Their Improbable Past and Promising Future* (Chicago: University of Chicago Books, 2008). Minow told me a telling story about when, as Chair of the Federal Communications Commission, President Kennedy asked him what he should say in a speech about television to a meeting of broadcasters. "Well, I think, Mr. President," Minow told Kennedy, "you ought to compare the way the free world allows broadcasters to cover a space launch with the Russians who do not allow any radio or television to see what their doing. . . ." When President Kennedy gave his speech to the broadcasters, Minow recalls, "It was a perfectly crafted five-minute speech about the difference between a free society and closed society. That as a free society, we invited the world to see through radio and television what was happening in our effort to send a man into space; and in a closed society, nobody knew what happened. He did this off-the-cuff perfectly."

16. See, Bakan, *The Corporation,* chapters 1, 2, and 6.

17. This account of corporate involvement at We Day is based upon Janet Newbury, "We Day: The Corporate Selling of Progressive Ethics and Hope to Youth," October 28, 2010, *Rabble.ca* (http://rabble.ca/news/2010/10/we-day-corporate-selling-progressive-ethics-and-hope-youth). Long lists of corporate sponsors for each city's We Day events can be found at the We Day website (Vancouver's, for example, are at http://weday.freethechildren.com/sponsors/vancouver/. Notable are brands that specifically target children, such as Club Penguin and Cadbury).

A description of the joint campaign by McDonald's and Conservation International can be found at www.conservation.org/discover/partnership/corporate/Pages/mcdonalds.aspx.

Index

Page numbers beginning with 177 refer to notes.

Index

Index

Index